Saving Shame

DIVINATIONS:
REREADING LATE ANCIENT RELIGION

Series Editors

Daniel Boyarin
Virginia Burrus
Derek Krueger

A complete list of books in the series is available from the publisher.

Saving Shame

Martyrs, Saints, and Other Abject Subjects

Virginia Burrus

PENN

University of Pennsylvania Press
Philadelphia

Published by
University of Pennsylvania Press
Philadelphia, Pennsylvania 19104–4112

Printed in the United States of America on acid-free paper

10   9   8   7   6   5   4   3   2   1

A Cataloging-in-Publication record is available from the Library of Congress.
ISBN-13: 978-0-8122-4044-3
ISBN-10: 0-8122-4044-8

for elliot

Contents

Preface: My Shame

Merely to write the words "my shame" is to perform a subtly transgressive act, albeit one already native to writing itself. What, the reader may wonder, with an impending sense of *vicarious* shame, is this author about to *reveal*? (Shame is peculiarly infectious.) Writing, however, is a place where we hide as well as reveal ourselves. Be reassured—and warned.

I am a fifth-generation Texan, as measured along at least one line of genealogy. In my case, this is to say that I am a child of both the U.S. South and its Western frontier—on my mother's side, the descendent of Baptists who arrived in East Texas as cotton mill workers, on my father's side, the descendent of Church of Christ folk who made their living in or alongside the vast ranches of the sun-baked Panhandle. Named for my two grandmothers, I am marked more than nominally by their doubled legacies.

From my maternal grandmother, I learned all too early of the dangers harbored within my very body, which seemingly could never be scrubbed clean enough—outside or in (don't ask). I learned too about the damp stain of shame that seeped through the gaping cracks of poverty (alternately, love of luxury) and ignorance (alternately, false pride in "book learning"), the treacherous betrayal of a grammatical lapse, an ill-chosen garment or ill-appointed house, the unseemly display of female sexuality, or the more typically masculine thirst for drink or gambling. ("Your body is the temple of the Lord"—a favorite proof text of Southern Baptists.) From the embarrassed silence that surrounded the topic of her husband's Cherokee descent, I now also apprehend with hindsight the particular (and particularly destructive) vulnerability of Southern whiteness to shame. That she had been divorced from her husband at her own initiative was something we likewise simply pretended not to know.

I learned much from my maternal grandmother, not to mention the many aunts, uncles, and cousins frequently joined under her matriarchal hospitality, about the joys of shamelessness as well, though these lessons were more difficult to decipher. Indeed, as a child, I was often slightly puzzled by the family habit of publicly recounting distinctly humiliating stories about a past located on the wrong side of the railroad tracks. My perplexity was increased by the fact that the stories—even the sentences of which they were comprised—were rarely finished before the laughter began, laughter that eventually left everyone gasping for breath and wiping their eyes with paper napkins. Wondering about the apparent fineness of the line that separated hilarity from tears, joy from humiliation, wondering too about the mysterious gaps in the stories themselves, I was torn between joining in the laughter and cringing away from it. (Having grown up in the city rather than the town, I was already obscurely aware of a certain awkward gap of culture, as well as class.) The laughter was generous, overwhelmingly so— and so too were many of the bodies. The very flesh that was seemingly the source of shame was also quite matter-of-factly in evidence. We were encouraged to pile plates high with ham, macaroni and cheese, starchy vegetable casseroles, jello salad, banana pie made with vanilla wafers—comfort foods for comforting and comfortable bodies that were simultaneously ashamed and shameless (not particularly modest), judgmental and forgiving at once. Sometimes I took refuge in them; sometimes I shied away—a fact of which I am still slightly ashamed, an ambivalence I still carry in my own body.

From my contrastingly understated and dry-eyed paternal grandmother, I learned different and more delicately communicated lessons—the importance of holding one's tongue, guarding privacy as well as modesty, practicing self-restraint and respecting difference, most often by tactfully overlooking it. Tellingly, it is harder for me to write about her. We did not pick the wild flowers, but she taught me their names. We did not make pets of the dogs or cows, but we gave them names. Talk was likely to be about the weather, which was no laughing matter. We carefully avoided each other's eyes in unvoiced solidarity when my grandfather complained (as he often did) about the "niggers," the "Yankees," or the "hippies." (I still of course cringe with shame—my own, in more than one sense.)

Paradoxically, perhaps, it was my Southern grandmother (a determined churchgoer and great respecter of God's judgment, which always seemed to coincide rather exactly with her own) who taught me how to strive for independence and freedom from social constraints—though she's not at all sure she approves of the results of my efforts, to say the least. The higher culture she once strained for seems to have destined her for betrayal, a matter of lingering shame for me. It was, on the other hand, my Western grandmother (whose relationship with God was nobody's business but her own) who taught me how to accept love as a gift and also how to resign myself to desire's sharpest disappointments in stoic silence. "The good Lord giveth and the good Lord taketh away"—that much was clear. We gave fervent thanks for the Lord's palpably "tender mercies" even as we wondered more quietly about His wisdom otherwise.

On both sides of the family, however different the cultures, however differently Christian, shame simultaneously threatened and stood guard, even after some of us had fled to the city, where we might just hope to escape the divine Eye. On the one side (at least in my own peripheral vision), the awareness of shame was communicated through the proliferating, very nearly exhibitionist rhetoric of prohibition and judgment, matched by equally prolific laughter that seemed to acknowledge uneasily both the power and the inevitability of transgression. On the other side, sensitivity to shame was marked by a dignified reticence that itself spoke volumes concerning both the need for caution and the possibility that we might yet hold ourselves safe. Standing at the intersection of these two paths, I could only try to make sense of them. I am still trying, of course, as so many of us are.

For me there is, finally, no place to stand outside shame, though it has always been clear that there are many places—"many mansions"?—within this variegated domain. (To be honest, I may once have hoped there was some place *else*: alone of all the members of my known extended family, I left Texas, apparently permanently. This is an embarrassment for me when I return to visit and am treated like . . . a visitor.) Neither, however, have I experienced shame as a sheerly destructive or paralyzingly inhibiting force—on the contrary. If I have, admittedly (and unremarkably), gone to great lengths to avoid dwelling on or in shame in the past, I now find myself in middle age (perhaps equally unremarkably) rather sharply interested in it. This interest in large part impels the current book, which will take me on a detour down far more distant passages of historical recollection.

My students are among those who have accompanied me on this path. Often they have done so, paradoxically, by refusing to follow my lead. In what seems by now a predictable gesture, they have recoiled from the manifestations in ancient Christian texts of self-hatred expressed above all in the loathing of the flesh. The students who voice such concerns respect and even powerfully identify with the yearning for transcendence, transformation, and freedom also evident in those same texts. But they resist—they struggle to resist—transcendence bought at the expense of the shaming of the body (above all the sexual body), transcendence that produces the flesh in and through shame, inscribing it as a matter of shame—the shame of matter itself. Many of them do not fail to note that women, sexual and racial minorities, and the poor or uneducated seem to carry more than their fair share of the burden of such shame, or that the planet itself groans with the painfully destructive effects of the shame that nature is forced to bear. Armed with the doctrines of divine creation and incarnation, desiring to affirm the goodness of materiality, the poignancy of transience and finitude, the gift of sentience, my students still often seem to fight a losing battle against a theological tradition that remains to this day marked by its shameful shame of the flesh. Sometimes they are ashamed of their failures to resist the force of tradition, are ashamed even of the passion conveyed by their very strength of conviction; but most of them continue to struggle nonetheless, shamelessly, against the weight of shame, in the face of their own shame. They struggle for their very spiritual survival, it often seems to me.

I am of course not so different from my students. Perhaps those who read this text will also find that they—*you*—can relate not only to the experience of shame, not only to the desire to resist shame, but also to the intuition that shame, in all of its complexity, may yet have much to teach us. The hunch I am pursuing is this: there is no escape from shame but there may be many possibilities for a productive transformation of shame and through shame. There is no escape from shame because we are always already marked by shame. Might it be that this is not merely the tragic effect of a fallen history but also an inherent aspect of creaturely finitude and relationality? That is a question that may be impossible to answer, though an affirmative response lures me. If the enormously destructive potentiality of shame is undeniable, whether accidental or inherent to human existence, salvation may lie in recognizing that shame is also the source of courage and humility, the opening to joy and grace. Within the transformation of shame, the possibility of love emerges. To be sure, shame can and often does stifle love. While some ancient Christians may have positively courted shame, few of us will want to take that particular risk. But if we simply refuse shame, we may find that we have also refused love—in all of its vulnerable exposure—as well. Can we afford such a refusal?

Introduction: Outing Shame

> When the ancients speak, they do not merely tell us about themselves.
> They also tell us about us.
>
> —Bernard Williams, Shame and Necessity

Shame is an emotion of which we frequently seem deeply ashamed. Famously the great inhibitor, shame at once suppresses and intensifies other affects with which it binds.[1] Shame can even bind with shame: "Shame, indeed, covers shame itself—it is shameful to express shame."[2] Evidence of this (if we needed any) is the fact that, until lately, shame has been a taboo topic even among psychoanalysts, psychotherapists, and psychologists, who have been "trained to celebrate guilt and demean embarrassment as its vaguely indecent sibling," as Donald Nathanson notes. In recent decades, however, the tide has begun to turn, exemplified by the work of scholars such as Silvan Tomkins, Helen Block Lewis, Leon Wurmser, and their various disciples, who, observes Nathanson, have "outed shame and declared it the issue of our era."[3]

If shame has come out of the closet, we are perhaps just beginning to apprehend its scope and complexity. Affect psychologists suggest that it emerges in the early stages of infancy, manifesting in response to a failure or break in the circuit of mirroring gazing that joins a child to another. "During mutual gaze we feel attached. In the moment of shame, we feel shorn not just from the other but from all possible others."[4] Tomkins associates the inhibition of the connective gaze with an encounter with the strange or unexpected—finding oneself looking at a stranger or being looked at by a stranger, for example, or experiencing one who is familiar as suddenly strange. He observes further that shame is necessarily incomplete in its inhibiting effect: "In shame I wish to continue to look and to be looked at, but I also do not wish to do so."[5] Eve Kosofsky Sedgwick and Adam Frank gloss Tomkins's point: "Without positive affect, there can be no shame: only a scene that offers you enjoyment or engages your interest

can make you blush. . . . Shame is characterized by its failure ever to renounce its object cathexis, its relation to the desire for pleasure as well as
the need to avoid pain."[6] Shame arrives, then, in the rush of self-consciousness in which the spontaneity of curiosity or joy is interrupted and rendered
problematic, marked by a sense of danger or risk, but thereby also made
sharply visible to the self and thus, it would seem, effectively augmented in
the process. In shame, desire, whatever its object (and in Tomkins's theory
at least, there is no privileging of the sexual, much less the heterosexual,
object),[7] is not so much decisively blocked as tantalizingly arrested, caught
like a deer in the headlights of (self-) scrutiny. The moment is open: what
happens next perhaps makes all the difference.

Shame is typically viewed as a quintessentially public affect. In this
context, it is frequently—and somewhat misleadingly—contrasted with
guilt and the interiorized conscience.[8] Yet shame is also the most intimate
and internal of emotions. "Shame strikes deepest into the heart of man,"
Tompkins proclaims.[9] Arguably, it often strikes still deeper into the heart of
woman.[10] Downcast eyes, a dropped head, or the sudden spread of a blush
all mark the site of encounter between public and private, inter- and intrasubjective realms, as the face broadcasts sharp awareness of its own visibility
and the self subsequently turns inward in a gesture of hiding. "Awareness
of the face by the self is an integral part of the experience of shame."[11] Here
"face" does not signify the sheer externality of shame's origination but
rather marks the mutually constitutive and transforming meeting point of
self and other—of all that is alien—at the limits of mutual exposure. Shame
is "the place where the *question* of identity arises most originarily and most
relationally."[12] It arises not only in relation to others but also, and perhaps
more crucially, in the relation of the self to itself. If common parlance associates shame with face, etymology links it with skin.[13] Shame is the site of a
subjectivity articulated at its thin-skinned limits. Indeed, it challenges the
very distinction between inside and outside. "Shame, as precarious hyper-
reflexivity of the surface of the body, can turn one inside out—or outside
in."[14]

Tompkins suggests that "shame-humiliation," as he terms it, encompasses realms of feeling commonly described as shyness, shame, and guilt.[15]
Wurmser likewise observes the linguistic multiplication that attends the articulation of shame, referencing "its cognate feelings of embarrassment and
put down, of slight and humiliation, or of shyness, bashfulness, and modesty."[16] He further proposes that shame—however we may name it—"really
covers three concepts." Wurmser specifies, first, the fear of disgrace or dis-

honor; second, the internalization of shame as "the affect of contempt directed against the self"; third, the "overall *character trait* preventing any such disgraceful exposure, an attitude of respect toward others and toward oneself, a stance of reverence" that encompasses "respect and a sense of awe."[17]

Shame manifested as fear of shame itself is frequently what keeps us in the thrall of conventional mores or moralities—Nietzsche's notorious "Thou shalt," in which guilt and shame are arguably scarcely distinguishable. The internalization of shame as self-contempt potentially intensifies such bondage, weakening the self's capacity for excitement, joy, risk, and creativity—likewise the target of what Wurmser dubs Nietzsche's "war against shame."[18] The third concept of shame emerges, Wurmser notes, as "almost the antithesis of the second one." Here, a sense of shame—or, perhaps more precisely, an empathic awareness of our capacity both to shame and to be shamed—serves as a guard against the violence of shaming, protecting privacy and dignity, cultivating not only tact but a positive sense of awe in the face (and again, "face" is crucial) of what is at once most vulnerable and most sacred in human existence.

Analysis of shame blurs at many points with what might be framed as an analysis of shamelessness. Shamelessness is always at least as ambivalent as shame itself, balanced between a refusal and a willful embracing of shame. Whatever it is, it is not simply outside shame but is at once resistant to and continuous with it. Cultivating courage, shamelessness engages the fear of being shamed and thus also exposes the coercive force of shaming: as eye meets eye, defying shame's inhibition, shame is itself shamed. Yet the power of such challenging and transgressive ocular intimacy—the power of a reclaimed desire—derives from the same source as the inhibition itself.[19] Shamelessness also engages self-humiliation, transforming it into a poignant, even defiant, acceptance of human finitude and vulnerability. At the same time, humility reflects not only the acceptance of limits but also an aspiration to exceed one's own limits. As philosopher Bernard Williams puts it, we feel "ashamed because we have contemptibly fallen short of what we might have hoped of ourselves."[20]

Viewed through the lens of shamelessness, Wurmser's three concepts of shame begin to reveal their coherence and interdependence. For it is at the very point where courageous resistance and deep humility meet that a shame conceptualized as the guardian of privacy and protector of awe is likewise productively engaged. Emerging at the intersection of safety and vulnerability, secrecy and exposure, shame both acknowledges the pressing need for the protection of privacy and puts the self-isolation inscribed by privacy at risk. What is potentially effected through the risk is not, however, an eradication of awe at the threshold of the sacred but an intensification of awe experienced in the crossing of thresholds—in the risking of intimacy as well as of social or political resistance—and also an explosion of creativity. Joseph Adamson and Hilary Clark note "the often compulsive relation between shame and creativity." We see this with particular clarity in the act of writing, "which allows one to hide and reveal oneself at the same time."[21] Writing is arguably both a prime instance of and a powerful trope for communication between subjects, in all of its shameful impossibility and desirability. It is thus no accident that literature long preceded the discipline of psychology in its relentless explorations of the creative dynamics of shame.[22]

Shame is thus not, it would seem, something we need *simply* to mitigate or try to get over. Shame is arguably something we need to take more seriously, in its productively transformative as well as its destructively inhibiting effects—in its unavoidable ambivalence. Shame is at the heart of the anguished awareness of human limits at the point where those limits are exceeded, conveying the power as well as the danger of relationality itself. For some, relationality may be too tame a term. Less tamely, Georges Bataille speaks of the violently self-sacrificial experience of the dissolution of disparate or "discontinuous" subjects in which shame is implicated.[23] For others, the term may be too apolitical, though the erasure of politics is scarcely my aim. Shame underlies and nourishes our complex and differentiated, self-transgressing and self-transcending capacities for intimacy and empathy, creativity and sociality, ethical response and political action. It is the affect that checks narcissism and monitors interpersonal relatedness and communal commitments.[24] Shame arises where we humans both honor and overflow our limits, where we recognize the limits of autonomy—where we observe, with no little alarm, the spreading stain of our mutual implicatedness. It is in and through shame that we risk trust and also that we acknowledge (and frequently shrink from) the risk of trust. If shame strikes deep into our hearts, it also necessarily attends the opening of our stricken hearts—or rather, it reveals that the heart is always already broken by, and thus also opened to, the advent of love.

A historian—which is what I am by profession—must confront her own shame when engaging embarrassingly universalizing theories of human nature, typically disdained by the discipline. Yet, as Sedgwick and Frank observe, there may be much to gain from deferring "the confrontation between any cross-cultural perspective" sharply keyed to difference and the hypotheses offered by such bold and subtle universalizers as the theorists of shame just briefly surveyed.[25] The subsequent chapters of this book will explore the distinctive cultural legacy of shame conveyed by ancient Christian literatures of martyrdom and asceticism, christology and confession. I hope, of course, to remain closely attuned to the particularities of the ancient texts that will engage me, honoring their distance and difference. Nonetheless, as is already clear, my interpretations will inevitably involve a shameless transgressions of limits as well, limits not only of time and cultural space but also of scholarly disciplines. How could it be otherwise?

For some readers, the very framing of the topic *Christian* shame may seem surprising. It has become a truism that Western cultures are characteristically guilt cultures, Eastern cultures shame cultures—a view both exemplified and made influential by Ruth Benedict's post-World War II monograph *The Chysanthemum and the Sword*.[26] Frequently Christianity is viewed as crucially implicated in the conversion of ancient Mediterranean cultures from shame to guilt and thus in the emergence of the characteristic emphasis of the modern West on guilt as *opposed* to shame.[27] This view has received significant nuance in the more recent discussions of cultural anthropologists who have explicitly rejected "the idea of reifying the distinction between guilt and shame and attaching it specifically to one culture or another." Such anthropologists nonetheless retain the perception that Christianity historically "related the sentiment of honor to a conscience free from guilt" wherein "true honor was only in the eyes of God" and "the subjective aspect was essential."[28]

I have already implicitly raised the question of whether the Christianized, if also secularized, modern West has, by becoming ashamed of shame, in fact effectively evacuated shame; that question will continue to incite my curiosity and color my readings. So too will the complex relation between shame and guilt within Christian tradition. Of equal importance to the historical inquiry, however, is the refusal of the blatant, and rather blatantly ideological, anachronism so often operative in the projection onto ancient Christians of a modern sensibility of guilt imagined to be morally superior to the contrastingly "primitive" affect of shame. As New Testament scholars influenced by the studies of anthropologists have been arguing for some time now, ancient Christians were participants in a culture for which honor and shame remained pivotal values and in which social conflict frequently took the form of an attempt to redefine what was honorable and what was shameful.[29] The work of historically minded philosophers of ethics suggests, moreover, that shame and guilt cannot be simply separated, much less opposed, in the analysis of either ancient or contemporary cultures. "Shame continues to work for us, as it worked for the Greeks, in essential ways," argues Williams.[30]

Yet it is also not my position that Christianity made no difference in the history of shame. At the close of her remarkably sensitive and insightful study of the early imperial Roman culture of honor and shame, historian Carlin Barton gazes somberly at the horizon of change that also draws my attention. Prior to the ascendancy of Christianity, Rome had *already* lost its balance by becoming an empire, suggests Barton, beginning the fall into a world—a world that would soon become Christian—in which conscience willfully submitted to a higher authority and thereby evaded the demands of public scrutiny and accountability that had formerly characterized a delicately sustained culture of honor and shame. With the unraveling of communal cohesion and collective identity in the expansively heterogeneous society of the empire, shame became ever more difficult to manage, even as there were ever more causes for shame in an ever more brutal world. Consequently, people looked for "ways of having self-consciousness without being alienated from oneself, of having honor apart from shame, hope apart from fear; life apart from death, soul apart from will."[31] The new Roman of late antiquity, argues Barton, was the "honest" man or woman, unshamable because (in theory, at least) utterly self-restrained, transparent, and autonomous—answerable only to an all-seeing god or a divinely appointed law.[32]

Barton has insightfully exposed a legacy of Rome that reverberates ominously in current American culture, and I find myself persuaded by both her subtle historical analysis and her astute cultural criticism. In addition, I share with her a reluctance to divorce a sociocultural analysis of honor and shame from a psychological approach to the affective dimensions of shame, when engaged in the demanding and necessarily creative enterprise of interpreting ancient texts. Historians have typically been more open to importing insights from the field of anthropology, which have the advantage of arising out of an attention to cultural particularity yoked to an explicitly comparative methodology. Yet anthropologists who have concerned themselves with the analysis of honor and shame (a disciplinary interest that arose at roughly the same time as did interest in shame in the field of psychology) have themselves often been open to the insights of psychology. As J. G. Peristiany and Julian Pitt-Rivers acknowledge, shame embraces not only "reputation" but also "sentiment," and "honor is too intimate a sentiment to submit to definition; it must be felt."[33] How indeed can the analysis of cultures be separated from the analysis of emotions or "mentalities" when one is dealing with a phenomenon like shame?

At first glance, affect may nonetheless seem far less available to historical investigation than culture. However, literary texts—the primary sources for historians of antiquity—arguably give us no more direct access to ancient cultures than to an ancient person's feelings. As an interpreter of texts, the historian does not simply throw open a window onto the past; even if she could, culture would remain a matter of interpretation every bit as much as would feeling. Rather, the study of history demands a sensitivity to the complex *texture* of the written documents that are often virtually the sole relics of that distant past. Many academic disciplines may prove worthy allies in such a task of textual interpretation that seeks to breach a perhaps unbreachable gap, so long as all disciplines are practiced with humility and openness to unforeseen possibilities. As Sedgwick puts it, "To perceive texture is never only to ask or know What is it like? nor even just How does it impinge on *me*? Textural perception always explores two other questions as well: How did it get that way? and What could I do with it?"[34] Feeling for texture, the historian inevitably and necessarily also brings with her the intricate texture of her own provisional knowing of cultures, societies, emotions, bodies, and more. Touch is, after all, always a two-way encounter. As readers, we leave our traces like invisible fingerprints on the ancient pages, just as the texts leave us "feeling" differently: even our fingerprints are not as immutable as they seem.

Taking Barton's interpretations of the subtle texture of Roman honor and shame as my point of departure, then, I ask whether there might not also be *another* Roman legacy, *another* story to be told. I ask too: How did it get that way? and What could I do with it? Approached from a slightly different angle, the writings of these later Romans—the Christians who interest me—may yet reveal a few secrets about the endurance as well as the transformability of shame. It is, moreover, just possible that this may constitute some kind of good news. Ancient Christianity does indeed innovate in relation to prior Mediterranean cultures of honor and shame, and Barton's work casts new light on the complex forces that drive such innovation, at once shaping Christianity and accounting for its increased influence. I want to explore the possibility, however, that Christianity innovates less by replacing shame with guilt than by embracing shame shamelessly. Where

Barton senses the yearning for an "honor apart from shame," I also detect the emergence of a shame that no longer desires honor.

Here my argument both builds on and supplements not only Barton's historical analysis but also the analyses of those anthropologists who have argued that the interpretation of honor and shame must take into account the place accorded to divine grace. Adding grace to the mix has fruitfully complicated the understanding of honor, not least by accommodating the role of religion and theology in negotiations of cultural values and social status. At the same time, this new emphasis has tended to keep shame still more tightly subordinated to honor by shifting focus to the collusion of grace with honor. In Pitt-Rivers's words, "Honor stands before the event; his honorable qualities produce the victor. Grace stands behind it; the will of God is revealed in the outcome. Each is therefore the precondition of the other."[35] Grace may indeed be helpfully understood to secure honor—or, in the late Roman terms explored by Barton, a sense of transparent "honesty"—by superhuman means. However, as Pitt-Rivers also acknowledges, it typically does so by paradoxically demanding that one "renounce one's claims to honor as precedence."[36] I would press this point farther: in ancient Christian texts, divine grace is invoked through the shameless courting of *dis*grace. Shame may well become most interesting (not least in relation to grace) precisely where it exceeds and disrupts the honor-shame system—and also perhaps thereby exceeds and disrupts the models of structuralist anthropology.

Among ancient Christians, I shall argue, shame is no longer primarily the source of admonishing exempla that fortify the honorable will. Instead, an extravagant—even gratuitous—embracing of shame puts honor itself into question. Rather than simply converting (one culture's definition of) shame into (another sub/culture's definition of) honor, ancient Christians lay claim to their own shame, at once intensifying it and converting it into a potent source of identity—and, paradoxically, also of identity's dissolution. In the shame culture of the early Christians, the defiant edge of cultural and political critique combines with the generative power of an excessive self-humbling that offers in exchange for the sacrifice of face a joyous opening of the subject within grace.

Honor, in both its sociocultural and psychic dimensions, is thereby rendered extremely ambivalent, to say the least. Martyrdom is the initial site at which shame is converted into a defiant shamelessness, giving rise to a performatively queered identity that retrieves dignity without aspiring to honor. Chapter 1 ("Shameless Witnesses") engages both martyrological and hagiographical texts in which spectacles of shame become stages for the politics of identity. Martyrdom is also where the sacrificial death of the self exemplified by Christ's crucifixion is performed most explicitly. The articulation within incarnational christology of the crucified flesh—and of corruptible materiality more generally—as the matrix of a shameful yet joyously transporting abjection is the focus of Chapter 2 ("An Embarrassment of Flesh"). Chapter 3 ("The Desire and Pursuit of Humiliation") explores in turn how ascetic practice plumbs the depths of bodily, emotional, and social self-abasement, thereby audaciously—indeed, shamelessly—cultivating a sensibility of extreme humility that is transformed into a positive source of spiritual as well as social metamorphosis. Finally, Chapter 4 ("Shameful Confessions") considers the practice of confession as a performance of abysmal self-exposure that reveals the continuities of an interiorized and crucially also generalized guilt with a shame that is rendered transformative precisely through its shameless disclosure. Confession is closely linked with martyrdom, and this last chapter will curve back toward the public arena where we begin. Now, however, it is the ear rather than the eye that must give witness to shame. Curving back toward Chapter 1, Chapter 4 also enfolds Chapters 2 and 3, which play on the more intimate senses of touch, taste, and smell associated with the flesh and the shame that lies close to the flesh.

The very notion of an innovatively shameless turn toward shame is, admittedly, fraught with paradox. Historically speaking, shamelessness is already amply in evidence in the finely tuned honor-shame code of the early Roman empire, as Barton's study reveals. It is at once that which seeks to elude the chastising force of shame and that which is potentially convertible to honor. Moreover, it is by no means easily distinguished in every case from the capacity for transgressive risk that conditions honorable actions themselves. The historical shift that interest me is, then, inherently subtle and slippery, entailing a set of incremental, but cumulatively perhaps momentous, adjustments in the late ancient calculus of honor and shame by which shame is partly unlinked from honor and more closely than ever wed to grace. The result of these adjustments is only very imperfectly captured in a supersessionist narrative announcing the advent of the guilty conscience. Rather than proclaiming their newfound guilt, I hope to "out" the persisting shame of the ancient Christians.

Chapter 1
Shameless Witnesses

To view performativity in terms of habitual shame and its transforma-
tions opens a lot of new doors for thinking about identity politics.
—Eve Kosofsky Sedgwick, Touching Feeling

First Perpetua was tossed, and fell on her loins; and when she saw her
tunic torn from her side, she drew it over her as a veil for her thighs, more
mindful of her shame than of her pain. Then she was called for again,
and she bound up her dishevelled hair; for it was not seemly for a martyr
to suffer with dishevelled hair, lest she should appear to be mourning in
her glory.
—Passion of Perpetua 20

The centrality of spectacle and performance in imperial Roman
culture is widely acknowledged. The spectacles of the arena in particular—
ranging from gladiatorial combat to fights with wild animals to mock military battles to various forms of dramatized execution—have exerted a
powerful fascination for modern readers, as for ancient spectators. In the
arena, rites of sacrifice to the gods, displays of military triumph over non-
Romans, assertions of social order through the punishment of criminals,
and manifestations of aristocratic munificence all converge in symbolically
saturated performances that embrace (in principle at least) the breadth of
a highly differentiated society at once energized and dangerously pressured
by the demands of empire.[1] As the emphasis on Perpetua's display of modesty (*pudor*) reminds us, shame—and the possibility of its varied mutations
and glorious transformations—pervades the performative violence of the
arena and accounts for much of the gripping suspense that captivates its
spectators, then and now. To be made a spectacle, to be subjected to the
gaze of so many eyes, to be publicly marked as a criminal, captive, or slave,
to be costumed or stripped, even to have one's very body ripped open and

exposed, was to be made vulnerable to shame in a most extreme and visceral manner. It was also, consequently and paradoxically, to be endowed with a circumscribed but potent agency, to be made an actor, a performer—to acquire a public "face," even (possibly) to attain glory. "In a fundamental way," notes Carlin Barton, "the arena reconstructed the traditional conditions of honor. . . . The arena, which seems to epitomize Roman 'decadence' when seen through modern eyes, also offered a stage on which might be reenacted a lost set of sorely lamented values."[2] Indeed, the power of shame and its transformations here draws our attention in large part because it promises to explain what often seems otherwise difficult to explain—namely, the extent to which the most violent public stagings of submission or defeat so frequently metamorphize into effective assertions of identity while also mediating complex mirrorings of identity between victors and vanquished, those watching and those being watched. In the process, "the traditional conditions of honor" are not only retrieved but also significantly shifted.

Writing in a scholarly context seemingly far removed from Roman cultural history, literary critic Eve Kosofsky Sedgwick has recently argued for the close relation between shame, performativity, and identity. In making the link between shame and identity, she draws on the work of Silvan Tomkins and other affect psychologists who find shame first and paradigmatically manifested in the response of an infant to the jarring interruption of the mirroring gaze that attaches him or her to another. "Shame floods into being as a moment, a disruptive moment, in a circuit of identity-constituting identificatory communication. . . . But in interrupting identification, shame too makes identity."[3] For Sedgwick, the paradoxical power of shame lies in "the double movement shame makes: toward painful individuation, toward uncontrollable relationality." This does not imply, however, that the individuation effected within shame grounds a stable or "essential" identity. Rather, shame is the place where "the *question* of identity arises most originarily and most relationally."[4] And it is a question that arises repeatedly and with particular urgency whenever one presents oneself "to the spectating eye": "the stage is set (so to speak) for either a newly dramatized flooding of the subject by the shame of refused return, or the successful pulsation of the mirroring regard." Thus, for Sedgwick, even more explicitly than for the many other theorists who have also emphasized the visual context and gestural repertoire of shame, shame "*is performance.*" She adds: "I mean theatrical performance. . . . Shame is the affect that mantles the threshold between introversion and extroversion, between absorption and theatricality, between performativity and—performativity."[5]

Of particular interest to Sedgwick in her treatment of shame and performativity is the actor as activist—specifically, "the activist in an identity politics."[6] Recounting the story of her participation in a political demonstration organized by a coalition of black lesbians and gays, she notes the demonstrators' reliance on the twinned forces of "shaming and smuggling." Playing to the audience of news reporters and the broader audiences mediated by their cameras, the demonstrators were effectively shaming the reporters into rendering visible precisely those people normally denied public visibility—and thereby implicitly if not also explicitly shamed. In (almost) the same gesture, the demonstrators were not merely demanding "representation" elsewhere—in this case, by protesting the refusal of a local PBS station to air a film about black gay men in the U.S.—but already giving body to self-representation, performatively smuggling "onto the prohibitive airwaves some version of the apparently unrepresentably dangerous and endangered conjunction, queer and black."[7] Sedgwick recalls carrying a sign (a "willed assumption of stigma"), though, interestingly, she does not remember what the sign said.[8] At the center of her recollection is the memory of fainting in front of the television cameras, a memory fully retrievable only through the lens of those cameras, which recorded the image of a supine figure, "motionless, apparently female, uncannily gravid with meaning (but with what possible meaning? what usable meaning?)" that was "available to everybody there except herself."[9]

In Sedgwick's riveting vignette, we observe the particular confluence of shame and shamelessness at the point where cultural queerness and the activism of identity politics meet. While shame is apparently a pervasive (even universal) affect, it differs, notes Sedgwick, not only across cultural contexts but also in the intensity of its grip on individuals within a shared context. There are those "whose sense of identity is for some reason tuned most durably to the note of shame"—for a reason, that is, that cannot be predicted in advance (does not designate an essence) but "remains to be specified."[10] "I want to say that at least for certain ('queer') people, shame is simply the first, and remains a permanent, structuring fact of identity, one that . . . has its own powerfully productive and powerfully social metamorphic possibilities."[11] The inherently performative politics of identity emerges, then, at the charged site of shame, in Sedgwick's account. Moreover, shame constitutes identity "as to-be-constituted, which is also to say as already there for the (necessary, productive) misconstrual and misrecognition."[12] What possible meaning, what usable meaning will it yield? is the question that ever arises. Forged in and through shame, identity is potently visible—visibly potent—to the very extent that it remains open and contested.

Sedgwick's analysis creates space for a fresh cultural-historical interpretation of some of the most spectacular performances of ancient Christians—performances staged for the eye of posterity in the literatures of martyrology and hagiography. Famously persecuted not for any specified crimes, but rather "for the name," Christians of the pre-Constantinian era represent themselves as perversely embracing the very preposterousness (as they frame it) of their persecution. Tertullian paints the scene with characteristic vividness: " 'I am a Christian,' the man cries out. He tells you what he is; you wish to hear from him what he is not. Occupying your place of authority to extort the truth, you do your utmost to get lies from us. 'I am,' he says, 'that which you ask me if I am. Why do you torture me to sin? I confess, and you put me to the rack. What would you do if I denied? Certainly you give no ready credence to others when they deny. When we deny, you believe at once.' " Tertullian concludes with the flourish of a rhetorical question: "How is it you do not reflect that a spontaneous confession is greatly more worthy of credit than a compelled denial?" (*Apology* 2). Indeed, confession is a credit that the Christians are more than willing to draw upon. Although threatened with the most brutal and humiliating forms of torture and death in the arena, where spectators alternately jeer and express grudging admiration, they refuse to relinquish the "name"—and thus shamelessly refuse to evade their shame. The literature of martyrdom (zooming in with all the sensationalizing voyeurism of a news camera) consistently portrays Christians plunging defiantly toward their deaths not for the sake of someone or something *else*—not even for the sake of justice—but for the sake of their own identity with Christ and as Christians. (This is a fact that consistently perplexes, frustrates, and even angers my social justice oriented seminary students, and understandably so: in our contemporary American context, Christian identity *requires* justification.)

Queerly—spectacularly—marked by shame, "demonstrating" their defiance of political authorities, "smuggling" their witnessing bodies onto the ancient equivalent of the "prohibitive airwaves" of network television, the ancient martyrs transform shame into the source of an oddly pure identity politics. Both the content and the evaluation of that identity remain open to question, reconstrual and misconstrual, recognition and misrecognition. As Tertullian charges, the very indeterminacy of the name ensures "that men may have no desire to know for certain what they know for certain they are entirely ignorant of" (*Apology* 2). Nonetheless, the existence of an identity that can be claimed and reclaimed—"I am a Christian!"—is secured in and through iterative spectacles of shame. Even as shame is transformed into glory "in the picturings of imagination" that see beyond the earthly to the heavenly arena, the performance of the Christians—like that of the gladiators—transforms its earthly spectators as well: "They have pleasure in those whom yet they punish; they put all slights on those to whom, at the same time, they award their approbation; they magnify the art and brand the artist" (Tertullian, *On the Shows* 30, 22).[13]

That these spectacles and the pleasure they excite in their viewers outlast the period of persecution is evidenced by their eventual displacement, in the post-Constantinian era, onto the stage of ascetic performativity. It is evidenced too by the fact that some of us still read the texts of martyrdom, as well as the Lives of saints, and do so not infrequently with a thrilling flash—or embarrassed flush—of self-recognition.

Prelude: Apocalyptic Shame

Indeed, for many, the figure of the martyr has become so familiar as to be almost domesticated: already assured of her glory, we may miss the fact that this glory is thickly lined with shame. I want to begin, then, with consideration of a text—John's Apocalypse—that not only appears to predate the fixing of martyrdom as a cultural given but also focuses our eyes on a shame we cannot miss—the shame of the whore of Babylon. A queer witness indeed: but let us call her to the stand. Or rather, let us gaze with eager anticipation as the curtain rises on the theater of her brief but exhilarating performance.

Anticipation is crucial, as it happens: without it, we will miss half the show. As is always the case with spectacles of martyrdom, we must observe the scene with doubled vision—encompassing, in this case, the split view of Babylon's present shamelessness and her future shaming, mirrored by our own initially shameless, but subsequently shamed, gawking.[14] (We both do and don't want to look. . . .) In one line of vision, we are carried with our narrator John into the wilderness (*erēmos*), guided by an angel to see "a woman sitting on a scarlet beast" that has "seven heads and ten horns"; she is "arrayed in purple and scarlet, and bedecked with gold and jewels and pearls, holding in her hand a golden cup full of abominations and the impurities of her fornication" (17.3–4). The beast, we have been told, is "full of blasphemous names" (17.3) and the woman herself, like so many figures in this graphically dense—indeed performatively palimpsestic—book, is tattooed with a name as well. "On her forehead was written a name of great mystery: 'Babylon the great, mother of harlots and of earth's abomination'" (17.5). Still eying the woman curiously, we observe further that she is "drunk with the blood of the saints and the blood of the martyrs of Jesus" (17.6). A marvel (*thauma*) as well as a mystery! But one quickly dispelled by the know-it-all angelic interpreter, who reveals the embarrassing shamelessness of our gazing—"Why marvel?" (17.7)—though it was he who initially directed us to look. The angel discloses not only the woman's identity—"the woman that you saw is the great city which has dominion over the kings of the earth" ("Rome!" is here our cue) (17.18)—but also her fate. Now a second line, or temporality, of vision opens up. The beast on which she sits, together with his ten "horns" (client kings, the angel patiently explains), "will make her desolate and naked, and devour her flesh and burn her up with fire" (17.16). Here is yet another all too arresting spectacle that is hard to look at and also hard not to look at, despite the warning that we should not marvel. As Christopher Frilingos argues, the Apocalypse here and elsewhere both exploits the attraction of monstrous spectacles and displays distinct unease regarding the power of amazement provoked by such strange sights: "angelic sanction or no, the seer is drawn to wonder at the grotesque figure."[15]

Lady Babylon is not usually viewed as a particularly ambivalent figure; she appears, rather, thoroughly condemned and contemptible, as feminist critics in particular have pointed out.[16] Yet, as we have seen, the text is rife with the ambivalence inhering in the spectacle of the whore, in the gaze of a spectating eye that is lured at once by her shamelessness and by the shame that it enfolds—the shaming that will, we are assured, unfold. This ambivalence is further intensified by a subsequent series of heavenly speeches in which satisfied vengeance at Babylon's anticipated fall is strangely mixed with the strains of grief, echoing and parodying the response to Jerusalem's shame in the biblical book of Lamentations. The polyglossal performance of the Apocalypse refuses reduction to a single or simple perspective. True, it is two angels (surely reliable witnesses) who both predict and performatively pronounce the destruction of Babylon—"Fallen, fallen is Babylon the great!" (18.2)—whereas "worldly" kings, merchants, shipmasters, and sailors are assigned the role of Babylon's mourners, tarred by the brush of empathy with the whore's own shame. Clearly, the text intends to align its readers with the exulting angels, not the lamenting rulers and merchants: "the extratextual audience is not supposed to sympathize with the suffering of Babylon."[17] However, once again the very performative power of the Apocalypse seems to complicate its own chastening intentions: the seductiveness of the grotesque figures and violent scenes displayed exceeds the control of the text. We may find ourselves sympathizing with the whore, even if we are not supposed to, sharing "John's own disquieting brush with the paralysis of amazement."[18] It is not insignificant that the anticipated lamentations are cited from the mouth of one of the angels;[19] moreover, the heavenly ventriloquist pulls off the act with poignant verisimilitude: "Alas! alas! the great city, Babylon the mighty city!" (18.10); "Alas, alas! the great city that was clothed in fine linen, in purple and scarlet . . . !" (18.16); "Alas, alas! the great city where all who had ships at sea grew rich by her wealth!" (18.19). Here, in the queered present of past predictions of future grief, time "slows down and invites listeners/readers to enter into the disappointment of Babylon's judgment and collapse."[20] Indeed, how can we readerly spectators *not* be moved by such articulate mourning of Babylon's shame, even as we are thereby tainted with the shame of our own ambivalence? (an ambivalence, we note, that repeats the earlier ambivalence of the "marveling" gaze upon her shamelessness).[21] This is all the more the case, given the odd way in which the angelic predictions of Babylon's punishment, on the one hand, and the cited lamentations, on the other, seem to bleed into each other. The first angel's speech in particular hovers ambiguously between vengeful satisfaction and lamentation—"Fallen, fallen is Babylon the great! It has become a dwelling place of demons" (18.2)—whereas the sea merchants end their lament with a cry to heaven to rejoice, "for God has given judgment for you against her" (18.20).

It might be enough to identify the infectious ocularity of shame as the source of the ambivalence that proliferates around the figure of Babylon: made painfully conscious of our own desirous gazing, we seem to catch the whore's shame like a contagious disease. (The implicit—angelic—moral of the story? That we be cured of our shame and released from the desire to look.) But there is perhaps still more to be said about the ambivalence of Babylon, and thus finally about the persisting, arguably incurable, ambivalence of martyrdom's shame—of the shame of a "martyr" herself drunk on the blood of martyrs. Babylon, we should remember, is not the only figure in the text to catch our eye, though she is arguably the most arresting. As is often noted, her performance anticipates the arrival of a sharply contrasting female figure, the chaste bride Jerusalem, establishing an opposition between harlot and virgin—between worldly and heavenly cities—that would seem calculated to dispel ambivalence. (We know exactly which woman we *ought* to prefer.) What is less frequently noted is that Babylon also echoes and mimics the complexities of another larger-than-life female figure who has appeared in an earlier scene—the mysterious birthing woman who is "clothed with the sun, with the moon under her feet, and on her head a crown of twelve stars" (12.1).

This heavenly mother, like Babylon, is accompanied by a red beast—in her case, a dragon—who also sports "seven heads and ten horns" (12.3). Whereas Babylon initially seems to dominate the beast but is (or will be) subsequently devoured by it, the heavenly woman is beset from the start by the dragon, who intends to devour her child (12.4). When the newborn child is whisked away to a safe place in the heavens but she is not, she subsequently evades the dragon by fleeing (actually, by flying, having been handily supplied with eagle's wings) to the wilderness (*erēmos*) (12.6, 14)—the very place where we will encounter Babylon in regal control of the beast. The wilderness first nourishes and later protects the winged lady: "the earth (*gē*) came to the help of the woman" by swallowing the river vomited by the dragon in an attempt to flood the woman out—earth's devouring thus perversely miming, and thereby undermining, the dragon's menacing voraciousness, in this text of proliferating mimicry (12.15–16). In contrast, the wilderness becomes, through angelic intervention, the passive site of Babylon's shameful exposure, as we have seen. The one woman, a survivor of beastly persecution (surprising in this bloodthirsty text), is (less surprisingly) the mother of martyrs (12.17), born of her own torturous labor (12.2). The other, shamefully inscribed as the "mother of harlots"—much as the Jesus of the gospels is mockingly marked as "King of the Jews"—is exposed, tortured, and slain by a beast. Each is, then, almost (but not quite) a martyr. Viewed as doubles, seen through split vision, the two arguably represent the almost (but not quite) suppressed ambivalence of martyrdom as a transforming witness of shame.

I use the term "martyr" both loosely and advisedly. Although, as I have already noted, a full-fledged discourse of martyrdom postdates this text, the term martyr or "witness" does appear with specific reference to the testimony of those white-robed souls "slain for the word of God"; such ones, we are told, have "washed their robes and made them white in the blood of the Lamb (6.9; 7.14). These apocalyptic martyrs are closely identified with the figure of the slain Lamb (5.6–14), soon to be married to the heavenly bride Jerusalem, who is "clothed with fine linen, bright and pure" that reflects the gleaming righteousness of the "deeds of the saints" (19.8). The futuristic fantasies of the Apocalypse are far more elaborate than those of later martyrdom literature, and its stagings of military combat and fights with beasts take place not in the arena but in the imaginary theater of the cosmos itself, as empires are humiliated and the Lamb enthroned in everlasting glory, in the most dramatic possible turning of the tables of power. Nonetheless, this text is at least proto- if not even hyper-martyrological. In the apocalyptic performance, slain victims have not merely become ambivalent victors. They seem to have been purified of shame altogether, as shed blood is alchemically transformed into cleansing whitewash, the darkness of night bleached by the blinding light of the lamplike Lamb pulsing through an eerily ethereal city that admits only "glory and honor" without the taint of a blush or the hint of either modesty or humility: indeed, the servants of the Lamb gaze boldly on his face (21.26, 22.4).[22] Such are the symptoms of a particular "Roman inheritance" that seems to resurface ominously in our own day, as Barton notes: "It is an attempt to be as pure and complete as the man or woman who has chosen death without actually being dead—by willing not to will." She adds: "The ideal of the stable, simple, autonomous, honorable human being of our culture bespeaks the long, tormented history it has sought to efface and overcome; it articulates a ferocious hope, and silences a terrible pain."[23]

Yet, however much it may strain after absolute purity (and strain it does), the Apocalypse cannot, in the end, completely efface and overcome the very shame from which "glory and honor" arise—and neither, perhaps, can we, as Barton hints. In a text that repeatedly, almost obsessively, showcases the literalized stigmatization of identity (all those tattooed bodies!), it is difficult to imagine that the Lamb—slain but still living—is not eternally marked by the scar of his wound. Marked too by his "wrath" (6.16), he carries more than a trace of the beast; yet he is also, as Harry Maier remarks, an improbable—even subversively ironic (I would add, obscurely shamed and shaming)—substitute for the imperial or messianic hero we might expect.[24] As for his apparently colorless urban bride, she is haunted not only by that other city Babylon, whose spectacular blaze of shame prepares the way for (and possibly also ironizes) the unveiling of her own crystalline purity,[25] but also by the third woman of this text—a woman who is *not* a city, who is claimed by both heaven *and* earth, whose wings span the distance between heaven and earth. If the show-stealing Babylon carries the burden of Jerusalem's disavowed shame, as well as the audacity of her shamelessness, the third woman, arriving first, bears her discarded modesty. This modesty—which has frequently thwarted interpreters who imagine her "erased from the text"[26]—enfolds the ambivalence of the shame doubled and intensified in Babylon—interjected too by the menacing figures of dragon and beast, splotching the text with a hot flush of red. Caught in the spotlight—or rather, the sun-, moon- and starlight—in the very act of giving birth, deprived of her child, chased by a gape-mouthed dragon, the woman finds refuge from so much overexposure in the wilderness, whence she disappears "for a time, and times, and half a time" (12.14). Mantled in deliberate obscurity (a strategic encryption), she is crucially not devoured by her shame. She will, it seems, reappear, but in the meantime ("a time, and times, and half a time") she, unlike either Babylon or Jerusalem, remains a difficult figure to read—and also, it would seem, an easy figure to appropriate through exposure to strong re-readings. Suspended between hiddenness and visibility, safety and danger, shamelessness and shame, this star-spangled, sun-bedecked, moon-cradled, and also desert-secreted woman gives modest, nameless witness to shame as the matrix of a performative identity—one that will repeatedly give birth to productive misconstruals and misrecognitions, whether as goddess or crypto-goddess Mary.[27]

Shame and Shamelessness in the Arena: Four Spectacles of Martyrdom

Whereas the Apocalypse makes an arena of the world, subsequent accounts of martyrdom bring us into the world of the arena, where (for those with the eyes to see it) the public display of suffering and death gives birth to a truth that is at once a confession of faith and a forging of self-identity. Here we view four well-known—indeed, virtually classic—literary performances of Christian witness that span a century and circle the Mediterranean from Syria to Asia Minor to Gaul to North Africa. The first of these, Ignatius of Antioch's *Letter to the Romans*, most likely written in the early years of the second century, stands at the cusp of the crystallization of the Christian discourse of martyrdom.[28] Ignatius's significantly innovative—and highly idiosyncratic—self-fashioning as one who can only truly become a Christian through death in the arena is complemented by consideration of the mid-second-century *Martyrdom of Polycarp*, a text associated with the Ignatian literary corpus (which includes a letter to Polycarp) and drawing heavily upon the gospels, as well as 2 and 4 Maccabees, for its representation of the witnessing death of a Christian subjected to public execution. In many respects, the *Martyrdom of Polycarp*, which evidences the first apparently technical use of the terminology of martyrdom, sets the model for subsequent third-person, "eye-witness" martyrdom narratives. These include the *Letter of the Martyrs of Vienne and Lyons* (circa 177) and the *Passion of Perpetua* (circa 203), texts in which the representation of martyrdom as a spectacle of the arena reaches dramatic new heights, as the sentenced Christians—especially, and intriguingly, the women among them—are now more explicitly than before represented not merely as condemned criminals but as gladiatorlike combatants.[29] The *Passion of Perpetua* also returns us in one significant respect to Ignatius, as it includes Perpetua's own self-envisioning as a martyr. In each of these texts, the foregrounding of the arena as the stage of martyrdom allows us to observe with particular clarity the varied and complex operations of shame in the performative production of Christian identity.

Ignatius of Antioch: Perfecting Shamelessness

For Ignatius, the arena, which he has not yet reached, is viewed through the anticipatory eyes of his imagination: he will be at once director, spectator, and spectacle in this performance.[30] In the figures of the military guard who accompany him from Syria to Rome—transformed by Ignatius's fantasy into "ten leopards"—he is already "fighting wild beasts . . . who become worse when they treat me kindly" (*Letter to the Romans* 5.1). "Let me be food for the wild beasts," he urges, looking forward to his arrival in the arena of Rome. "Entice the beasts so that they become my grave and leave behind nothing of my body" (4.2). He repeats the forceful terms of his seductive desire: "I wish to profit from the wild beasts that have been prepared for me. . . . I will even entice them to devour me quickly, not like some whom they, being cowards, did not touch. But in case they do not want to act out of free will, I shall force them" (5.2). Ignatius demands a good show (requiring, among other things, strong supporting actors and effective props) that will yield him the glory of a spectacular death; indeed, he will settle for no less. "Let fire, cross, groups of wild beasts, the scattering of bones, the cutting up of limbs, the grinding of the entire body, and the devil's evil punishments come upon me, so long as I may attain Jesus Christ" (5.3).

Perversely aspiring to be "hated by the world" (3), Ignatius appears to model a shame that has been thoroughly converted into shamelessness. For this reason, his *Letter to the Romans* continues to embarrass those many readers who find it . . . well, too *extreme*. As Elizabeth Castelli notes, scholars have persistently "distanced themselves from the self inscribed by the discourse of this soon-to-be martyr" while overlooking the very inventiveness of Ignatius's self-inscription. "Who is the 'I' who speaks here?"[31] In his performative "self-writing," Ignatius enacts the anticipated mutation of his visible body into a purely invisible witness through the digestive metamorphosis—better yet, transubstantiation—effected by the devouring beasts (4.2). What the *Apocalypse* aggressively inflicts on Babylon, Ignatius actively desires. "His is a self in the process of multiple transformations," as Castelli puts it. "In short, he is laboring to write himself out of corporeal existence in the hopes of achieving a transformed and wholly spiritual existence."[32] Here invisibility is not so much protection against a shaming visibility as it is the conversion through shame's visibility of an earthly spectacle into a heavenly mystery. Once again, double vision is required for the viewing of a martyr: in an imaginary carnivore's gory meal we are invited also to see a Christian's glorious transformation. When Ignatius's body has disappeared—when his shaming has been perfected—his identity will be rendered transparent: "For if I prove to be a Christian, I can also be called one, and be faithful then, when I am no longer visible to the world" (3.2). In the arena, he will give birth to himself (6.1)—an articulate word (2.1), pure light and true man (6.2), one who, imitating God's suffering, carries that God within him (6.3). It is, finally, what passes beyond sight that lures the spectating eye of this fantasy.

Whereas the Apocalypse tries, and fails, to perform a glory purified of shame, Ignatius's motto—surfacing other, barely submerged, narratives of the Apocalypse—might be "no shame, no gain."

Polycarp of Smyrna: Modest Witness

In the account of the martyrdom of Polycarp of Smyrna, the conversion of shame to shamelessness takes a detour through a dignified modesty that Ignatius, like Babylon, seemingly entirely lacks. When a crowd of spectators already gathered in the arena call for Polycarp, he initially withdraws from the city "in deference to the wish of many" (*Martyrdom of Polycarp* 5.1). Pursued to his hiding place as if he were a bandit or rebel rather than a respected bishop, he refuses, however, to flee again. Instead, shaming shame, he greets his pursuers graciously and offers them food and drink while he prepares himself with a lengthy prayer that leaves even his enemies marveling at the old man's godliness (7.1–3). The officials to whom he is subsequently conducted entreat him to preserve his public reputation by performing the required offering to the emperor, but Polycarp stubbornly refuses (8.2). This refusal is the pivotal moment on which the narrative turns (arguably, on which *every* narrative of martyrdom turns): Polycarp, like Ignatius, *will not* evade humiliation. Shame immediately colors his skin like a blush—or rather, a bruise—as the elderly bishop, now pushed roughly from the carriage that has brought him to the arena, injures his shin. Ignoring both the indignity and the pain, he turns eagerly—shamelessly—to meet the jeering crowd that awaits him in the stadium (8.3).

Polycarp, unlike Ignatius, has actual spectators to witness as well as to provoke his performance. Like Ignatius, he also plays to a divine audience: as he enters the stadium, a heavenly voice cheers him on, "Be strong, Polycarp, and be a man" (9.1). As Castelli observes, "Thus begins a tradition whereby the martyr's endurance comes to be linked explicitly with masculinity and tied also to images of masculinized athleticism and militarism."[33] His is a virtuoso performance, laced with an irony that doubles meaning while also splitting vision, in this act that spans heavenly and earthly arenas. Asked both to renounce and denounce his Christianity by proclaiming "Away with the atheists!" Polycarp obliges, solemnly scanning the crowd before pointing a finger in their direction and uttering the required words (9.2). Once again shaming shame, this elderly trickster smuggles his witness onto the airwaves, making his confession to a magistrate who perversely desires not a confession but a denial: "I am a Christian!" Polycarp insists (10.1). What the Apocalypse so often inscribes graphically and Ignatius performs liturgically, Polycarp utters performatively—an uncompromising witness of identity that, paradoxically, remains to-be-constituted. Polycarp does, interestingly, offer to instruct the magistrate in the "word of Christianity," but when the proconsul responds that it is the people who must be persuaded, Polycarp declines to explain himself before such an unworthy crowd (10.2). As for the spectators, they both do and don't understand Polycarp's witness, and words again bend with the ambivalence of double meaning: "This is the teacher of Asia, the father of the Christians, the destroyer of our gods, who teaches many not to sacrifice or worship" (12.2).

As ever, spectators play a large role in shaping the spectacle, even as the spectacle has its way with them. Calling for a lion, the crowd is informed that the beast fights have already been concluded; they demand in response that Polycarp be burned alive (12.2–3). Violence accelerates, as Polycarp's nearly unflappable dignity intensifies the crowd's desire to shame him; conversely, the more shame is heaped on him, the more opportunity Polycarp has to demonstrate his shameless imperviousness to shame. Yet the tension between shame and shamelessness, humiliation and dignity, is equally revealed in the modest details, here as earlier in the reference to the bruising of the old man's shin. Having been led to the pyre, Polycarp strips off all his clothes, but it is less his shameful exposure than his poignant fumbling with his shoes that reveals the inherent vulnerability of dignity to shame, the dependence of dignity on the possibility of shame, of shamelessness on shame's actualization: he was, we learn, "not previously in the habit of doing this, because all the faithful were always eager to be the first to touch his flesh" (13.2). As Polycarp is burned at the stake, our vision remains split and doubled: Is this the shameful execution of a common criminal or the glorious sacrifice of a splendid ram? (14.1). Is the old man's body being devoured by the flames or is it baking like fragrant (eucharistic) bread? (15.2). In a deliberately shaming denial of proper burial, Polycarp's corpse is subsequently cremated. Unlike Ignatius, Polycarp has not, however, been rendered entirely invisible through his witnessing death. Instead, his frail body, like his shame, has been converted through the testing of fire into an enduring treasure: what remains are his bones, "more valuable than precious stones and finer than refined gold" (18.2). Yet we note too the contrast with the Apocalypse's culminating and totalizing vision of a heavenly Jerusalem constructed of jewels and gold. When the curtain falls on the martyrdom of Polycarp, what we see are fragments of glory, broken glimpses of beauty, modest flickerings of dignity, immodest flashes of shamelessness displayed in an arena of shame.

Blandina: Taking It like a Slave Woman

The refusal of burial is a narrative motif that also caps the account of the martyrs of Vienne and Lyons, whose cremation yields no relics of bone. Small matter, perhaps: this text is reliquary enough, searing the eyes of its readers' imaginations with the vision of the elaborately tortured bodies of the Gallic martyrs, even as it zooms in on one body in particular—that of the slave woman Blandina, "through whom Christ proved that the things that humans think cheap, ugly, and contemptuous are deemed worth of glory before God" (Eusebius, *Ecclesiastical History*, 5.1.17). This is, then, a literary work not only unusually preoccupied with the spectacle of torture but also unusually focused on those "whose sense of identity is for some reason tuned most durably to the note of shame," as Sedgwick puts it.[34]

That a slave woman should be a particularly shameable subject scarcely requires explanation: such a one is, as it were, already shamed in advance. That she should also be—or rather become—a peculiarly powerful witness to a culturally "queer" identity is less self-evident (even, perhaps, for readers of Sedgwick) but also not inexplicable.

Page duBois's work illuminates the juridical practices by which an earlier Greek society marked the body of the slave as a privileged site for the production of truth through torture: "The slave on the rack waits like the metal, pure or alloyed, to be tested. The test, the touchstone [*basanos*], is the process of torture. . . . The *basanos* assumes first that the slave always lies, then that torture makes him or her always tell the truth, then that the truth produced through torture will always expose the truth or falsehood of the free man's evidence."[35] If the free man meets torture with a noble silence and indeed is not finally a torturable subject, the tortured slave has no choice but to "break" into a truth that he or she contains but does not possess. Defined by torture, the slave *cannot* witness freely; correspondingly, the slave *must* give witness when coerced, but this witness belongs wholly to the free man. DuBois goes on to explore the ways in which the slave body, typically scarred, branded, or tattooed, resonated with ancient Greek images of the text or writing tablet as a site of truth's inscription.[36] She also notes that the tortured body containing a hidden or buried truth was associated with "female space, with the containment and potentiality of the female body." Indeed, on duBois's reading of a constellation of cultural tropes, "the female is analogous to the slave."[37] If, in the Roman imperial period, distinctions between slave and free had been problematized and destabilized both juridically and culturally, even as masculinity itself had been rendered more ambivalent, this merely injected the traditional, implicitly gendered discourse of slavery and torture with both fresh anxiety and increased imaginative flexibility.[38] This is perhaps nowhere more evident than in the *Letter of the Martyrs of Vienne and Lyons*.

Although the text initially spotlights Vettius Epagathus, a "distinguished" man who comes forward voluntarily to make his bold confession, our attention is quickly directed elsewhere, in a movement that implicitly relativizes the value of the free speech of the honorable man by displacing it with the coerced witness of the shamed body of the tortured slave woman. There are three major moments in the competing presentation of torture's witness, each constituting a scene of public humiliation and physical mutilation of Christians in the arena. The first scene establishes the relation between slavery, torture, and truth in such a way as to relocate the slave's subjectivity within this ancient configuration. Crucial is the scene's framing with an account of the arrest of pagan slaves as part of a process of investigating their Christian masters. Fearing and seemingly evading torture, the servants readily agree to implicate their owners in the crimes of cannibalism and incest (5.1.14). Later, however, a woman named Biblis (thus, at least nominally, an inscribed "text") is tortured and, under the condition of torture, "comes to her senses" and denies the charge of cannibalism, confessing herself "from then on" a Christian (5.1.25–26). Although Biblis is not explicitly identified as a slave or as one of the domestic servants initially arrested, the text seems to invite, if not require, this interpretation, according to which Biblis's performance becomes a critique of the false witness of her fellow slaves. The slaves who speak from fear but without the coercion of physical torture speak falsely, the letter suggests, whereas the one who is tortured sees clearly, not only denying the false charges but also giving witness to her own identity as a Christian. The classical reading of the coerced speech of the slave is thereby invoked, but with a crucial interpretive shift: the truth revealed in Biblis's confession is not only a truth about her real master (Christ) but also a truth about herself. The power of judgment claimed by the torturer is wrested from him, as the narrative places the persecutor himself on trial and shamelessness once again shames shame.

Within this frame occurs the first public spectacle of torture of four Christians—Sanctus, Maturus, Attalus, and Blandina. The performances of Blandina and Sanctus are highlighted, and again the text both exploits the connections between slavery, torture, and truth and contests the traditional terms of a discourse that awards the slave's truth to her owner. It is here that Blandina is explicitly presented as a symbol of social reversal, in which contemptibility is converted into glory (5.1.17). This reversal is made concrete in the context of torture, as we are informed that Blandina's mistress, who is also among the accused Christians, feared that she would not be able to confess her faith due to the weakness of her body, while the slave "Blandina was filled with such power that even those who were taking turns to torture her in every way from dawn to dusk were weary and exhausted" (5.1.18). If the examples of Blandina and her mistress seem to privilege the shame of slavery over the honor of free status in the context of torture, Sanctus's subsequent performance teases, raising the question of whether an apparent reversal of slave and free status does not constitute a dissolution of these very categories: "he would not even tell them his own name, his race, or the city he was from, whether he was a slave or a freedman; to all of their questions he answered in Latin, 'I am a Christian'" (5.1.20). Here, extorted speech is simultaneously the true speech of the coerced slave and a kind of "no-speech," the silence that traditionally distinguishes nobility from slavery in the context of torture. The response of the persecutors to this asserted ambiguity is more torture, an excruciating reinscription—indeed branding—of slave status: "they finally tried pressing red-hot bronze plates against the tenderest parts of his body" (5.1.21). Sanctus's broken body—"being all one bruise and one wound, stretched and distorted out of any recognizably human shape"—proves nonetheless eloquent, no hollow container of spoken truth but rather itself a revelation of "Christ suffering in him" (5.1.23). And indeed, that carnal truth continues to amaze its spectators: "his body unbent and became straight under subsequent tortures" (5.1.24). Sanctus's broken witness is not at the torturer's disposal but brings salvation to the body of the slave itself.

A second scene explicitly invokes the comparison of the martyr to the professional fighter of wild beasts, while at the same time turning the tables and suggesting that it is not the Christians but their persecutors who are made a shameful spectacle when the martyrs are matched with animals in the arena. "Maturus, then Sanctus, Blandina, and Attalus were led into the amphitheater to be exposed to the beasts and to give a public spectacle of the pagans' inhumanity, for a day of gladiatorial games was expressly arranged for our sake" (5.1.37). Again, the performances of Sanctus and Blandina are highlighted. Sanctus is once more subjected to multiple tortures, including maulings by beasts and culminating finally in a second fiery branding of flesh via the "iron seat." Again, the slave witness refuses to "break" into the truth sought by his torturers but instead continues to repeat his monotonous profession of Christian identity: "from Sanctus all they would hear was what he had repeated from the beginning, his confession of faith" (5.1.38–39). Blandina is reintroduced, once more in an interpretive context that gives christological significance to social reversal: "Blandina was hung on a post and exposed as bait for the wild animals that were let loose on her. She seemed to hang there in the form of a cross, and by her fervent prayer she aroused intense enthusiasm in those who were undergoing their ordeal, for in their torment with the physical eyes they saw in the person of their sister him who was crucified for them" (5.1.41). In this text, the doubleness of earthly and heavenly spectacles seems to collapse in the gaze of the "physical eyes." Blandina's gender once more becomes fraught with significance as she is scripted not only as the crucified Christ but also as a second Eve: "for her victory in further contests she would make the condemnation of the crooked serpent irrevocable, . . . for she had overcome the Adversary in many contests" (5.1.42). Finally, in this second scene, slave status and tortureability are again explicitly destabilized, as Attalus is paraded through the arena like a slave, only to be removed when it is discovered that he is a Roman citizen (5.1.43–44).

The third scene of public torture and humiliation circles back to the opening portrait of Vettius Epagathus, as one Alexander is introduced as a second figure of honorable male speech: "He had been standing in front of the tribunal and by his attitude he had been urging the Christians to make their confession." Alexander's maleness, however, is almost immediately disrupted as he, like Ignatius, is depicted as making his own confession "as one who was giving birth"; his free status is likewise compromised when the letter records that the governor "flew into a rage and condemned him to the beasts" (5.1.49–50). Ambiguity about social status persists as Alexander, though subject in a torturous spectacle, remains silent—the response of a noble man. In parallel, Attalus, reintroduced into the arena despite his earlier identification as a citizen, seems to claim his freedom not through the noble silence exhibited by Alexander but through speech: like Sanctus, he employs Latin, the language of his persecutors, ironically turning their accusation of cannibalism back on them as he sniffs his own roasting flesh (5.1.50–52). Finally, Blandina reenters, proving herself the ultimate virtuoso of torture. Her witness dissolves into a purely nonverbal utterance, which may be read not only as the noble refusal to speak the torturer's truth (and thus to accept her own humiliation) but also as the tortured slave's insistence on speaking the Christian truth through the shamed body. "Duplicating in her own body all her children's sufferings," Blandina finally dies, a distinctly maternal (as well as transiently bridal [5.1.35]) figure of christological recapitulation. As the text notes, "the pagans themselves admitted that no woman had ever suffered so much in their experience" (5.1.55–57).

It is Blandina, then, not Vettius Epagathus, who claims the center stage in this spectacle of shame's transformation, suffering most and dying last, in a final displacement mediated by the intervention of the free man Alexander, who explicitly appropriates the personae of both the birthing woman and the publicly tortured slave. In Blandina, truth proves best articulated not through the speech of the honorable man but through the silent confession of the coerced female slave: torture is converted into the pangs of labor through which the truth of Christian identity is born. Blandina is not simply made "noble": her power resides in her bottomless capacity for shame as both a woman and a slave. Her witness is the mute speech of a body that has become a queerly open text, awaiting a cycle of reappropriations by subsequent readers invited to identify with the Christ figure made accessible in the flesh of a female slave.

Perpetua: What's in a Name?

When the young Carthaginian Perpetua—no slave but a respectable matron—is arrested as a Christian, it is her father who initially tests her by his vigorous attempts to convince her to deny her faith. Perpetua records their initial dialogue. " 'Father,' I said, 'do you see, for example, this vessel lying here, (and is it) a little pitcher or something else?' And he said, 'I see (it).' And I said to him, 'Can it be called by any other name than what it is?' And he said, 'No.' 'So too I cannot declare myself anything else but what I am, a Christian' " (*Passion of Perpetua* 3). Perpetua's simple comparison, introduced "for the sake of discussion (*causa verbi*)" and punctuated by her father's minimalist affirmations (*video, non*), wobbles intriguingly. If the identity of the pitcher is secure, this is because it is "seen" ("do you see?" "I see"), and indeed one can easily imagine that it might be "called" by more than one name: Perpetua herself, afterall, refers to it as both "vessel (*vas*)" and "little pitcher (*urceolum*)." In subtle contrast, the name of a Christian is fixed (she cannot and *will* not be called anything else!), whereas its significance remains open to interpretation: it remains to be *seen*. The remarkable literary text known as the *Passion of Perpetua*, a third-person, purportedly eyewitness account of Christian martyrdom in which are enfolded two first-person narratives, layers the name *Christiana* with a series of performative interpretations that sometimes collude and sometimes contest one another unsettlingly. At the center of this complexly polyglossal text is the spectacle of a young woman's repeatedly exposed body.

The first exposure is a modest one and not *overtly* either shaming or shameless. Describing her days in prison, Perpetua matter-of-factly reveals her milk-laden breasts.[39] Initially suffering not only physical discomfort but anxiety on behalf of her son, she rejoices when the child is brought to her in prison: "I nursed my infant, now enfeebled with hunger," and "the dungeon became to me as it were a palace" (3).

Subsequently Perpetua is granted a vision in the form of a dream, the first of three that she will record in her diary. "I saw a golden ladder of marvelous height . . . and very narrow . . . ; and on the sides of the ladder was fixed every kind of iron weapon. There were there swords, lances, hooks, daggers; so that if any one went up carelessly, or not looking upwards, he would be torn to pieces and his flesh would cleave to the iron weapons." At least one character in this vision appears to have wandered in from the pages of John's Apocalypse: "And under the ladder itself was crouching a dragon of wonderful size, who lay in wait for those who ascended, and frightened them from the ascent." Perpetua's fellow prisoner Saturus is the first to climb the ladder; having reached the top, he turns to her with words of encouragement and caution. She apparently needs neither: "And I said, 'In the name of the Lord Jesus Christ, he [the dragon] shall not hurt me.'" Nor does he, as this New Eve neatly turns the table on woman's ancient foe in a decisive triumph also granted Blandina but denied (or deferred) in the case of the winged woman of the Apocalypse: "And from under the ladder itself, as if in fear of me, he slowly lifted up his head; and as I trod upon the first step, I trod upon his head." Here Perpetua—like Blandina, Eve's "seed" (Gen. 3:15), if not the son we might have expected—becomes through her own vision an explicitly christological figure.

At the top of the ladder Perpetua discovers a garden, "and in the midst of the garden a white-haired man sitting in the dress of a shepherd, of a large stature, milking sheep; and standing around were many thousand white-robed ones"—perhaps played by the same extras who filled similar roles in the Apocalypse. Welcoming Perpetua, the man gives her a little cake of cheese, as the densely intertextual dream metamorphizes the figure of a breast-feeding mother into that of a venerable shepherd, and Perpetua is identified not as the feeder but as the one fed. "I received it with folded hands; and I ate it, and all who stood around said Amen. And at the sound of their voices I was awakened, still tasting a sweetness which I cannot describe" (4). This milky feast celebrated at the threshold of Paradise seems to constitute a first eucharist for the newly baptized woman. It also supplies her with a heavenly "father" at once benevolent and dignified. In contrast, her earthly father (who is also her spiritual adversary) is publicly humiliated in a scene beheld by her waking eyes shortly following her public confession of Christian identity before the magistrate: "And as my father stood there to cast me down from the faith, he was ordered by Hilarianus to be cast down, and was beaten with rods" (6). Later, her father will again humiliate himself before Perpetua, throwing himself on the ground and tearing at his beard (9): her consistently compassionate response renders him not merely her adversary but also a poignantly failed martyr, destroyed rather than saved by his shame.

Perpetua's breasts yield one more vision, in which a thirsty child (her deceased younger brother) is given water to drink (7–8), but not before her own child—now withheld by her father—has been miraculously weaned: "And even as God willed it, the child no long desired my breasts, nor did they cause me discomfort, so that I was not tortured by concern for my infant or by pain in my breasts" (6). It is, however, Perpetua's third and final dream that claims our attention, even as it brings Perpetua into the arena.

In this scene, where Perpetua is finally fully exposed to the gaze of spectators (both those in the dream and those who read the text), her breasts—indeed her very femininity—are artfully concealed. "Then there came forth against me a certain Egyptian, horrible in appearance, with his assistants, to fight with me. And there came to me, as my assistants and supporters, handsome youths; and I was stripped and became a man (*et expoliata sum, et facta sum masculus*). And my supporters started to rub me down with oil, as one does for a combat." Much has been made, for good reason, of Perpetua's gender-bending in this dream,[40] but we should also pause to take note of the visual impact of the scene. Perpetua might have simply represented herself as a man from the start of the dream. Instead, she *shows* us the moment of her transformation. We watch with bated breath as a woman is shamefully, shamingly stripped of her clothes, but immediately our gaze is confounded, less by what we don't see than by what we do see, namely a "masculine" body. This moment of visual confusion may linger, as we are invited to watch that body being rubbed down with oil by handsome youths. Soon, however, the excitement of the contest takes over. The action takes place between Perpetua's feet and the Egyptian's head, in a replay of her first dream, where she treads on the head of the serpent. As the Egyptian fighter grabs at her feet, she kicks his face, and continues to do so as she is lifted into the air. Finally, she succeeds in getting a lock on his head with her intertwined hands and hurls him to the ground: "He fell on his face and I stamped on his head."

Following the details of the fight, we may forget to wonder what we *see* when we look at Perpetua's body—a question perhaps easier to evade for a modern reader whose eyes are preoccupied with the text than for an ancient "reader" more likely to have heard the text read aloud, leaving the eyes of the imagination free to wander. As Augustine remarks, with respect to the liturgical reading of this text: "all those things, recounted in such glowing words, we perceived with our ears, and actually saw with our minds" (Sermon 280.1).[41] The body thus seen is a masculinized body, as we have been told, but it is also still Perpetua's body, as the unabashedly direct style of the first-person narrative (together with the echoes of her prior dream) will not allow us to forget. Moreover, as soon as her triumph in the arena is complete, Perpetua's femininity resurfaces when the official (evoking memories of the good shepherd who has given her cheese) offers her a "green branch with golden apples," kisses her, and calls her "daughter" (10).[42] Perpetua's final dream, with which her prison diary concludes, thus performs her Christian "identity"as a complex *subversion* of identity, raising the question of *who* this "daughter" *is*—insisting on the question, rather than offering an easy answer. The complexity and openness of identity is conveyed through the performative ambivalence of her gender, yet only on the stage of shame does that gender becomes visible. Expecting to see a female body humiliated by its exposure to the public eye, we see instead the shameless display of the oiled body of a male athlete. Or, rather, we see both. We see that both are somehow the same and also not the same. In the process, the spectating eye is itself challenged and transformed, trained to see the shamelessness inhering in shame and the shame inhering in shamelessness—or, in Sedgwick's terms, the "powerfully productive and powerfully social metamorphic possibilities" of shame.[43]

Perpetua does not, however, have the final word in this textual performance of her passion. If her last dreamed vision repeats and replays her first, it will in turn be echoed by the narrator's account of her waking arena performance. Yet here, as a different eye guides our own seeing, the narrative echoes betray as much dissonance as resonance. When a twin figure, the slave Felicitas, is introduced, gender itself becomes both a more dominant and a less fluidly constituted trope while femaleness and slavery are realigned, as in the *Letter of the Marytrs of Vienne and Lyons*, in such a way as to return shame to the woman. Felicitas is pregnant and through divine intervention is enabled to deliver her child prematurely so that she will be allowed to join her companions in martyrdom. Unlike Perpetua, the slave woman bears a daughter, and this final section of the *Passion* becomes almost parodic in its exaggerated—and rather explicitly eroticized—strategies of feminization. The self-dreamed Perpetua is made male in order to meet an intensely masculinized adversary, but in the realm of the insistently "literal," the doubled female figures of Perpetua and Felicitas face a "mad heifer," an adversary that the narrator assures us "was an unusual animal," "chosen that their sex might be matched with that of the beast" (20.1). Stripped and enmeshed in nets, the bodies of the martyrs remain resolutely female, the one—Perpetua—notably fragile and the other—Felicitas— dripping with milk, their vulnerability arousing a horrified excitement in the spectators (20.2). In a teasing performance, the women are reclothed, only to have Perpetua's body again exposed in her first tussle with the cow. Perpetua's performance recalls Polycarp's modest witness—his witness of modesty—as she re-covers her thighs and re-pins her disheveled hair (20.3–5). Undefeated and therefore by the logic of martyrdom not yet victorious in relation to the female beast, Perpetua and Felicitas subsequently die by the sword. Indeed, Perpetua has to direct the faltering, misguided weapon of the gladiator to her own throat. Judith Perkins reads this gesture as a sign that "the 'unruly woman' is in control until the end."[44] Barton sees in it "the gladiator's gesture of baring the throat."[45] One might also note that the throat is the site, as Nicole Loraux has argued, where the demands of classical tragedy dictate a woman must meet her peculiarly female death.[46] Despite the narrator's chastising reinscription of the woman's shame (a shame only dubiously transformed by her vaunted modesty), Perpetua's recounted death still opens a multi-faceted window through which to observe a performance of identity that exploits the ambivalence of the martyr's gender and thus also both draws on and challenges the distinct femininity of her shame. If martyrdom is "linked explicitly with masculinity" as Castelli (among others) points out, masculine identity is itself rendered queerly malleable and unstable by its explicit linking with the suffering endurance of women.[47]

Interlude: Surviving the Arena

Perpetua's dream of her fight with the Egyptian in the arena ends not with her death but with her release: "I began to go gloriously toward the Sanavivarian gate"—the gate of health ("salvation") and life (10). Intriguingly, a roughly contemporaneous stele preserving the images of two female gladiators, labeled Amazonia and Achillia respectively, includes the caption "they were set free."[48] Manumission of arena performers as the reward for an unusually impressive performance was rare but not unheard of in Roman antiquity. In a Christian context, the possibility of liberation resulting from triumph in the arena could be put to the service of theological affirmation, conveying the promise of release into the eternal life of the resurrected saints, whose deaths were celebrated as birthdays and who were not infrequently, as we have seen, represented as giving birth through their suffering to their identity in Christ. In fact, for Christians, the failure to achieve a spectacular death was likely to represent a thwarting of hopes for liberation.

Perpetua's prophetic dream of release was, after all, fulfilled—as she knew it would be—by her death in the arena.

Yet this was not always so. Many who confessed their faith survived public torture to go on to become authoritative figures in the Christian community—frequently to the irritation of the bishops who had to compete for power with these revered witnesses. Clement of Alexandria, for one, felt that true witness consisted at least as much in the life lived as in the death died (*Miscellanies* 4.4). Sometimes, though not often, the story of a survivor was even worth telling. Sometimes an arena performance was so spectacular that the failure of the performer to die hardly mattered. Such is the case with the "martyrdom" of Thecla, a legendary first-century heroine whose adventures are recounted in the late second-century *Acts of Thecla*. In the story of Thecla, the shameful exposure of a female body, conveying threats of sexual aggression, is even more vividly depicted than in the *Passion of Perpetua*, and the woman's shamelessness, moreover, endures beyond the arena.

According to the *Acts*, the trouble begins when the apostle Paul arrives in Thecla's hometown of Iconium, preaching "the word of God concerning continence and the resurrection" (5). As Thecla listens to Paul's preaching through a window of her home, her virginal chastity is already threatened by her impending shamelessness, as her mother recognizes when she questions "how a maiden of such modesty" can be so strongly affected by the words of a strange man (8). Thecla's fiancé Thamyris swiftly joins forces with her mother, attempting to call the young woman to her senses: "Turn to your Thamyris and be ashamed!" he urges (10). Thecla ignores them both. Indeed, by the time Paul has been arrested and imprisoned for corrupting the wives, and prospective wives, of the Iconian men (15), Thecla appears to have shed her modesty like an unwanted garment. Sneaking out of the house in the middle of the night, she bribes Paul's guard, giving him a silver mirror (18)—a symbol, we might imagine, of the internalized gaze that she now effectively renounces. She shamelessly kisses Paul's chains, the sign of his own humiliation, now also hers. When morning dawns, she is scandalously exposed in Paul's prison cell, "so to speak, bound with him in affection" (19). At this point, even her mother calls for Thecla's death: "Burn the lawless one! Burn her that is no bride in the midst of the theater, that all the women who have been taught by this man may be afraid!" (20). Mounting the pyre, Thecla is no more touched by the flames or destroyed by her shame than is Polycarp. In her case, moreover, a miraculous rain quenches the fire and saves her life (22).

Surprisingly, when Thecla subsequently rejoins Paul, who has been banished from the town, he expresses doubts about the strength of her Christian conviction. Like Perpetua, Thecla imagines herself a virtual man: "I will cut my hair short and follow you wherever you go." In Paul's eyes, however, she remains a beautiful woman, likely to be tested again and likely also to demonstrate unmanly weakness in the face of such testing. For this reason, he refuses to baptize her just yet (25). Thecla, in Paul's view, is still the captive of her feminine vulnerability to shame.

Shame, as it turns out, is a test that Thecla will pass with flying colors. Baptism too is a prize she will seize shamelessly with or without Paul's co-operation. When the two travelers enter the town of Antioch, Alexander, one of its most notable citizens, is overcome with desire for Thecla, whom he mistakes as a sexually loose woman and thus literally up for grabs: he "embraced her on the open street." Thecla shames shame, loudly protesting Alexander's public assault on her dignity as well as her body. "And taking hold of Alexander she ripped his cloak, took off the crown from his head, and made him a laughing-stock" (26). Impelled to vengeance by both his thwarted desire and his "shame at what had befallen him," Alexander accuses Thecla before the governor, who condemns her to the beasts (27). In this rather explicit contest of mutual shaming, the women of Antioch—in marked contrast with the women of Iconium—take up Thecla's cause: with a slight shift of context, Thecla, who initially seemed a threat to female modesty, now embodies a female modesty threatened by shame. Thecla is stripped and led into the arena. There, a lioness dies protecting her from the attack of a male lion, in a rather obvious redramatization of Thecla's resisting of Alexander's sexual assault (we are even told that the beasts "belonged to Alexander") (33), while female spectators evidently well schooled in the arts of taming male passion hurl perfumes into the arena to lull the ferocious beasts, so that "they did not touch her" (35). In between these two episodes, Thecla baptizes herself in a pool of apparently dangerous seals, who are immediately struck dead by lightening, even as the freshly baptized Thecla is given new clothes: "there was about her a cloud of fire, so that neither could the beasts touch her nor could she be seen naked" (34). Later, when the governor declares that Thecla be set free, we are again reminded of her nakedness as well as her divine garb. The governor has her clothes brought and orders her to don them; she does so, but not before declaring defiantly, "He who clothed me when I was naked among the beasts shall clothe me with salvation in the day of judgment" (38). Both shamed and unashamed—splendidly shameless—Thecla, who has been granted a heavenly wardrobe, scarcely requires the modest covering of female attire. In fact, shortly after exiting the arena, she performs an explicit act of self-refashioning, modifying her cloak to conform to a more manly style (40). Like Perpetua's transgendering, Thecla's transvestitism marks her as both woman and man: shamed like a woman (shamed *as* a woman) through her bodily exposure and vulnerability to sexual assault, she is now able to display shamelessly the perverse virility of a woman "who is no bride."

The Desert a Theater

When Constantine put an end to the persecution of Christians, the arena shut its gates on the performances of martyrs—though heretics might still have their chance to enjoy the ambivalent glory resulting from political suppression or even, on rare occasion, the spectacle of a public execution. The tales of martyrdom were, however, scarcely silenced, and the post-Constantinian era gave rise in particular to highly eroticized stories of girl martyrs,[49] even as the emergent cult of saints likewise enshrined—and rendered once again "present"—the martyred heroes and heroines of a bygone age. At the same time, some Christians began a drift toward the wilderness, discovering that the desert (as the author of the Apocalypse already knew) might be transformed into a stage for ongoing live performances of shameless witness.

As a number of scholars have pointed out, ascetic practice is inherently performative.[50] Indeed, asceticism, like martyrdom, seems to require a spectator—somewhat paradoxically, given the movement of withdrawal that is also inherent to the practice. Who sees in the wilderness, one might well ask. How is the desert transformed not only into a monastic "city" (as Athanasius famously claimed it was), but also into a theater that might be observed even by spectators who are not part of that city? Georgia Frank has highlighted the crucial significance of the exposing eyes of the ancient pilgrims who traveled to see not merely holy places but also holy people—or, alternately, of the armchair travelers who followed the pilgrims' progress by perusing their literary traces.[51] The rise of asceticism was accompanied by the explosion of a distinctly voyeuristic literature encompassing travelogues and collections of mini-biographies as well as hagiographical monographs, all of which enabled readers to view holy men and women in exotically remote locations like Egypt or Syria without having to undergo the rigor or expense of an actual journey to the wilderness. As with martyrology, the literature of asceticism allowed for the staging and restaging of spectacles before the eyes of the imagination.

Shame colors and excites such literary performances in a number of ways. So obvious as to be easily overlooked is the transgressiveness of the ascetic performances themselves: were the holy men and women of the wilderness not dramatically flouting social convention, and thus also tempting shame by acting shamelessly, there would have been little worth seeing. As with martyrdom, the glory achieved in asceticism is typically routed through shame, and the success of a performance of shamelessness is never assured: not all shame is transformed or transformative, and there are failed ascetics as well as failed martyrs. (I will have more to say in Chapter 3 about the positive *courting* of shame and failure that is vital to the pursuit of humility in ascetic discipline.) In addition to the shame attending ascetic performance itself, there is something shameful in the very viewing of such a spectacle, exceeding even the embarrassment that always attends the witness of another's shame. To gaze upon an ascetic is to look at something that should not be seen, to invade the privacy and violate the modesty so elaborately cultivated by the holy man or woman. Writers and readers of ascetic literature, like the persistent pilgrims crying out at the doorway or peering into the chinks of an ascetic's cell, are thus positioned as so many "peeping Toms," and the writers of travelogues and hagiographies not only frequently betray awareness of the ocular transgression inherent to their literary endeavors but also sometimes seem to exult in the very shamelessness of these acts of exposure.

The affinities of ascetic and martyrial literatures are not exhausted by the shared aspects of ocularity, performativity, and shame. Of special relevance here is the way in which ascetics, like martyrs, are represented as combatants in the spectacles of the arena. Sometimes the "beasts" with which they contend are wild animals that inhabit the desert. Occasionally those animals, like Thecla's lionness, are rendered improbably docile in the face of the holy person's power. More often, however, these beasts are demonic adversaries. Not infrequently, it is difficult to tell the difference between a "real" animal and a demonic apparition. The demons may also take the shape of armed fighters. What is crucial, however, is the element of agonistic spectacle. As David Brakke puts it, "demonic appearances, whether in experience or in literary description, . . . made visible a normally invisible combat; monks or their admirers could see what took place in the mind or soul."[52]

The *Life of Antony*, apparently innovative and unquestionably influential, remains paradigmatic in its representation of ascetic combat with demons. The hagiographical text maps a holy man's journey from his native village ever deeper into the Egyptian desert. It also plots the intensification of his fights with demons: as his training in the discipline advances, Antony, like a skilled gladiator, is pitted against ever more formidable opponents. Initially, the demons attack the youthful Antony, as they attack so many adolescents, with thoughts of sexual desire; Antony laudably blushes, while strengthening himself with prayer and fasting. This encounter, seemingly interior, is described as a visible contest: "even the onlookers saw the struggle which was going on between them." The devil is humiliated by his inability to sway Antony: "all this was a source of shame for his foe" (5). When a slightly more mature Antony subsequently shuts himself inside a tomb at some distance from his village, demonic attacks increase in ferocity as well as sheer physicality. A friend who delivers bread finds that Antony has been beaten senseless by the whips of the demons. He carries Antony's corpselike body to the village, but when Antony recovers consciousness he demands to be carried back to the tomb (8). Now the demons shift their game. The contest is not with armed fighters but with beasts. "And the place was suddenly filled with the forms of lions, bears, leopards, bulls, serpents, asps, scorpions, and wolves." Despite the enclosure of the tomb, the reader of the *Life* can "see" the spectacle of Antony's fight with the beasts. More plausibly perhaps, from the vantage point of one outside the tomb, the reader can also *hear* them: "altogether the noises of the apparitions, with their angry ragings, were dreadful." Antony, once again, is wracked with bodily pain but unbroken in spirit as he verbally mocks the demons (9).

Emerging from the tomb, Antony travels farther into the desert, where he walls himself up in an abandoned fort that is "full of creeping things"; however, "the reptiles, as though someone were chasing them, immediately left the place" (12). Antony remains hidden from the sight of the visitors who pursue him, but they are alarmed to hear the clamor of combat inside the fort. Thinking that "there were some men fighting with him," they finally peer through a hole in the wall of the fort and perceive that the combatants are demons. As they cry out in fear, Antony hears them and offers words of reassurance before sending them on their way (13). Antony, meanwhile, gets stronger and stronger. When, after twenty years in the fort, he finally emerges to view (for his friends, having grown impatient, tear down the door), he is not emaciated by fasting or soft from lack of exercise, "but he was just the same as they had known him before his withdrawal" (14). By the time Antony reaches his final dwelling place on a mountain in the inner desert, the fights with gladiators and beasts—the latter both "real" and demonic—have become practically routine. "There then he passed his life and endured such great wrestlings." Visitors hear the clamor of voices and the clash of arms and see the mountain at night "become full of wild beasts and him also fighting as though against visible beings" (51).

As Brakke remarks, the figure of the monk as combatant appears distinctly—even stridently—masculine, as if defending against the threat of gender ambiguity introduced with the male ascetic's abdication of the traditional social roles of familial patriarch or civic leader. The masculinist cast of monastic combat comes out even more strongly in a militant text like the Life of Martin, the soldier monk of Gaul.[53] Indeed, the element of combat pervades the very writing of male hagiographies, each of which competes with its precursors to display the superior power of its saint. Yet, as Brakke also observes, ascetic women could be represented as combatants too and might even be privileged figures of combat, as we have seen in earlier accounts of martyrs. "One of the virtues of female monks was that they could make dramatically visible the masculinization that demonic combat and ascetic struggle produced in the monk in a way that male monks could not: they started out as female and could be 'made male.'" In addition, the spectacle of women's struggle brought home the vulnerability of the ascetic: many ancient texts construct the female body as "an interior space that the demonic had invaded and made its home," as Brakke notes.[54] Yet if every ascetic could hope to be "made male," every ascetic also faced the inevitable—and peculiarly "feminine"—shame of temptation's invasion. Gender bends and reverses itself repeatedly in the struggle for virtue. We should not miss what the combat imagery partly, but only partly, covers up: for the ascetic, there is no battle without temptation, no temptation without some degree of succumbing, and no succumbing to temptation, however fleeting, without a blush of shame. The contest itself involves a shameless confrontation with shame, and victory is achieved less by dominating than by learning to submit. The ascetic is not so much a warrior on the battlefield as a captive in the arena of his own psyche: there shame is unavoidable but also transformable.

No surprise, perhaps, that the shame that haunts the spectacle of ascetic performance surfaces most clearly in the relatively rare—but potent—representations of women visibly combating demons. It is almost palpably embarrassing, for example, to read of Amma Sarah, one of the very few ascetic women of antiquity actually credited with sexual desire, that "for thirteen years she waged war with the demon of fornication." A pornographic spectacle indeed! Shamelessly, "she never prayed that the warfare should cease" (*Alphabetical Sayings*, Sarah 1). We read subsequently that two venerable old men of the desert plot together, saying "Let us humiliate this old woman." Their visit is not merely a test but a set-up: by coming to see her, they intend to expose her pride in receiving visitors. "So they said to her, 'Be careful not to become conceited thinking to yourself: "Look how anchorites are coming to see me, a mere woman."'" Sarah's answer is cleverly indirect: "According to nature I am a woman, but not according to my thoughts."

As a woman (she does not deny it), she is particularly vulnerable to humiliation on account of her pride, a mark of temptation especially contemptible in a female already humbled by her very sex. The shame of "nature," however, only strengthens "thoughts" honed in combat, as she also suggests. In the meantime, if Sarah refuses to take pride in the visit of two such shamefully mean-spirited monks, she does not seem to have renounced confidence in her own ascetic discipline: her shameless self-certainty shames their shaming. Amma Sarah is reported to have said to other "brothers" (or was it the same two?): "It is I who am a man, you who are women" (9). This assertion perhaps goes beyond the conventional goading of men into more honorable behavior by implying that what a mere woman can do, they should be able to do even better. Just as Blandina was a better martyr than Vettius Epagathus, not despite her status but precisely because she was both a slave and a woman, so too Sarah may be a better ascetic *because* she is a woman, naturally susceptible to the shame of temptation and thus also naturally capable of shameless defiance. She is, in other words, among those "whose sense of identity is for some reason tuned most durably to the note of shame." Another of the sayings attributed to Amma Sarah is as follows: "If I prayed God that all men should approve of my conduct, I should find myself a penitent at the door of each one" (5).

Postlude: Peformance Art in the City

Not every ascetic made the journey from the town to the desert. The seventh-century *Life of Symeon the Fool* tells the story of one sixth-century monk who reversed the trend: after having lived for nearly thirty years in the Syrian desert, Symeon left the desert for the town in order to perfect his ascetic discipline. His entry into Emesa could scarcely have been more dramatic or bizarre: dragging a dead dog on a rope to the accompaniment of children's chants ("Hey, a crazy abba!"), Symeon effectively initiated his career as an urban fool—in current parlance, a performance artist—while also punningly signaling his affinities with prior countercultural traditions of "doglike," or Cynic, shamelessness (*Life of Symeon* 145). As Derek Krueger has shown, implicit references to the legendary Cynic founder Diogenes of Sinope proliferate in the *Life*, including depictions of Symeon defecating in public, eating copious quantities of beans, consuming raw meat, and generally pestering and scandalizing the good citizens of Emesa with his deliberately offensive—indeed, apparently insane—acts.[55] Queer antics for a Christian saint, indeed!

However, as Krueger also shows, Leontius of Cypriot Neopolis, the author of the *Life*, persistently balances his descriptions of Symeon's outrageous conduct with apologetic protestations that the holy man's motivations were utterly pure, his folly sheerly strategic. Krueger sums up Leontius's message: "By pretending to be crazy, Symeon converts heretics, Jews, fornicators, prostitutes, and other sinners; and by this method he is also able to keep his holiness concealed."[56] In keeping with other traditional uses of the motif of "concealed sanctity," Symeon's abominable behavior is, according to his hagiographer, but a mask for his interior holiness, already established in his long years of desert asceticism. Leontius is, in effect, not celebrating his hero's seeming transgressiveness but "outing" his actual virtue. "Symeon is a saint," notes Krueger, "not because of his shamelessness, but rather in spite of it."[57] In this he differs from prior Cynic cultural critics like Diogenes, for whom shamelessness would appear to be precisely the point.

Krueger has skillfully uncovered both the logic of Leontius's apologetics and the lure of the hagiographical payoff that justifies the risk of introducing such a seductively naughty saint. Nonetheless, we may still find ourselves asking whether Leontius has entirely succeeded in explaining away Symeon's shameful behavior. Has something of the Cynic's shamelessness not, after all, been smuggled onto the "prohibitive airwaves" that constrain even late ancient hagiography? If so, perhaps Leontius has "outed" not only Symeon's sanctity but also the cultural-political critique conveyed, to varying degrees, by all ascetic performances.[58] Like Diogenes, Symeon "paid no attention to what might be judged disgraceful conduct either by human convention or by nature," as Leontius puts it (148). Squatting in the marketplace to defecate, stealing and gorging himself on beans, running naked into a women's bathhouse, and flirting outrageously with prostitutes as well as respectable matrons are, moreover, acts that significantly exceed what might be required to conceal holiness while at the same time demonstrating little *direct* utility for the saving of lost souls. The same might be said of the following Leontian list: "For sometimes he pretended to have a limp, sometimes he jumped around, sometimes he dragged himself along on his buttocks, sometimes he stuck out his foot for someone running and tripped him" (155). If pointless as measured by the standards introduced by Leontius, such performances do, nonetheless, make us laugh. We laugh at Symeon, but more importantly we laugh with him. For Symeon's queer shamelessness, has, to our readerly delight, shamed the shamers by exposing the arbitrary tyranny of *every* naturalized social convention. Symeon, for his part, throws in his lot with those who bear the heaviest burden of shame: Christ's place, he knows, "is among the beggars, especially among the blind, people made as pure as sun through their patience and distress" (167).

Ironically, perhaps, in our own day "cynicism" has come to be associated with a defensive "attempt to avoid a painful feeling of vulnerability to rejection and to shame," as psychotherapist Michael J. Bader phrases it.[59] If the self-protective (and deeply self-critical) scorn of the modern cynic exposes any form of idealism to shame, the deliberately defiant behavior of the ancient Cynic similarly shames all conventional values and authorities. The crucial difference perhaps lies in the ancient Cynic's cultivation of shamelessness as a means to transform shame rather than simply internalize or deny it. Yet a question remains regarding the social or political efficacy of such acts of shamelessness, a question that may press more urgently still when we are dealing not with the acts themselves but with their subsequent narration. As Krueger observes in another context, "Telling about defecation in public is not the same as defecating in public."[60] Stories of Cynic shamelessness mobilized humor to dissipate social tension in the late Roman empire "by giving those who shared the stories and the system an opportunity to achieve critical distance and to laugh." Nonetheless, Krueger argues, even the unmitigated bawdiness of the tales of Diogenes "bolstered a largely conservative agenda": "Cynic tales did not propose an alternative structure for society; instead their critical perspective recast the status quo."[61] Does such "recasting" not, however, open the imagination to the possibility of alternatives? Indeed, Symeon the Cynic saint arguably avoids both the naivete and the idealism implicated in a proposal for reform while modeling precisely the "ridiculous childlike vulnerability" that Bader calls for as an antidote to the depressive political paralysis induced by contemporary cultures of cynicism.[62]

Conclusions

The very term "identity politics" highlights the fact that identity only becomes visible when put into question—in Sedgwick's terms, when raised *as* a question—in the public eye of the political arena. This is why it appears that only some people have an identity—on the surface an absurd, even suspect, notion. The performative politics of identity are inseparable from the complex dynamic of shaming, in which shame rebounds on the shamers, even as those shamed both shamelessly *accept* their shame and transform it into *something else*. But what? Not honor exactly: for where the forces of shaming are powerful enough, honor may be rendered not merely elusive but positively undesirable; in other words, where shamelessness shames shame, it also shames honor.

If it is not honor that is retrieved through shamelessness, perhaps it is pride. While anthropologists typically speak of honor-shame cultures, affect psychologists refer to a shame-pride axis.[63] Frequently understood as the emotional antidote to shame or stigmatization, pride is explicitly thematized within our own culture in festively ritualized demonstrations of shamelessly asserted identity such as the Gay Pride parades celebrated in many urban centers. More discreet, even secret, gatherings of shamed communities convey little expectation, perhaps also little wish, of achieving honor, but have much to offer in the thrill of defiantly claimed pride that reverberates like a private transcript audible, for those with ears to hear, even on the seemingly repressive stages of public performance. Yet pride can also harden identity into a rigid essentialism, just as defiance can reveal itself to be no more than an inversionary strategy for turning the tables in the competition for honor. *Dignity* might therefore better name the effects of a performative claiming of worthiness that converts shame to shamelessness while refusing the temptation of triumphalism.[64]

What was at stake for the martyrs and those ascetics who transposed the martyrs' shameless acts into the cultural key of a later antiquity, as well as the many others who witnessed these varied performances with excitement and pleasure? Identity and dignity forged within and through shame—and also a transformed sense of community. This is perhaps most evident in our ancient texts in the challenge to the patriarchal family and civic mores as well as to the politics of empire (or even of an imperial Christianity), frequently—though by no means inevitably—resulting in rather dramatic destabilizations of gender roles as well as class status. However, what such assertions of identity meant, and what they might still mean, was and remains open and unpredictable—ever "to-be-constituted." Perhaps that *is* the point: at its most productive, the performance of a shamed and shameless identity opens up hitherto closed spaces, challenges prevailing assumptions, and thereby creates new social and political possibilities. Arguably those possibilities are less thoroughly constrained by triumphalism and vindictiveness—less sheerly inversionary in their fantasies—than they are often interpreted to be. Shame does indeed fuel vengeful anger but it also breeds compassion. Shame constitutes a space of painful differentiation— even the very site of individuation—but also of deep commonality. For ancient martyrs and ascetics, their shamed shamers were "adversaries" (like Babylon) but they were also, lamentably, failed witnesses, unable (quite) to effect the spectacular transformation of their shame into . . . *something else.*

Chapter 2
An Embarrassment of Flesh

The time of abjection is double: a time of oblivion and thunder, of veiled infinity and the moment when revelation bursts forth. Jouissance, in short. . . . Jouissance alone causes the abject to exist as such. One does not know it, one does not desire it, one joys in it. Violently and painfully. A passion.

—Julia Kristeva, "Approaching Abjection"

And being found in human form, he humiliated himself (etapeinōsen heauton), *becoming submissive to the point of death, even death on a cross.*

—Philippians 2.7–8

"Why, then," they ask, "did the divine stoop to such humiliation (pros tēn tapeinotēta tautēn)?*" Our faith falters when we think that God, the infinite, incomprehensible, ineffable reality, transcending all glory and majesty, should be defiled by associating with human nature, and his sublime powers no less debased by their contact with what is abject. . . . "What death," they urge, "could be more shameful than that on a cross?"*

—Gregory of Nyssa, Catechetical Oration 14, 32

One spectacle of shame remains yet to be disclosed—the shameful spectacle of Jesus' death on a cross. Unlike death in the gladiatorial or martyrial arena, execution by crucifixion offered little possibility for glorious transformation: arguably, even the canonical gospels fail to make a triumphant spectacle of the cross. Mark's Jesus, executed along with two bandits and mocked mercilessly by his spectators, does not, after all, defiantly proclaim his divine identity but instead poignantly pronounces his God-forsaken abjection (15.34). The earliest narratives of crucifixion seem already to require the supplemental account of resurrection to secure Jesus' undying glory in the face of his inglorious death. But they cannot quite efface the taint of shame that clings to the pierced and bleeding flesh of the Lord. They cannot *quite* erase the disturbing presence of the shrouded (unseen) corpse.

Indeed, the ancient christological hymn cited by the apostle Paul seems to exult in Christ's humiliation. Christians of later antiquity remained well aware of the shamefulness of death on the cross, as the citation from a catechetical treatise written by the fourth-century theologian Gregory of Nyssa demonstrates. Yet the same source also reminds us that the early Christians were even more preoccupied by a prior, encompassing shame, the shame of incarnation itself. That God should be *crucified* was a shocking proposition that nested within a proposition more shocking still—that God should be *born* and thus "defiled" and "debased" by subjection to the frailty of mortal flesh. To be born was, after all, already to begin to die. From the perspective of incarnational christology, flesh was, then, itself a source *of* shame while also representing that which could be marked *by* shame—*stigmatized*, in fact. Paul boasts shamelessly: "I bear the stigmata of Jesus on my body!" (Gal. 6.17). Ancient theologians frequently, and notoriously, tried to cleanse Christ of the embarrassing effects of so much messy contact with carnality—birth, death, and all the passionate travails that lay in between. Equally frequently, however, they positively rejoiced in the scandal of divine incarnation, thrilling at the shame of a flesh that was always already dying and also always already becoming divine.

But why should flesh be distinctly vulnerable to shame and even itself a cause of shame? Why, furthermore, should that shame be so thrilling to either ancient theologians or their current readers? Shame is an affect closely linked with sensation, and this in itself binds it tightly to the flesh. Psychologist Helen Block Lewis remarks on the unusual intensity and breadth of shame's sensory register, noting that shame "seems to rest on an increase in feedback from *all* perceptual modalities" and observing that it "usually involves greater body awareness than guilt."[1] Shame plays across our senses, then; indeed, it is largely an effect of heightened *sensitivity*. Furthermore, among the senses that both excite and are excited by shame, touch may be at least as significant as sight. We carry shame, after all, not only in our downcast eyes but also on our burning skin. If it seems to come from somewhere deep inside us, it registers most vividly on the exposed surfaces of our flesh. Shame arrives *as a feeling*—the hot spread of a blush, the damp seepage of sweat. It also *attends feeling*, hovering protectively over the contact zones that open us to the ambivalence of irresistable self-fragmentation and uncontrollable connectivity: for if to be touched is always to be touched in a part it is also to be joined, however fleetingly, to an other.[2]

It is also in shame that flesh is conceived as the passionate site of pleasure inseparably wedded to pain, joy bound up with its own thwarting. As Silvan Tomkins remarks, we frequently feel shame when our physical wants are not satisfied. I would add that we also frequently feel shame when they *are*: what is perhaps crucial to shame is the very exposure of our fleshly wanting, of the immensity of human need. Moreover, continues Tomkins, the body itself becomes a source of shame when its physical capacities fail to match our appetite for joy or excitement.[3] "Old age is the prime occasion of shame . . . because there is both a heightening of the zest for life and a heightening of all the impediments to the enjoyment of life to which the aging body is vulnerable."[4] Birthing, childhood, illness, and torture are other "prime occasions." In shame we become aware of our limits—the limits of mortal flesh itself. We encounter our own transience and finitude, our innate corruptibility. We encounter, then, also a lack of limits, an excess of materiality, a propensity for debasement, a slide into dissolution—a monstrosity of *abjection*, in short.

Julia Kristeva's psychoanalytic concept of abjection cannot simply be mapped directly onto the concepts of either shame or flesh. It does however take us considerably farther in understanding the particular relation of shame to flesh. Kristeva defines abjection as the primal gesture by which a nascent subject separates itself from that which is borderless, undifferentiated, or chaotic. Shame is the partner of desire in this movement, which gives rise to both the bounded subject and its excluded abject: "A certainty protects it [the desiring subject] from the shameful." Such "certainty" is, however, always fractured with ambivalence—an ambivalence harbored in shame, as we have seen—as the subject of desire is "drawn toward an elsewhere as tempting as it is condemned."[5] And drawn it must be, for, if the shameful abject is endlessly threatening to the subject, it is also the abysmal matrix of creativity, love, and joy, at once the necessary precondition for desire and the cause of desire's undoing, the "elsewhere" in which both subjects and objects ever die and rise again. It is also, I would add, the site of a flesh excluded by the constructed borders of the body. As literary theorist Lynda Hart puts it: "The 'flesh' is a place toward which we reach that always exceeds our grasp, that indeed *must* elude us for it is the site beyond (or before) the 'body' that permits us to continue *making* reality even as our desire disavows it."[6] Flesh manifests in Kristeva's writing with particular vividness as the abjection of decay and excrement: "Refuse and corpses show me what I permanently thrust aside in order to live. These body flu-ids, this defilement, this shit are what life withstands, hardly and with diffi-culty, on the part of death. There, I am at the border of my condition as a living being. My body extricates itself, as being alive, from that border."[7]

For ancient Christians, the abjection of the flesh went hand-in-hand with the exaltation of divinity. The lure of a transcendence that promised to rescue the spirit from the mire of shameful carnality was powerful, to be sure. But so too was the lure of the shameful. Indeed, it is not always easy to distinguish between the disintegrating depths of shame and the dissolv-ing heights of ecstasy within Christian discourse. If "the abject is edged with the sublime," as Kristeva puts it,[8] this is due in part to the fact that both the abject and the sublime evade objectification and exceed the bounds of mere selfhood or body. "Abjection is a resurrection that has gone through death (of the ego)," Kristeva also suggests.[9] Such a possibility illumines the logic of ancient fantasies of a resurrected glory that did not—and could not—relinquish its purchase on fleshly corruption. Christ's scandalous car-nality continued to stagger the ancient imagination, even as the limits of cosmological reflection were stretched. The weight of materiality appeared at once unbearable and inescapable for those who sought salvation. Seem-ingly in flight from the flesh, Christians also enfolded themselves in its shameful embrace, not least by embracing a savior who had already touched them with the tender violence of his passion—who had revealed the secret collusion of mortal shame with sublime *jouissance* that lies, per-haps, at the heart of every resurrection.

Taste Me, Touch Me, But Don't Hold Me: Jesus in the Gospel of John

The Gospel of John is notoriously, even infamously, transcendentalizing. In this text we encounter the most ethereal, the least mundanely human—therefore also, one might think, the least shameful—of Christs. Yet John's gospel is not only the gospel of the sublime Logos but also the gospel of the Enfleshment; it is the gospel of Love as well. Here divinity touches flesh, even as flesh reaches toward the divine. In the mutual touch, there is a joy-ing. In the joying, there is both a shaming abjection of flesh and a passage through the boundlessness of abjection into the infinitude of sublimity. Put otherwise, John's gospel discovers in the shameful death of the contained and ordered body a resurrection that is itself a fleshly abjection edged with the sublime. In fact, it is already there in the beginning.

The well-known opening verses of this gospel align God's creative Word with both life and light. "In the beginning was the Word. . . . It was in the beginning with God; all things came to be through it. . . . In it was life, and the life was the light of humanity. And the light shines in the darkness (*skotia*), and the darkness did not lay hold of it (*ou katelaben*)" (1.5). The point is repeated, even as the language shifts subtly: "It was in the world (*kosmos*), and the world was made through it, yet the world did not know it. It came to its own, and its own did not receive it (*ou parelabon*)" (1.11). A further iteration anticipates the "good news" that will resolve the cosmic predicament: "and the Word became flesh (*sarx*) and dwelt amongst us. . . . And from his fullness we have all received (*elabomen*)" (1.14, 16). The parallelism of these three sets of verses, together with the wobbling of verb tenses, suggests both a sequential unfolding of narrative episodes and a spiraling repetition of what is (almost) the "same" story: "in the beginning" the light that is in the Word "shines in the darkness" (1.5); it was "coming into the cosmos" (1.9); it "became flesh" (1.14).

Darkness : *cosmos* : *flesh.* How are we to understand the relation of these three structurally linked terms? Genesis 1, the scriptural text that John here exegetes, advances from one primal, plenitudinous, and undifferentiated darkness (Gen. 1.2) toward a separation of light from darkness that initiates the cosmic order (Gen. 1.4).[10] John's midrash seems to shuttle between the two "darknesses," and much hinges upon the reading of the phrase "it [the darkness] did not lay hold (*ou katelaben*) of it [the light]." Both the intertextual tug of the second verse of Genesis, in which we read that "darkness was upon the face of the deep" over which the divine Spirit was hovering, and the parallelism with closely related words in John 1.11 (*ou parelabon*: "they did not receive") and 16 (*elabomen*: "we received") suggest that the posited failure of the darkness to "lay hold of"—to grasp or comprehend—the light is tragic. God desires that darkness "comprehend" or "receive" the light.[11] However, a later passage in the gospel implies just the opposite, in terms that exceed even the tidy separation inscribed in the fourth verse of Genesis, by seeming to reject darkness altogether: "Walk while you have the light, lest the darkness lay hold of you (*katalabe*); the one who walks in the darkness does not know where he goes" (John 12.35; cf. 8.12, 12.46). In this context, it appears desirable that the darkness *not* grasp or overwhelm the light, even that light ultimately overwhelm darkness. Yet how can light shine if there is no darkness to illumine? Appropriately, given its exegetical matrix, "cosmos" displaces "darkness" in the text of John's prologue just as it does in the performative narrative of Genesis

1.[12] If the world does not receive the Word any more than the darkness lays hold of the light, this is now *clearly* marked as tragic. Yet the Word does not cease coming into the world, despite its initial failure to be received.

Indeed, the Word finally enters and inhabits the world as *flesh*. Does it not then also come into the world as the *darkness*—the *abjection*—that does not grasp or extinguish light but both receives and gives rise to all cosmic orders of differentiation that emerge in ongoing processes of dissolution and reassembly? A depth "opening to that less-than-nothing which is not nothing—light."[13] If only the world—they, we—could recognize this. John does, and he is showing us: the divine Word has become flesh; it exists in and as the eternal becoming of flesh's fullness. This is the scandalous mystery at the heart of both creation and redemption.

What more can we say about Johannine flesh? From the prologue we have learned that it is not the source of the creative will (1.13) but it *is* the site of the divine becoming within the world (1.14). In a subsequent passage, John's Jesus seems, however, to reject the flesh in favor of the spirit, as he schools the literal-minded Nicodemus in the distinction between fleshly and spiritual birthing: "That which is born of the flesh is flesh, and that which is born of the Spirit is spirit" (3.6). Subsequently he asserts, in a similar vein, "It is the spirit that gives life, the flesh is of no avail; the words that I have spoken to you are spirit and life" (6.63). Yet, shortly before this latter statement, Jesus has made a more surprising claim, namely, that his own flesh is bread given "for the life of the world." "Truly, truly, I say to you, unless you eat the flesh of the Son of man and drink his blood, you have no life in you; the one who eats my flesh and drinks my blood has eternal life. . . . For my flesh is food indeed, and my blood is drink indeed. The one who eats my flesh and drinks my blood abides in me, and I in him" (6.51–56).

Attention has sometimes focused on the violations of kashrut observance implicated in such a bloody meal, but the shock is perhaps still greater than that. John's Jesus offers his flesh and blood as the very nurturance of spiritual life, thus jamming binary distinctions made elsewhere in this gospel between flesh and spirit, much as the ambiguity initially attending darkness complicates subsequently asserted oppositions of darkness and light. Flesh already wedded to divinity—the abject always edged with the sublime?—is the only food that matters, and it matters precisely because it gives the lie to *merely* bodily or worldly existence. Flesh precedes, saturates, and exceeds the cosmos. Excluded in the gesture that gives rise to the contained and ordered body, it is crucial to both the making and the unmaking of the body, constituting the womb as well as the ongoing source of nurturance for "eternal life." ("The time of abjection is double.") In eternal life, moreover, clear-cut boundaries of psychic and somatic identity dissolve along with plot-lines of temporality: Jesus abides in those who eat him, and they abide in Jesus. This is a point that apparently bears both repetition and expansion: "I am in my Father, and you in me, and I in you" (14.20); "even as thou, Father, art in me, and I in thee, [I pray] that they also may be in us" (17.21). As Luce Irigaray notes, "Porosity and its fullest responsiveness, can occur only within difference. A porosity that moves from the inside to the outside of the body."[14]

The Gospel of John appears strangely preoccupied with the matter of eating and drinking even in passages where "flesh" is only implicitly invoked.[15] Jesus converts water to wine at a marriage celebration (2.1–11). He desires both to receive a drink from and to give a drink to a Samaritan woman whom he meets at a well (4.5–42);[16] furthermore, in the midst of that episode, he himself refuses to eat when his disciples beg him to do so, explaining, "My food is to do the will of the one who sent me" (4.34). He offers himself to his followers as "the bread of life" (6.35) and presents his heart as the source of rivers of "living water" that will satisfy all thirst (7.37–38). He announces his own thirst as he hangs from the cross but receives only vinegar (19.28–29). In his final resurrected appearance, he feeds his disciples fish and bread and admonishes Peter to "feed my lambs" (21.13, 15).

What is the import of all this performative ingesting in which food and drink are repeatedly offered and consumed? Kristeva suggests that Christianity "identified abjection as a fantasy of devouring,"[17] and certainly a dominant fantasy of John's gospel is the devouring of the food offered by Jesus—the food that is, moreover, identified with or as Jesus' own flesh. Jesus' nourishment lies in being consumed, his followers' in consuming Jesus. If eating results in their virtual identification (I in you and you in me), it also results in a mutual and ongoing transformation of identity. Flesh as food traverses bodily boundaries and brings us again to the threshold of the boundary-dissolving abject—that which "disturbs identity, system, order," which "does not respect borders, positions, rules."[18] It thus brings us also to the threshhold of the boundless sublime—"a *something added* that expands us, overstrains us, and causes us to be both *here*, as dejects, and *there*, as others and sparkling."[19] Both here and there, transported in a eucharist of love: "I in them and thou in me, that they may become perfectly one, so that the world may know that thou hast sent me and hast loved them even as thou hast loved me" (17.23). "Hence a jouissance in which the subject is swallowed up."[20]

The erotic joying that pervades this gospel, in which subjects dissolve into one another like food on the tongue, is most vividly enacted in the relationship of Jesus to the mysteriously unnamed "beloved disciple."[21] Here, perhaps tellingly, a tasting that may threaten to devour begins to give way to a touching that is definitively not a grasping. As Karmen MacKendrick argues, knowledge of John's Jesus "is faith alone; not grasp, but touch."[22] In an intimate meal-time moment charged with intimations of betrayal as well as promises of faithfulness, "one of his disciples, whom Jesus loved, was lying close to the breast of Jesus." Skin to skin, they share confidences, leaving the other disciples to participate as mere onlookers and eavesdroppers (13. 23–26). Later, when "the disciple whom he loved" is standing near Jesus at the crucifixion (almost but not quite touching him, then), Jesus names him momentously as the son of his own mother (19.26–27).[23] Maternal flesh—not paternal disembodiment—is thus rendered an indispensible place of mediated touch between loving "brothers." And why not? The "immeasurable, unconfinable maternal body" is so often the psychic and cultural repository of uneasy awareness of the erotic fluidities and continuities, the myriad "touchings," that both underlie and disrupt subjective as well as cosmic differentiation: "The other is inevitable, she [the mother] seems to say, call it a God if you wish, it is nevertheless natural, for such an other has come out of myself, which is not yet myself but a flow of unending germinations, an eternal cosmos."[24]

All the same, John's Jesus is apparently wary of being "swallowed up" in the *jouissance* represented by feminine flesh. He wants to be tasted, but not devoured. Facing Mary of Magdala in the tombside encounter where he reveals his resurrected body for the first time, Jesus famously warns the woman, "Do not hold me (*me mou haptou*), for I have not yet ascended to the Father" (20.17). Ascent to the sublime Father is here balanced against descent into maternal abjection, as Jesus' paternally mediated self-certainty protects his desire from what is thereby excluded as shameful—the embrace of a woman.[25] In the process, Mary is already subtly burdened with a shame that will blossom in a later tradition that construes her as a repentant prostitute. Yet maybe Jesus has misrecognized the Magdalene's intentions. As if caught in an embarrassing play of projection, he seems to fear her desirous grasp—the grasp, perhaps, of a "darkness" that threatens (so he imagines) not merely to "receive" but to "lay hold of" him. Might it not be, however, that Mary offers him no more (or less) than the trusting gift of mutually transformative touch, in which there is no more (or less) shame than that incurred in the touch of the beloved disciple who lay close to his breast? Or, for that matter, in the deeply intimate touch of the dubious Thomas, whom Jesus subsequently approaches boldly by walking through walls, his uncanny flesh traversing all borders and also opening itself receptively, as he invites the disciple to press his fingers into the piercings in his hands, to lay his own hand within the wound of Jesus' side (20.26–27).

As the ever-more-porous resurrected Jesus[26] seems poised, in the closing verses of this gospel, to merge back into the flow of the "unending germinations" of eternal life ("call it a God if you wish"), he responds to Peter's oddly abrupt and seemingly inconsequential question about the status of "the disciple whom Jesus loved, who had lain close to his breast at the supper," with a shimmeringly enigmatic question of his own: "If I desire that he remain until I come, what is that to you?" (21.20–22). The lover will come, the beloved will wait to receive him: perhaps their positions are even reversible—I in you and you in me. In such a joying suspense of erotic communion, the gospel—itself pointing toward an "immeasurable, unconfinable" expanse of materializing writing "that the world itself could not contain" (21.25)—does not so much end as open. But to what does it open itself—to the sublime or the abject, to glory or shame? (To the father or the mother?) The Gospel of John deconstructs such oppositions, or very nearly so. When Word becomes flesh, shame is no longer the brittle defense of desire against the threat of the abject but rather the expansive gateway of a nearly intolerable exposure to erotic transformation from within the depths of abjection—as gloriously manifested in the wild openness of fleshly touch, the fluid exchanges between bodies and subjects, the sublime boundlessness of eternal resurrection(s).

Unblushing Apologetics: Tertullian's Defense of the Flesh of Christ

Tertullian of Carthage, writing at the cusp of the third century, enthusiastically embraces the challenge presented by Christianity's most controversial teachings regarding the divine incarnation and fleshly resurrection, which (as he does not tire of reminding us) defy the common sense of his day. With unsurpassed rhetorical verve, he follows John's lead by boldly placing *flesh* at the center of his theological construction, thereby offering himself as a defiant witness to a truth that others find disgraceful. Flesh thus becomes the site of a deliberately offensive, explicitly countercultural faith articulated in the exotically alien language of scripture. As Thomas O'Malley notes, Tertullian "is quite aware of the otherness of biblical words," not least the Latin *caro* ("flesh") that features so prominantly in the Gospel of John.[27] Tertullian positively glories in his own shameless biblicism. Indeed, it is not just an implicitly shamed flesh but an explicitly named shame that Tertullian makes central to his soteriologically-driven christology. In a humiliation at once Christ's and the Christian's, salvation unfolds. The paradoxical framing of this embrace of what is shameful—most famously encoded in the phrase *credibile est quia ineptum est* ("it is believable because it is absurd" [*On the Flesh* 5.4])—has rendered Tertullian a particularly controversial theologian.[28]

Tertullian opens his treatise *On the Flesh of Christ* by observing that, although there is general agreement among Christians about Christ's spiritual nature, "his flesh is questioned." To question Christ's flesh is to interrogate his birth since, as Tertullian notes, "there is no nativity without flesh, and no flesh without nativity" (1.2). Painting a vivid scene of gestation and childbirth, Tertullian performatively invokes the abjection of flesh, even as he skillfully displaces the defensive affect of shame onto others. Thus he represents his opponents as declaiming "against the uncleanness of the generative elements within the womb, the filthy concretion of fluid and blood, or the growth of the flesh for nine months long out of that very mire." He urges them tauntingly to "inveigh now likewise against the shame itself of a woman in travail" and imagines their horror "at the infant, which is shed into life with the embarassments which accompany it from the womb." Rhetorically throwing all of this bloody mess into the face of Marcion, a favorite theological rival, he addresses him challengingly: "You detest a human being at his birth; then how do you esteem anybody?" (4.1–2).

Indeed, esteem or love is at the heart of all this "matter" for Tertullian. Love is what manifests in Christ when he becomes flesh: "Christ loved that one who was condensed in the womb in the midst of its uncleannesses, the one delivered through its shameful parts. . . . Loving man, he loved both his nativity and his flesh" (4.3). Following Jesus, Tertullian refuses to turn nativity and flesh into cause for blushing. If Christ takes on and reanimates our mortal flesh, "does he blush to be born in it?" Surely not (4.4). Tertullian exults in the appropriated Pauline "folly" of his own shameless refusal to blush at belief "in a God born, and that from a virgin, and of a fleshly nature too, who wallowed in all the before-mentioned humiliations of nature" (4.6).

To refuse to be ashamed of birth is also to refuse to be ashamed of suffering or death. Tertullian's christological aesthetics links nativity tightly to mortality: "For what is more unworthy of God, what more likely to cause a blush, to be born or to die? to bear flesh or cross? to be circumcised or crucified? to be cradled or coffined? to be laid in a manger or in a tomb?" (5). Tertullian reiterates his own unblushing faith in folly. "Why," he asks, "do you destroy the necessary disgrace (*dedecus*) of faith? Whatever is unworthy of God is helpful to me. I am saved if I am not ashamed (*non confundar*) of my lord" (5.3). Tertullian continues to develop his audacious argument that Christ's shameful shamelessness will save him. Only the born and dying God can render him "well in shamelessness and happy in foolishness (*bene impudentem et feliciter stultum*)" through his own christologically mediated "contempt of shame (*rubor*)." "The Son of God was crucified; it does not shame because it is shameful (*non pudet quia pudendum est*)" (5.4). Indeed, precisely because his faith in a God enfleshed *is* shameful, Tertullian can be made shameless. His shameless love of the flesh, miming Christ's own love, is the source of his salvation.

Although only Matthew's and Luke's gospels provide narratives of Christ's birth, it is John's gospel that seems to animate Tertullian's defense of Christ's native flesh. Indeed, the phrase "verbum caro factum est" (John 1.14)—all the condensed nativity that either John or Tertullian requires—repeats like a refrain throughout the later chapters of the treatise. Addressing the question of the origin of the Word's flesh (did it arise from the paternal seed or the maternal womb?), Tertullian invokes John 3.6—"what is born in flesh is flesh"—in order to demonstrate conclusively the Word's nativity from the woman. This is a somewhat surprising exegetical move, given that the cited Johannine passage emphasizes the superiority of spiritual birth over fleshly birth. Tertullian himself acknowledges that John's Jesus goes on to say that "what is born of spirit is spirit," but he discovers in this an affirmation of Christ's paternally generated divinity that complements rather than contradicts the prior affirmation of his maternally generated flesh (18.5). "Thus just as he is spirit from the spirit of God, born of God, he is also a human from the flesh of a human, generated in the flesh" (18.7).

Tertullian goes on immediately to tackle another potentially problematic passage from the prologue of John's gospel: "He is born not of blood, nor of the will of the flesh, nor of the will of a man, but of God" (John 1.13).[29] Crucial for Tertullian is the fact that the verse does *not* deny that Christ was born "of the substance of flesh." Nor, he insists, should we imagine that "blood" here refers to the substance of flesh in a general way, "but only of the matter of the seed," since, in the terms of ancient medical theory, sperm is a heated froth of blood (19.3). The point, then, of John's repeated denials that the Word is made flesh from *blood* or the *will* of either flesh or man is to emphasize that his birth was *virginally* conceived: "what is denied is the Lord's birth from sexual intercourse (*ex concubitu*) . . . not from the participation of the womb (*ex vulvae participatione*)" (19.4).

Tertullian has thus interjected into John's gospel the vivid presence of a maternal womb to which John himself does not, of course, refer directly. Intertextual exegesis continues to allow that womb to grow and swell within Tertullian's own fertile composition. Earlier he has noted the pleasing symmetry between an original creation of humanity from the virginal earth and the new birth of "the most recent Adam" from Mary's virginal womb (17.4; cf. Gen. 2.7, 1 Cor. 15.45), highlighting as well the neat reversal of Eve's diabolical misconception brought about by Mary's divine conception: "Eve believed the serpent; Mary believed Gabriel" (17.5; cf. Gen. 3.1–6, Luke 1.26–38).[30] Now he draws on Psalm 22.9–10 in order to develop a distinctly uterine perspective on the flesh of Christ: "You are the one who tore me from my mother's womb; my hope since the breast of my mother, on you I was cast from the womb; from the womb of my mother you are my God" (20.4). If Christ was "torn" from the uterus, he must have once been firmly fastened to it, bound to the maternal womb by the umbilical cord, reasons Tertullian.

He is at pains to show that the connection between maternal and filial flesh could not have been more intimate: "Even when one strange matter amalgamates with another, it produces such a communion of flesh and viscera (*concarnatur et convisceratur*) with that with which it amalgamates, that when it is torn away, it takes with it from the body from which it is torn a certain consequence of the severed union and bond of mutual joining (*coitus*)" (20.5). "A mother is a continuous separation, a division of the flesh," notes Kristeva, in seeming sympathy with Tertullian's point. "What connection is there . . . between my body and this internal graft and fold, which, once the umbilical cord has been severed, is an inaccessible other?" she asks. "No connection except for that overflowing laughter where one senses the collapse of some ringing, subtle, fluid identity or other, softly buoyed by the waves."[31] No connection except for that "certain consequence" conveyed as a trace of the other, an overflowing of boundaries within flesh itself, a fluidity of identity sucked like milk from maternal breasts that, according to the scientific authorities cited by Tertullian, bear testimony to the (severed) union of mother and child: the womb "could not have had a source to supply milk," he proposes, were it not for the bleeding that resulted from the tearing away of its own flesh in birth (20.6).[32] No connection except for that discovered in rupture, where the son's tearing away is also the opening up of the mother's self-enclosure: "If a virgin conceived, in her delivery she became a bride. For she became a bride by the very law of the opened body, in which it made no difference whether it was by the power of the masculine entering or exiting; the same sex unsealed the body"(23.3–4). A "mutual *coitus*" indeed![33] "To say that there are no sexual relationships constitutes a skimpy assertion," observes Kristeva, "when confronting the flash that bedazzles me whe I confront the abyss between what was mine and is henceforth but irreparably alien. Trying to think through that abyss: staggering vertigo. No identity holds up."[34] Christ's flesh, like all flesh (indeed, like his mother's flesh), is drawn—torn—from the dizzying abyss of abjection that is at once womb and tomb, the source of both natality and mortality and the site of the union as well as its severance—of identification as well as difference—among human creatures.

Christ's flesh, for Tertullian as for John, is also the fecund matrix of divine love and thus of eternal resurrection. This is an argument developed particularly in a second treatise entitled *On the Resurrection of the Flesh*. While his opponents deliver an "invective against the flesh" (4), he offers instead a "eulogy," urging that "the flesh begin to give you pleasure, since its creator is so great" (5). Here, under the sure touch of divine love, shame opens onto joying. In the very beginnings of creation, the humble "clay" from which humanity is fabricated is embued with glory by the "hands of God": "so often then does it receive honor as it experiences the hands of God, when it is touched by them, and pulled, and drawn out, and molded into shape" (6). In the restorative rituals practiced by Christians, it is the flesh that is washed, signed with the cross, illumined by the imposition of spirit-laden hands, "fattened" on the body and blood of Christ. In martyrdom—which is, for Tertullian, the quintessential transformative rite of Christians—flesh is crucified with Christ, subjected to countless deprivations in prison, "dragged out into public view and exposed to the hatred of all" and, thus exposed, "racked by every kind of torture that can be devised" until brought to the point of an agonizing death (8). In all this unspeakable suffering—in all this carnal passion—the worthiness of the much-maligned flesh surfaces like a flush on skin brushed by God's loving touch. "He will love the flesh which is, so very closely and in so many ways, his neighbor—although infirm . . . , although disordered . . . , although not honorable . . . , although ruined . . . , although sinful . . . , although condemned . . ." (9). Tertullian proclaims the power of God "to rebuild and restore the edifice of the flesh" (11). This is less a power exercised over or against nature than one inhering in the nature of flesh's eternal becoming. "All creation is instinct with renewal," he insists. "All things begin after they have ended. . . . The whole, therefore, of this revolving order of things bears witness to the resurrection of the dead" (12).

The dignity of flesh is thus manifested through the power of God inhering in creation's renewal, a process of corrective transformation that strains toward a telos in which flesh will be "exempted from all humiliation, and all loss, and all injury, and all disgrace," ultimately acheiving a state of "integrity and perfect resurrection" (58). Here Tertullian seems finally to relax the productive tension of his paradoxical embrace of shame, revealing, perhaps, the limits of paradox.[35] Shame still has a role to play, however, even in the resurrection. The lure of a flesh exempted from disgrace is not, evidently, adequate explanation for the necessary "integrity" of the resurrected body. Tertullian supplies an additional rationale: "the judgment seat of God requires that the human be kept entire"—even the most shameful parts (60). Justice, accomplishing creation's fulfillment through the chastening correction effected by judgment, requires that the wedding of soul to flesh be eternally preserved in the marriage of humanity to divine spirit, "fitted together as bride and bridegroom," that takes place when the Word of God becomes flesh. "By drinking in evermore the resurrection of the flesh, you will be satisfied with the refreshing draughts" (63), Tertullian assures his readers, in a final felicitous mingling of Johannine images of fleshly consumption and metamorphosis.

Sophia's Shame: The *Apocryphon of John*

Other interpreters of both John and Genesis, roughly contemporaneous with Tertullian, take a rather different approach to the problem of fleshly shame. Indeed, these Christians number among those whose views Tertullian adamantly opposes. Yet a simplistic opposition of "orthodox" and "heretical" theologies not only threatens to domesticate Tertullian's purposefully outrageous and explicitly shameless incarnationalism while passing anachronistic judgment on those labeled "gnostic" by modern scholarly convention; it also elides the many similarities of thought discoverable across a range of ancient Christian writings that are, admittedly, nonetheless quite diverse. Focusing on the *Apocryphon of John*, we observe the dramatic staging of two intricately interwoven, mutually contesting narratives of divine creativity.[36] Flesh is therein made to bear the burden of a cosmic shame that is ultimately turned against the shamers—namely, the false creator "God" and his nefarious henchmen, who subject this world to the unjustice of their totalitarian rule. It is by shaming the shamers and thus exposing the ignorance and deception on which their claims to power rest that the *Apocryphon* unfurls its revelation and also discloses its revealer, the Christic Pronoia. It is also, however, through shame that repentance is made possible and salvation is effected. If flesh as such is arguably never redeemed in this text, the performative humiliation of human bodies ambivalently construed as prisons nonetheless plays a crucial role in the process of enlightenment that restores spirits to the "pleroma," or fullness, of divine creativity. At this point—the very point of material dissolution where abjection gives way to sublimity—the distinction that Tertullian makes between the "destruction" and the "transformation" of flesh (*On the Resurrection* 55) perhaps begins to blur.

In the *Apocryphon of John*, shame precedes and anticipates the creation of flesh. The shame is first and foremost Sophia's. An "aeon" of the divine pleroma, Sophia, or Wisdom, desires to think a thought of her own. On the face of it, this desire appears both natural and laudable, for it is of the character of the divine, as the *Apocryphon* portrays it, to generate the fullness of its own potentiality through intellectual conception. Indeed, we are told that Sophia's thought in some way proceeds not only from herself but also from "the invisible Spirit and foreknowledge," just as we might expect, based on the patterns already established for divine generativity—not to mention the typical role of Sophia as agent of creation in other Wisdom literature. Nonetheless, the *Apocryphon* shockingly disrupts such initial expectations by emphasizing the inappropriateness of Sophia's desire. "She wanted to bring forth a likeness out of herself without the consent of the Spirit—he had not approved—and without her consort, and without his consideration." The points of Sophia's failure to respect patriarchal authority evidently bear repeating: "And though the person of her maleness had not approved, and she had not found her agreement, and she had thought without the consent of the Spirit and the knowledge of her agreement, she brought forth" (9). Sophia's distinctly feminine and implicitly sexualized shame[37] quickly materializes in the shape of a fatherless, bastard progeny that bears no kind of likeness even to its mother: "Something came out of her which was imperfect and different from her appearance. . . . And it was dissimilar to the likeness of its mother." This unfortunate creature meta-morphizes into the monstrous figure of a lion-faced serpent whom Sophia swiftly banishes from the divine realm, attempting to hide it a cloud and giving it the name Yaldabaoth (10).

The humiliation of Sophia initially confirmed by the grotesque mani-festation of her misbegotten thought, further exposed in her very attempt to hide it from sight, is amplified in the subsequent narration of Yaldabaoth's creation of a cosmos that mimics and parodies the realm of divine full-ness.[38] The narrative itself seems to mimic and parody both Genesis 1–3 and John 1: in this, its hermeneutical tactics reflect its soteriology, seeking the realm of truth obscured by the distortions of both a fallen cosmos and a flawed scriptural text. Despite his monstrosity, Yaldaboath carries with him a trace of his mother's divine light. "And when the light had mixed with the darkness, it caused the darkness to shine. And when the darkness had mixed with the light, it darkened the light and it became neither light nor dark, but it became dim." Stumbling about foolishly in a dimness generated by this strong rereading of John's prologue, Yaldaboath boasts, "I am God and there is no other God beside me" (11). The knowing reader mocks such ignorance: satisfyingly, Yaldabaoth's absurd (and palpably derivative) hyp-ermasculine boast exposes him to shame. But the shame is also Sophia's, as is reflected in her visible agitation. "Then the mother began to move to and fro. She became aware of the deficiency when the brightness of her light diminished. . . . And she was overcome by forgetfulness in the darkness of ignorance and she began to be ashamed" (13). Unlike Yaldabaoth's, Sophia's shame is the beginning of her salvation, for it initiates her repentance. In intertextual terms, it is also the beginning of creation, as evoked by the echo of Genesis 1.2: "And the Spirit of God was hovering over the face of the waters." The *Apocryphon* continues: "And the whole pleroma heard the prayer of her repentance and they praised on her behalf the invisible, vir-ginal Spirit. And he consented" (14).

At this crucial turning point, the realms of the invisible Spirit and Yal-dabaoth are brought into still more complex interrelation. Now the divine pleroma begins to intervene actively in the imitative pattern of creation al-ready unwittingly initiated by Yaldabaoth, thereby gradually nudging demi-urgic mimicry in the direction of a true mimesis. Indeed, Sophia's creation will finally become an authentic "likeness" and thus a legitimate extension of the divine fullness—but this will only take place through her further ex-posure to shame. With the help of the pleroma, Yaldabaoth and his aeonlike archons are tricked into creating a human being who will bear the image and likeness not of Yaldaboath and his fellow rulers but of the divine pleroma itself. In a lengthy and intricate, even perversely loving process, the archons construct the human body, part by part. (It is not yet, however, a "fleshly" body.)[39] The end result embarrassingly exposes the limits of their power: "their product was completely inactive and motionless for a long time." Again the divine pleroma intervenes to fool Yaldabaoth, urging him: "Blow into his face something of your spirit and his body will arise." The false God falls for the trick: "The body moved and gained strength, and it was luminous" (19). Recognizing belatedly that the human whom they have created is now superior to them, the archons attempt to reassert their control by refashioning its body out of "matter": "This is the tomb of the newly-formed body with which the robbers had clothed the man, the body of forgetfulness; and he became a mortal man." The *Apocryphon* adds: "But the Epinoia of the light which was in him, she is the one who was to awaken his thinking" (21). Epinoia is here the name given to the luminous trace of Sophia that initially passed into Yaldabaoth and has now left him, becoming the life and light of the enfleshed human creature.

Placing the human in paradise, the archons desire to seal the tomb of its mortality by poisoning the creature with the fruit of "the tree of their life" (21). But there is another tree in the garden, "what they call the tree of knowledge of good and evil, which is the Epinoia of the light." The archons try to hide the tree from Adam "that he might not look up to his fullness and recognize the nakedness of his shamefulness." Through divine intervention, Adam is nonetheless persuaded to eat and thus enabled to know his own shame, which will (as with Sophia) initiate his redemption. Again the *Apocryphon* reads Genesis against its grain: "It is not the way Moses wrote." The archons cause the sleep of forgetfulness to fall upon Adam; they try to bring Epinoia out of his rib. The operation is unsuccessful: "But the Epinoia of the light cannot be grasped. Although darkness pursued her, it did not catch her" (22). Genesis is here once more interpreted through the filtering lens of John's gospel. When Adam awakes to behold Eve/Epinoia—who is also "our sister Sophia, she who came down in innocence in order to rectify her deficiency"—his true identity as a child of light is suddenly revealed to him like an image in a mirror.

Yet again Yaldabaoth attempts to gain control of the now ambiguously pluralized humans by humiliating them. In this iteration, humiliation takes the dramatically shaming form of rape. Desiring the luminous Eve/Epinoia—desiring to possess and control her—Yaldabaoth begets in her two sons, Eloim and Yave. Yet the divine foreknowledge has already "snatched life out of Eve" (24): thinking that he has impregnated Epinoia/ Sophia, the ignorant Yaldabaoth in fact plants his seed in the dim womb of mere carnality. (Ambiguity is later reintroduced when we are told that Yaldabaoth and the archons "committed together adultery with Sophia, and bitter fate was begotten through them, which is the last of the changeable bonds" [28]). Thus sexual intercourse inaugurates the production not of bodies but of fleshly tombs, "copies of the bodies . . . inspired with his counterfeit spirit" (24). However, if Yaldabaoth has apparently succeeded in tainting humanity with the dark shame of sexuality, the divine powers of light continue to mimic the mimicry in such a way as to purify and correct the likeness. A second, competing human genealogy is established when Adam begets Seth in the image of the divine son and "the mother" imbues his seed with divine spirit (25). The distinction between carnal sexuality and divine generativity both does and does not hold in this complex play of parallelism and mimicry.

At this point, if not before, it becomes evident that the two realms represented respectively by divine creation and demiurgic perversion occupy the same, contested space. It is within the race of humanity that the battle of light and darkness, knowledge and ignorance, freedom and imprisonment, true and counterfeit spirits, is waged. Ultimately, as the revealer who speaks through the text assures us, the deficiency introduced by Sophia will be healed "so that the whole pleroma may become holy and faultless" (25). The text ends with a distinctly Johannine discourse delivered by Christ-Pronoia, a figure ambiguously identified with Epinoia/Sophia. "I, therefore, the perfect Pronoia of the all, changed myself into my seed, for I existed first, going on every road. For I am the richness of the light; I am the remembrance of the pleroma." Echoing the structure of John's prologue, she describes her three-stage descent into the realm of darkness, ending with her incarnation: "And I entered into the midst of their prison which is the prison of the body." Her speech ends on another Johannine note: "And behold, now I shall go up to the perfect aeon. I have completed everything for you in your hearing. And I have said everything to you that you might write them down" (31).

The shame of Sophia, repeated and amplified in the humiliations suffered by her children, is thus ultimately productive. Shaming the shamers by exposing the fact that their exploitative rule rests on falsehood and ignorance, the *Apocryphon* enables its readers to claim their superior identities as creatures divinely begotten. Resisting the shame that oppresses and alienates, they become shameless witnesses—"martyrs," in Tertullian's terms.

They write their witness with each new reading. At the same time, the centrality of repentance in the narrative renders shame itself peculiarly ambivalent, arguably even more so than in Tertullian's account. Whereas Tertullian's embrace of shame rests heavily on a shameless rhetoric of paradox, the *Apocryphon of John* emplots a more intricate narrative in which the necessity of shame for salvation is subtly revealed.

Can anything, even shame, finally lie outside the ever-expanding fullness of the "all," from the perspective of this text? The divine Sophia transgresses shamelessly and must subsequently experience shame in order to learn humility. But does the invisible, virginal Spirit, source of the "all," not also perform a necessary act of repentance when it grants a consent initially withheld and thereby heals a rupture in which it has itself (perhaps) participated?[40] Without of course quite allowing the compromise of divine perfection, the *Apocryphon* nonetheless hints that the fullness of perfection encompasses vulnerability—that the generative nature of the divine entails a certain risk. Divine conception produces self-differentiation; thus does its fullness unfold infinitely. Yet what, if any, are the limits of containable difference, of sustainable "likeness"? At what point, if any, is "identity" broken, communion disrupted?

The narrative of the *Apocryphon* pivots on the acknowledgement that limits have been breached, initiating a break within being—a tragic "rupture," as Karen King puts it.[41] Sophia's shame marks awareness of this danger of transgression harbored within desire's very fecundity. It is, however, a shame that must finally be owned by the divine fullness. Only then can it be rendered redemptive. The externalization or chastening projection of shame onto the complexly gendered and sexualized figures of Sophia and Yaldabaoth can, therefore, only be transient. If bodies that have been perverted into prisons of mortal flesh must ultimately melt away, in the terms of this text, this happens less through the shaming of flesh itself than through the conversion of spiritual alienation inaugurated by Sophia's desire to conceive autonomously. The redemption of Sophia's desire must be accomplished through the recognition and renunciation of the demonic consequences of such desire, as these are manifested in Yaldabaoth's perverted will to dominate and control.

Through shame and repentance desire is converted, as Sophia/Pronoia passes through "the realm of darkness" (30). The redemption of Sophia's shame that is finally accomplished by her incarnation reestablishes the "likeness" at the heart of divine generativity and thereby rescues the cosmos from alienation. Likeness is the conceptual pivot on which salvation here turns. Indeed, the mimetic production of likeness is at the center of divine conception itself. So it is that the invisible Spirit—or "Father"—is manifested in a process of self-reflection that gives rise to the pleroma: "For it is he who looks at him[self] in the light which surrounds [him]" (4). "And [his thought performed] a deed, and she came forth, [namely] she who had [appeared] before him in [the shine of] his light. . . . This is the first thought, his image; she became the womb of everything" (5). Likeness arises in divine self-imaging but crucially it also gives birth to difference, and it is the play of identification and difference encapsulated in generative likeness that is the font of creativity—that *is* the erotic flow at the heart of being as well as language. Metaphor carries the play of identity and difference within language. In Kristeva's suggestive words, "*Metaphor* should be understood as movement towards the discernible, a journey towards the visible." In the terms of the *Apocryphon*, metaphoricity, or the production of likeness, characterizes the creativity of the invisible Spirit evidenced in a self-revelation that constitutes "a journey towards the visible." Kristeva adds, "The object of love is a metaphor for the subject—its constitutive metaphor."[42]

Within Kristeva's psychoanalytic framing, metaphor, likeness, and love are associated with the abjected, pre-Oedipal and pre-linguistic realm of the "material maternal," metonym, otherness, and desire with the Oedipal advent of the Father's linguistic "Law." The two realms and temporalities are, however, always already interpenetrating, as the *Apocryphon of John* also attests via its complex construction of dual narratives of creation. If, according to Kristeva, it is love for the m/other that portends the birth of subjectivity, the identification that is the movement of love is also the advent of difference and desire within a subject thereby rendered irreducibly heterogeneous. To identify metaphorically with the other is also to appropriate the desire of the other, a desire that points to objects beyond—that opens onto a theoretically infinite metonymic chain of displacement of desired objects that remain, finally, ungraspable. Metaphoricity, which begins with the movement of identification in which difference is always already implicated, thus extends itself in metonymy, which itself prolongs the movement of differentiation, even as love unfurls in desire. If this is a "fall," it is a fall into heterogeneity and creativity, a fall that is also a "flow." But if the fullness of divinity expands infinitely, must it also observe limits?

From the perspective of the *Apocryphon*, it must. Metaphor and love cannot be simply superseded by the metonymic operations of desire in the generative fall into difference. Pretemporal, they are also eternal; yet the eternal fecundity of the divine that sustains the cosmos can be partly (if never fully) thwarted, not least through the forceful repressions of abjection. Then, narratives dry up and time winds down, law becomes tyranny, affinity gives way to alienation, desire is no more than a futile defense against shameful lack, and creation, thwarted by its apparent arbitrariness, lapses toward nothingness: such, as we have seen, are the demiurgic nightmares that haunt the margins of the *Apocryphon*'s theological imagination like so many motherless fathers. When, in the *Apocryphon of John*, the cosmos recovers its likeness to the invisible Spirit, the fullness of divinity manifests the generosity of an overflowing creativity and endless communion across fluid difference, ultimately overcoming the arrogantly totalizing aspirations and "counterfeit spirit" of authoritarian regimes represented by the rapacious, hypermasculine desire of Yaldabaoth and his archons. At the same time, through Sophia's redemptive shame, the abjected maternal womb is healed of an alienation in which both Sophia and the invisible Spirit have arguably colluded through their mutual refusal of "consent." The maternal is now fully accommodated within the divine pleroma. Indeed, it is the incarnate Mother—Sophia, Pronoia, Christ—who has "completed everything."

Flesh as the Site of Divine Becoming: Origen of Alexandria

Not unlike the anonymous author of the *Apocryphon of John*, the third-century theologian Origen has often been suspected of a great—even possibly a heretical—shame of the flesh. Fourth-century polemicists such as Jerome found the fantasies of resurrection elaborated by Origen and his successors far too ethereal to satisfy their own shameless longings for an afterlife in which men would remain embodied as men, virgins, virgins— and whores, whores.[43] Many others before and since have shared the discomfort with Origen's insistently spiritualizing tendencies, despite the lure of his optimistic egalitarianism and the widespread admiration evoked by his philosophical and exegetical brilliance. As Rebecca Lyman puts it, "His Christian commitment was unquestionable, but his theological conclusions stimulated passionate apologetic or repudiation; he was too right to be wrong, or too attractively wrong to be ignored."[44] Even the staunchest contemporary scholarly defenders of the Alexandrian must face the embarrassing disdain for carnality conveyed by Origen's soteriology, which strains toward an end in which all differences will dissolve like flesh, as souls merge with God in a union of perfected love.[45]

One could, however, equally suspect Origen of a certain *imperviousness* to the shame of the flesh, as exemplified by his response to the pagan critic Celsus's energetic attack on incarnational christology. Celsus mocks Jesus outrageously as one "born in a certain Jewish village, of a poor woman of the country, who gained her subsistence by spinning, and who was turned out of doors by her husband, a carpenter by trade, because she was convicted of adultery" (*Against Celsus* 1.28). He goes so far as to taunt Christ directly: "The body of God would not have been so generated as you, O Jesus, were" (1.69). Faced with such provocation, Origen eschews the rhetorical flights of fancy and the glorying in paradox that animate Tertullian's explicitly shameless defense of the incarnation. The hyperverbal equivalent of the noble silence which, he professes, he would have preferred to maintain in imitation of Jesus before Pilate (1.1), Origen's eight long books *Against Celsus* seek to demonstrate—not least through their performative dignity—that shame does not belong to the incarnate Christ or his followers but to the irrational people who slander and persecute them. If Origen unquestionably admired and purportedly deeply desired martyrdom as the ultimate witness to such worldly opposition, he was not willing to run shamelessly naked into the streets in order to attain that goal (Eusebius, *Church History* 6.2.5). For Origen, Christianity demands an intellectual practice at once austerely disciplined and boldly speculative, meticulously exegetical and richly dialogic, wherein reason combines with inspiration in a witness that strives to transcend all shame.

But does it thereby transcend the flesh? I would argue that it does not. The divine Word lies at the center of Origen's theological construction,[46] and for Origen, I suggest, Word is always becoming flesh and flesh is always the becoming of Word. Both his cosmology and his christology hinge on this unabashed assertion, which is not only distinctly Johannine but also, as Mark Edwards has argued, less conventionally Platonic than most interpreters have recognized.[47] Yet it is also the case that for Origen, as for the *Apocryphon of John*, the narration of the Word's becoming flesh is necessarily complex and remains haunted by a subtle ambivalence—though not, in this instance, by an outright attribution of shame. In his early treatise *On First Principles*, Origen demonstrates that fleshly existence is part of a longer, larger process of creation, fall, and redemption. It is within materiality that divine transcendence is manifested. Yet materiality also marks a loss of unity with the divine. Origen's Logos gracefully accommodates this ambivalence, representing at once the perfect and incorporeal image of God *and* the site at which the One shatters into the "many differences and varieties," the "dispersion and division" of materiality (*On First Principles* 1.6.2,4). In the Logos, the temporal finitude of fleshly creation (the seeds of which are always already borne in the Word's womb) intersects with the eternity of divine generation.

The cosmic generativity of the Logos correlates directly with its linguistic fecundity. (This is an insight that Origen shares with many Valentinian Christians in particular, despite his strong resistance to certain aspects of Valentinian cosmology and soteriology.)[48] Origen observes that the Word, God's only-begotten Son, "is called by many different names" (1.2.1). He discovers in the Gospel of John striking evidence of the inexhaustible plentitude of divine epithets by which the Logos reveals itself to a differentiated creation: "Let no one be surprised," he exclaims, "if we have understood Jesus to be announced by the plural 'good things.' For when we have understood the things of which the names which the Son of God is called are predicated, we will understand how Jesus . . . is many good things" (*Commentary on John* 1.52).

On First Principles places particular emphasis on the "name" of Wisdom or Sophia as a signifier of the creatureliness as well as the creative power of the Son. "Now this Son was begotten of the Father's will, for he is the 'image of the invisible God' [cf. Col. 1.15] and the 'effulgence of his glory and the impress of his substance' [Heb. 1.3], 'the firstborn of all creation' [cf. Col. 1.15], a thing created [*ktisma*], Wisdom. For Wisdom herself says: 'God created me in the beginning of his ways for his works' (Prov. 8.22)," recites Origen (4.4.1). Eternally generated , this incorporeal *ktisma* is also, as Patricia Cox Miller reminds us, identified by Origen as one whose "desire was by means of this very emptying [cf. Phil. 2.6,7] to display to us the fullness of the godhead" (1.2.8). "What, then, is the invisible Wisdom, whose emptying reveals a pleroma?" asks Miller. Pointing out that *ktisma* can mean not only "creature" but also "foundation" or "building," she suggests that for Origen the Son who is both Logos and Sophia is "God's binding structure in which all things are made new."[49] In Sophia, "there was implicit every capacity and form of the creation that was to be . . . ; it contains within itself both the beginnings and causes and species of the whole creation," writes Origen (1.2.2). "In this Sophia . . . the creation was always present in form and outline" (1.4.4). Not made of "stuff," either intellectual or bodily, but rather constituting the something-else that underlies the process of individuation inherent to corporeal existence, Sophia/

Logos "provides a kind of intermediate, or mediating, structure within which *nous* and *soma* are associated in varying degrees."[50] The cosmic generativity of Sophia, like the linguistic fecundity of Logos, is an enactment of divine self-revelation in which God's presence is also, paradoxically, withdrawn, as unity gives way to multiplicity and incorporeality gives rise to flesh.[51]

At this point Origen's curious doctrine of the fall fruitfully complicates his Sophia/Logos-centered cosmology. Origen suggests that the differentiated mingling of intellect with body that constitutes the creation of the material universe occurs in tandem with the fall of souls created as pure intellect. Starting from one beginning, the souls "were drawn in various directions by their own individual impulses and were distributed throughout the different ranks of existence in accordance with their merit," as Origen imagines it (1.6.2). Thus, oddly enough, "the beginnings and causes and species of the whole creation" that are said to be always already contained in Sophia/Logos are *also* attributed to a lapse in creation itself—a lapse not located, as in the *Apocryphon's* myth, in the inexplicable surge of divine desire in Sophia but rather in its mysterious cessation in human souls that are crucially imbued with free will. Whether this lapse is due to negligence or to satiety or to some other cause, Origen cannot say for sure (1.3.8, 1.4.1), but is it not at least possible that human spirits, in imitation of the divine Sophia/Logos itself, positively *desire* difference?[52] Leaving such questions open, Origen is content to emphasize that it is in the midst of difference—a difference necessarily articulated within the materiality of both cosmos and language—that the Logos encounters humanity. This is a fact that apparently causes Origen no embarrassment whatsoever.

As Edwards argues, the common view that Origen argues for two "falls"—the one pre-cosmic, the other post-cosmic—is likely erroneous, as is the corollary notion that he proposed that human souls once existed in a purely disembodied state.[53] Origen does, after all, frequently assert that incorporeality is the exclusive characteristic of the divine trinity of Father, Son, and Holy Spirit. Edwards's case, however, turns primarily on the interpretation of several disputed passages in Origen's treatise; because of the problematic transmission of the text, which has survived in full only in Rufinus's fourth-century Latin translation, uncertainty regarding its original wording and meaning inevitably persists precisely at those points where Origen's thought has historically been most controversial. Nonetheless, I am willing to wager that Edwards is largely right on this point. What is distinctive about Origen's account, it seems to me, is not the controversial sequencing of two separate accounts of creation and fall but rather the intricate and delicate imbrication of the narrative of the creation of the material cosmos with the narrative of the fall of human souls.

Already, however, I begin to depart from Edwards's explicitly apologetic reading. I agree that it is not at all helpful to brand Origen anachronistically "heretical," but in that case we also need not defend his orthodoxy. Edwards notes that for Origen "The variety of the world arises . . . from the foreseen variety of human choices, not from any antecedent fall."[54] Divine foresight does indeed provide a tidy—and reassuringly orthodox—explanation for the creation of a differentiated cosmos already aptly accommodated in advance to the conditions of human fallenness, and Edwards's interpretation is well supported by the Latin text (2.9.6). Yet Origen's thought is perhaps not always so tidy; his intuitions are perhaps still more complex. Indeed, his Sophialogical doctrine of eternal creation, in conjunction with his doctrine of the fall, seems to suggest that materiality arises in a process of divine creativity that is also always already a falling of the divine One into multiplicity.[55] Cosmos, Christ, scripture—these are so many fertile incarnations of God's desire, unfurling as capacious schoolrooms housing the pedagogical formation of human souls ever moving toward fulfillment of creation's promise. The ascetic discipline pursued by souls caught up in this pedagogical venture thus does not emerge merely as a necessary correction of an unfortunate error; rather, it reflects the freedom of human participation in a divine intentionality that itself seemingly *mandates* a fall into difference. In other words, the processes of creation, fall, and redemption are not entirely separable in Origen's thought. The movements of falling and rising, departure and return are aspects of one and the same desire, a desire that is both divine and human—a desire that reflects, in other words, the image and progressively perfected likeness of God in humanity.[56]

The Logos as matrix of creation and the Logos as incarnate Christ, possessed of both soul and flesh, are also one and the same, or very nearly so. Here again, narrative temporalities are as much layered as sequential—though I would not deny, of course, that Origen also has resort to a more conventionally sequential account of salvation history.[57] Origen's distinctive teaching regarding the soul of Jesus positions the incarnate Logos as that which knits incorporeal divinity together with the flesh of the created world. Already the only-begotten Word, "the invisible image of the invisible God" through whom all things were made, is present in humanity according to a logic of differentiated rational participation: "each obtained a degree of participation proportionate to the loving affection with which that one had clung to him." The Word is, however, also uniquely present in one particular soul, which, "clinging to God from the beginning of creation and ever after in a union inseparable and indissoluble, as being the soul of the wisdom and word of God and of the truth and the true light, and receiving him wholly, and itself entering into his light and splendor, was made with him in a pre-eminent degree one spirit." This soul, Origen adds, was "a medium between God and the flesh. . . . For the Word of God is to be thought of as being more 'in one flesh' with his soul than a man is with his wife" (2.6.3). Christ as Word "married" to the enfleshed soul of Jesus thus animates the cosmos as a differentiated unity bound together by love.[58] Logos as written text animates and binds scripture as a differentiated unity as well. In the incarnate Christ, the materiality of both world and writing are revealed as manifestations of divine generativity and desire.

Both cosmos and scripture are, nonetheless, intensely ambivalent realms, for Origen as for the *Apocryphon of John* (though not identically): divine creativity exercised in genuine freedom is ever attended by suffering and alienation, and the material universe is the site of a contest of angelic and demonic powers, in the midst of which humans must struggle to achieve their potential as lovers of God. The Bible itself unfurls in Origen's interpretive gaze as a place of challenge and contestation, of hiding as well as disclosure, where the Logos lures souls through its very elusiveness. Put simply, the scriptures "have a meaning not such only as is apparent at first sight, but also another, which escapes the notice of most" (preface 8). But the task of interpretation is of course not simple at all, in Origen's view. The biblical text is rife with signification yet the release of meaning in the act of reading requires both diligent study and the gift of inspiration. As Miller describes Origen's textual sensibilities, "Words are active, . . . there is a play or an energy packed into language. The interpreter's task is to let words speak, not to perform an exegetical dissection upon them."[59]

If, from one perspective, the coming of Christ can be said to have removed the veil that had concealed the truth of the Mosaic law from prior interpreters (4.1.6), the unveiling of the divine Logos within scripture is nonetheless an ongoing process of revelation that requires active human participation—a fact that complicates (but does not eradicate) Origen's hermeneutical supersessionism.[60] "One cannot separate the interpretive and the revelatory modes," and the practice of exegesis "is, in some sense, an imitation of the historical event of revelation," as Elliot Wolfson observes with regard to kabbalistic hermeneutics,[61] a description strikingly apt for

Origen as well. Origen crucially understands the Bible as a cryptic text. The "splendor of its teachings" remains "concealed under a poor and humble style." If the aesthetic imperfections of scripture may seem to some a source of shame, for Origen these very imperfections reveal scripture as an "earthen vessel" that hides a treasure (4.1.7). By implication, a treasure is necessarily constituted as such via its very concealment.

The "earthen" text initially discloses a "fleshly" or self-evident meaning (4.2.4), but this is yet another veil. Here strategic deception leads indirectly to revelation. One must discern the lies in order to comprehend the truths hidden therein.[62] "The Word of God has arranged for certain stumbling blocks (*skandala*) and interruptions and impossibilities to be inserted into the midst of the law and the history" (4.2.9). Without the impediment of a shameful text, laced with both falsehoods and stylistic infelicities, the reader might continue to skim the surface and thereby fail to press beyond the literal sense. Stumbling over the scandal of implausible meanings, he or she may, however, be provoked to push beyond the veil of literal signification to glimpse the unity of spiritual meaning that inheres in the body of scripture.[63] "It all has a spiritual meaning but not all of it a bodily meaning, for the bodily meaning is often proved to be an impossibility" (4.3.5). Spiritual interpretation—the ultimate goal for Origen—is the result of agonistic striving, even taking the form of violent transgression: the text must be broken open if it is to reveal its hidden treasure. To this end, divine aid must be sought, as "God alone is able to 'break in pieces the gates of brass' [cf. Is. 45.2] that conceal them and to burst the iron bars that are upon the gates" (4.3.11).[64] Though the metaphor of breaking implies that the divine Word will ultimately be freed from the material vessel of the scriptures, this is apparently a telos that will be indefinitely deferred. The task of interpretation and thus the process of revelation is endless: "For however far one may advance in the search and make progress through an increasingly earnest study, even when aided and enlightened in mind by God's grace, one will never be able to reach the final goal of one's inquiries" (4.3.14). Origen's insight that interpretation always fails to exhaust the bottomless plenitude of the text yields what Miller has dubbed "a poetics of the abyss."[65] Scripture remains ever veiled, then, precisely because there is no end to the unveiling of meaning. Logos ever manifests in and as the suffering of the interpreted text, even as it also thereby ever eludes the reader's grasp. Or perhaps better yet: scripture is the veil without which there is no unveiling; the flesh of textuality is the indispensable site of passionate signification.

It is surely no accident that Origen's closing doctrinal recapitulation, immediately following his hermeneutical chapters, ends with a meditation on the status of materiality, a subject that he has already marked as particularly difficult in the preface to *On First Principles*. He finds no scriptural reference to "matter" as "that substance which is said to underlie bodies" (4.4.6). Nonetheless he argues that it is necessary to infer the existence of such an underlying substance (4.4.7). All creation partakes of materiality, insists Origen, and the definitive character of materiality is its radical mutability, which itself accounts for the diversity of created beings. Rational creatures—human souls—are always already changeable, thus always already differentiating, and thus always already becoming flesh. But will the materiality of creation ultimately be overcome? Here, again, the problematic transmission of Origen's work gives rise to perplexing contradictions, with the result that *any* interpretation represents a "strong" reading that must make the most of the very stumbling blocks implanted in the text, whether by Origen himself or by his subsequent transmitters. According to Rufinus's translation, "There will always exist, therefore, this bodily nature whose coverings must necessarily be used by rational creatures" (4.4.8). A Greek fragment avers, in apparent contrast, that when the restoration of rational creatures is perfected "these bodies are dissolved into nothing, so that this is forever happening."[66] Origen is clear that the end of creation is a return to the beginning, and I have already suggested that for him creation is always already materializing in and as flesh. Is flesh not then also always already becoming logos?

Origen proposes that the very mutability of materiality contains the promise of creation's perfectability, and according to the Greek fragment "this is forever happening." Here again Origen's complex understanding of temporality appears to be a stumbling block for interpretation that exceeds (and may also underlie) the difficulties that hinder textual reconstruction. The beginning that is also an end is perhaps best understood as the eternity enfolding and enfolded by time—and also the eternity unfolding *in* time, where the perfecting of creation "is forever happening." On this reading, the "covering" of bodily existence is also always the site of spiritual uncovering, much as the text of scripture is both the veil and the unveiling of Word. Materiality is "forever" dissolving into sublimity. As David Dawson puts it, "In Origen's view, salvation requires a radical transformation of body, but it cannot entail its replacement, even as an allegorical meaning requires deepening and extending, but not replacing, the text's literal sense."[67] While Dawson highlights Origen's emphasis on the continuity of bodily identity at the expense of the corruptible "flesh,"[68] I am suggesting that "flesh" or "matter" may also be seen as central to Origen's soteriological cosmology in so far as it constitutes the underlying substance that conveys the infinite convertibility of all bodily forms. Indeed, "flesh" arguably endures precisely where "body" does not and cannot. Just as the body of scripture is "broken" to disclose an abyss of plenitudinous signification, as Miller's interpretation of Origen suggests, so too creaturely bodies continuously open up to an abjection of flesh—an abjection "edged with the sublime"?—that is the matrix of creation's ongoing transformation.

Origen's *On First Principles* thus situates the divine Word at the beginning of a creativity that results—that is eternally resulting—in a fleshly cosmos, as well as a world of textuality, marked by multiplicity, flux, and difference, but crucially not by absolute alterity. The progressive perfection of the image of God in humanity uncovers within the mutability of materiality the source of human hope and the site of divine revelation. Here, again, Origen's perspective draws close to that of the *Apocryphon of John*, while resisting its more extreme pessimism regarding the physical universe. Regardless of whether the "fall" into flesh is assigned to an errant aeon within the divine pleroma (as for the author of the *Apocryphon*) or to the negligence of human souls (as for Origen), it doubles and therein both reveals and reveils the generative lapse within divinity, the eternal "falling" that *is* the Logos/Sophia. That *is*, in other words, the enactment of divine self-revelation in the ongoing process of divine incarnation—the trace of God in the world and of the world in God. If this lapse into carnality is not, for Origen, a matter of shame, it nonetheless constitutes a provocative scandal, the stumbling block on which all else turns. It is what folds humans back toward their own desire and at the same time propels them beyond themselves in the limitless reach of desire toward a God who ever eludes human grasp. Flesh, including the flesh of textuality, is the place of transformation and striving where time and eternity, difference and identity, multiplicity and unity fleetingly coincide through the ever-creative power of God's love. It is where the divinely generated and generative Word is eternally becoming.

The Ambivalence of the Two-Natured Christ: Athanasius of Alexandria and Gregory of Nyssa

The fourth-century theologians Athanasius of Alexandria and Gregory of Nyssa each played crucial roles in the articulation of trinitiarian theology.

Each also contributed significantly to the adaptation of incarnational christ-ology to the context of trinitarian thought via their early elaborations of a doctrine of two natures that would become the source of enormous contro-versy in subsequent decades—a controversy that of course continues to di-vide Christian communities to this day. Both Athanasius and Gregory work out of an Origenian tradition, yet they develop that tradition in strikingly different ways. With the elevation of the Word or Son to a position of essen-tial equality with the divine Father, the burden of cosmological and soterio-logical mediation rests more heavily than ever on the historical incarnation of Christ, even as the doctrine of the incarnation itself appears more pro-vocatively scandalous than ever. How is one to understand the uniting of the fully transcendent Son with the contrastingly abject flesh of humanity? For Athanasius, the shame of the flesh appears nearly unbearable: the incar-nation of the Word that effects the divinization of flesh thus operates as an antidote to shame, stabilizing a materiality that is otherwise ever sliding back into the abyss of nothingness. For Gregory, in contrast, the shame of the flesh is embraced with excitement: the incarnation of the Word repre-sents the infinite possibilities conveyed by a capacity for transformation fu-elled by the insatiability of desire. In other words, where Origen seems to balance an optimism about fleshly mutability with a vision of ultimate sta-bility within divine love, Athanasius sternly represses mutability in favor of stability while Gregory imagines a mutability without limit, manifested in the endlessly unfurling process of human perfection. Yet, for both, the in-carnation of Christ results in a distinctly hybrid subject who reflects the radical conjunction of essentially alien natures and wills also at work in human salvation.

Athanasius's treatise *On the Incarnation of the Word* opens with the acknowledgment that the doctrine of the incarnation is the object of scorn, mockery, and laughter on the part of "Greeks." (Jews for their part simply fail to see past the flesh.) Yet, insists Athanasius, it is precisely through his "supposed humiliation"—above all, the humiliation of the cross—that Christ demonstrates the power of his divinity and thereby turns false mock-ers into true believers. In order to persuade his readers that a doctrine that appears a matter of embarrassment is anything but that, Athanasius must demonstrate that the incarnation of the Word is in seamless—and seemly!—continuity with the Word's initial role in creation (1). The distinc-tiveness of Athanasius's perspective begins to emerge as he details that role in such a way as already to begin to rescue the Word from the taint of a shame that, for him, ever attends a fleshly nature created *ex nihilo*.

Protesting that it is a sign of divine power and strength that, through his Logos, God creates out of nothing, Athanasius is also preoccupied with the weakness of just such a creation, which is unable, "by virtue of its origin, to continue in one stay." Lacking stability, creation is ever inclined toward corruption, in a return to the nothingness from which it initially emerges. Thus it is that God, taking pity on humanity, gives "them a further gift"— namely "a portion even of the power of his own Word" conveyed in the bestowal of rationality. This is the significance of the scriptural statement that God made humans "in the image" of divinity. But even this "further gift" is not enough: "Knowing once more how the will of humanity could sway to either side, in anticipation he secured the grace given to them by a law" (3). This too, of course, proves insufficient to protect humanity from the forces of corruption and death that result from a transgression to which creatures are apparently always already inclined. "For transgression of the commandment was turning them back to their natural state, so that just as they have had their being out of nothing, so also as might be expected, they might look for corruption into nothing in the course of time. . . . Humanity is by nature mortal, in as much as it is made out of what is not" (4).

The power of the divine Logos sustaining creation and offering the potential for stability is thus tensely balanced against the "natural" tendency of creation to slide back into the "nothingness" signified by mortality or corruptibility. Change, one might say, is for Athanasius always for the worse. Yet it would be "unseemly "and "monstrous" were God to allow this weakness in creation to prevail (6). Thus the incarnation of the Logos, like the activity of the Logos in creation more generally, is not itself a matter of shame but rather a defense against the ever impending shame of material corruptibility. "For this purpose then, the incorporeal and incorruptible and immaterial Word of God comes to our realm. . . . He takes unto himself a body." This body is like ours yet "not merely so," for it comes "from a spotless and stainless virgin." "He prepares the body in the virgin as a temple unto himself." It is, then, a body that the Logos can don without shame, having its source in a most unnatural mother. The purposes of this incarnation are twofold: to satisfy and thus overturn the penalties resulting from the transgression of the law; and to renew and fulfill the promise of the divine image with which humanity was initially graced. "Whereas humanity had turned toward corruption, he might turn them again toward incorruption, and quicken them from death by the appropriation of his body and by the grace of resurrection, banishing death from them like straw from fire" (8). The renewal of humanity is a process at once ontological, accomplished through the transformative appropriation of flesh by the Logos, and pedagogical: "while he blotted out the death which had ensued by the offering of his own body, he corrected their neglect by his own teaching" (10). The Logos remains, however, uncompromised by the flesh: "he was not bound to his body, but was rather himself wielding it." "Not even when the Virgin bore him did he suffer any change" (17).

If Athanasius thus understands himself to have adequately defended the incarnation of the Word against those who mock it, the crucifixion still requires special apology. "Why, then, one might say, if it were necessary for him to yield up his body to death in the stead of all, did he not lay it aside as a man privately, instead of going so far as even to be crucified?" Surely this would have been more honorable than "ignominiously to endure a death like this." Or would it? As Athanasius sees it, it would have been far more shameful to die a natural death and thus succumb to corruptibility than to suffer a violence that exposes the profound unnaturalness of death for one imbued with the power of the Logos (21). It was, moreover, crucial to the revelatory role of the Logos that the death—and thus also the resurrection—of the body assumed be as public as possible (23). In the particular public display of the crucifixion, Christ spreads out his hands to signify the inclusiveness of his sacrificial death; he is lifted up, that the devil might be cast down (25). Meeting violent death at the hands of his enemies, Christ also reveals the inherently agonistic aspect of the incarnation, in which "death is destroyed and . . . the cross is become the victory over it" (27). If the cross has become a victory, it is the victory of the divine Word over the weakness inhering in flesh.

It is also rather explicitly a victory over shame, but in this perhaps a pyrrhic victory. "Banishing death from them like straw from fire," has Athanasius not virtually *annihilated* the very flesh that, on his own account, manifests the power and goodness of the divine Logos who creates *ex nihilo*? Of course, he has not done so—not quite—precisely because incarnation is made so central to his christology. Nonetheless, his incarnate Logos betrays the strain of an asserted "certainty [that] protects it from the shameful,"[69] in which we may hear the echoes of a primal repression that is also a primal abjection. In the beginning of creation, even before mimesis—that "further gift" of the Logos as "image"—comes the exclusion of a fluid and ambiguously maternalized mutability that is willfully mistaken for nothingness. "Even before being *like*, 'I' am not but do *separate, reject, ab-ject*," notes Kristeva, in a strikingly apt (if of course unintentional) reframing of the Athanasian doctrine. She continues: "The more or less beautiful image in which I behold or recognize myself rests upon an abjection that sunders it as soon as repression, the constant watchman, is relaxed."[70] Athanasius does not relax his guard. As a result, his incarnational christology remains haunted by the shame it attempts to refuse. Perhaps that haunting both hides and discloses the source of salvation in and for Athanasius's teaching.

Gregory of Nyssa's christology, as I have already indicated, demonstrates both striking continuities and striking contrasts with Athanasius's thought.[71] In his *Catechetical Oration*, Gregory, like Athanasius, positions himself as responding to non-Christian detractors of incarnationalism: both Jew and Greek, he claims, "will equally reject the plan by which God's word became human, as something incredible and unbefitting to say of God" (5). Like Athanasius, he emphasizes the continuity of the Logos's agency in creation and incarnation. Like Athanasius, he also emphasizes the inherent mutability of a creation that comes from nothing. "Everything that depends on creation for its existence has an innate tendency to change" (6). "Whatever derives from the noncreated nature has its subsistence out of nonbeing. Once it has come into being through change it constantly proceeds to change." Gregory's evaluation of this creaturely mutability, however, diverges sharply from Athanasius's. "If it acts according to its nature, this continued change is for the better. But if it is diverted from the straight path, there succeeds a movement in the opposite direction" (8).

Since, for Athanasius, all change is for the worse, the deterioration of mutable creatures is only to be expected and thus the fall scarcely requires explanation. For Gregory, on the other hand, as for Origen, the fall represents a dramatic perversion of creation that results from the freedom God grants to humans. The source of evil lies in the unpredictable convertibility of the will, not the inevitable corruption of the flesh (5). Yet even human freedom is not quite enough to account for the surprising inclination of humans to diverge from the goodness of their created nature. Thus Gregory invokes the myth of the angel (also a creature and thus mutable) who "falls" into envy upon perceiving the stamp of the divine image that humanity uniquely bears; he thereafter "cunningly deceives and cheats humanity by persuading it to become its own murderer and assassin" (6). (Gregory's fallen angel here evidences affinities with the *Apocryphon of John*'s Yaldabaoth.) "Nor would this deception have succeeded had not the fishhook of evil been furnished with an outward appearance of good, as with a bait" (21). The success of demonic deceit accounts for the fact that human "life is fleeting, subject to passion, mortal, liable in soul and body to every type of suffering" (5).

Like Athanasius, Gregory insists that the incarnation of the Word was not an unseemly but an altogether appropriate divine response to the condition of humanity—though, again, he attributes that condition not to the general mutability of created nature but to the particular (albeit also collective) perversion of human wills subjected to diabolical trickery. He insists that "there is nothing shameful" or alien to God in the flow of creaturely existence—"the birth, the upbringing, the growth, the natural advance to maturity, the experience of death and the return from it." Indeed, such things are "altogether free from shame" (9). Moreover, "the whole anatomy of the body is uniformly to be valued"—including the "generative organs" (28).

Nonetheless, the contrast between divine transcendence and human finitude cannot be denied. "Why, then, they ask, did the divine stoop to such humiliation?" (14). If the question is fair, the answer is also clear: "Our nature was sick and needed a doctor. Humanity had fallen and needed someone to raise it up. . . . The one who had ceased to participate in the good needed someone to bring him back to it. . . . The prisoner was looking for someone to ransom him" (15). Why, however, did God die? Because he was born, and so that he could be resurrected, answers Gregory (32). Gregory's rationale for the incarnation and crucifixion does not, perhaps, differ greatly from Athanasius's. It encompasses both the need for an ontological—indeed, vividly metabolic (37)—restoration of human nature effected by its healing (re)union with the divine Word, on the one hand, and the necessity that the devil be forced to relinquish his claim on humanity, on the other. Like Athanasius, Gregory understands that Christ had to redeem humanity from its enslavement to the devil in accordance with the dictates of justice (23), yet his account lays less stress on the oppositional logic of law and transgression than on the subtle forces of mutual deceit. Thus the incarnate Christ is repeatedly represented as the "bait" with which God "hooks" and thus deceives the one who has already "hooked" and deceived humanity. The Word veils itself in human nature so that the devil "might swallow the Godhead like a fishhook along with the flesh, which was the bait" (24). Swallowing the divine Word, the devil is like the Johannine "darkness" that once refused but now receives the light: "thus, when life came to dwell with death and light shone upon darkness, their contraries might vanish away" (24). "For he who first deceived man by the bait of pleasure is himself deceived by the camouflage of human nature." Once again, mutability is bent to the purposes of salvation, as even deceit can be converted to benefit. "The purpose of the action changes it into something good. For the one practiced deceit to ruin our nature; but the other, being at once just and good and wise, made use of a deceitful device to save the one who had been ruined. . . . He freed man from evil, and healed the very author of evil himself" (26).

Gregory's defense of the native goodness of creation thus considerably exceeds Athanasius's grudging affirmation of humanity's capacity to be saved from its shameful propensity for corruption. His optimistic view of creation eases the imaginative challenge presented by a doctrine of incarnation accommodated to the context of a fourth-century theology inclined to emphasize the distance that separates the transcendent and essentially divine Word from creatures derived from nothingness. It also powerfully inflects his soteriology, which appears to go beyond even Origen's thought in embracing creaturely mutability as the source of ongoing perfectibility. Christian life becomes for Gregory a continuous liturgy of transformation. In even an ordinary meal, bread and wine "become blood and flesh, since in each case the food is changed by the power of assimilation into the form of the body"; in the eucharist, bread and wine are simultaneously converted into the blood and flesh of Christ, so that Christ "unites himself" with the bodies of all believers who thereby come to share in "that immortal body" (37). Baptism too initiates a process of ongoing transformation, "for it is patent to everyone that we receive the saving birth for the purpose of renewing and changing our nature," insists Gregory. Convertibility is the hallmark of Christian identity, evidenced in "the way of life each chooses" (40).

Conclusions

The articulation of identity entails "the willed assumption of stigma," as Sedgwick puts it, in Kristeva's terms, the suffering of "a law that mutilates."[72] Through the shameless conversion of stigmatization, identity emerges in and as an ever contested and ever transformable performance that has its beginning in the subject's very vulnerability to shame. That is to say, identity is produced in the visible wounding of the subject by shame. (The subject is always already thus wounded.) The wound of identity is at once a shining scar that marks a tearing away from the other and a dark welling of blood that silently mourns a (nearly) lost connection. The defiant politics of identity illumined in Chapter 1 cannot, then, be separated from the ambivalent depths of abjection repeatedly touched upon in this chapter's explorations of the divine Word's enfleshment.

While the early Christian martyrs and later ascetics are seen to convert the spectacle of public humiliation into glory, transforming the shaming loss of face into a novel witness of identity, the incarnate Christ is understood to descend from the glory of his divine identity to take on the intimate shame of the flesh, in an abjection "from which identity becomes absent."[73] Yet if Christic abjection is the death of the subject it is also its glorious resurrection, as we have seen. The Word is the source of "eternal life" not despite but because of the fact that it is always shamelessly becoming flesh. Christ is the border of Word and flesh where death touches life and time coincides with eternity. The abject is also such a border. Initially produced by an annihilating act of exclusion, separation, and shaming, this border is ever again traversed by a shameless joying that disrupts identity and thereby allows it to be born again, *ex nihilo*—that is, from the ambiguously "maternal" abject, which is neither subject nor object. Resurrection emerges out of the dissolution inhering in a flesh that is always edged with the sublime precisely because it exceeds both "the subject" and "the body." In the shameless *jouissance* of abjection—in the shameful enfleshment of Word—the self is split from itself (it is both "here" and "elsewhere") and time is doubled: there is "a time of oblivion and thunder, of veiled infinity and the moment when revelation bursts forth."

John's gospel inaugurates what becomes an extended ancient Christian meditation on the incarnation of the divine Word, uncovering the hope for resurrection harbored within a fleshly abjection where "I" am in you and "you" are in me—where identity, in other words, ceases to hold and the communion of love takes its beginning. Both Tertullian and the *Apocryphon of John* work out of a distinctly Johannine matrix. Both also explicitly surface the shame that inheres in carnality and that must, moreover, be actively appropriated by human creatures who desire salvific transformation. However, their theologies also differ dramatically, differences that arise in part from an ambivalence already present in the Gospel of John. Tertullian glories in mimicking Christ by shamelessly celebrating the stigma of natal and mortal flesh and thereby securing the promise of eternal regeneration within a fleshly resurrection. The *Apocryphon,* for its part, construes flesh (or perhaps, more precisely, the ordered "body") as *both* the signifier of a shameful desire for autonomy and domination—the desire to "be" a subject by "possessing" an object—*and* the site of a humiliation of desire that ultimately gives way to the humility of repentence and the liberation of the cosmos from the imprisonment of embodied existence.

Origen, also deeply influenced by John's gospel, betrays affinities with the *Apocryphon*'s spiritualizing tendencies while simultaneously sharing Tertullian's conviction that materiality is the direct effect of divine desire and generativity, albeit an ambivalent effect. At first glance, Origen appears to bear the shame of abjection more lightly than the other theologians here considered, precisely because he seems to wear the flesh more lightly. Yet the very complexity of his thought, which is not only logocentric but also deeply incarnational, together with the sustained ambiguity of his texts regarding the nature of the resurrection, argues against such a view. Indeed, Origen may be among the most subtle of the ancient theorists to have explored the borderline of flesh and Word wherein the abjection of materiality discloses the sublimity of the spirit, as is evidenced not least in his incarnational hermeneutics. Word, for Origen, is always revealed in the flesh of text and the text of flesh. In the fourth century, Origen's legacy gives rise to a range of diverse incarnational christologies. Even the relatively similar christologies of Athanasius and Gregory of Nyssa demonstrate the richness and malleability of a tradition that would ultimately generate violent debate concerning the relation of the divine and human natures of Christ. Now the shame of the flesh created *ex nihilo* stands in starker than ever contrast to the transcendence of the essentially divine Word of trinitarian theology. Faced with the thrilling conflation of apparent oppositions enacted by the incarnation of the Word in Christ, Athanasius fantasizes the ultimate stabilization of flesh by Word, whereas Gregory imagines the endless perfectibility of a created nature ever malleably transformed by Word.

In all its many variations, far exceeding the sampling of texts here surveyed, incarnational christology, together with the cosmology to which it is tightly bound, reflects a common and ongoing preoccupation of ancient Christian thought with the abysmal fecundity of an abjection that is always edged with the sublime—a flesh that is ever disclosing spirit, a death that continuously gives rise to resurrection, a shame that is always being converted to glory. The enfleshment of the divine Word is the self-revelatory manifestation of divine creativity, and the inherent mutability of creation may result in either the perversion or the perfecting of God's generative desire. If creaturely perversion is construed as the source of shame, this is, paradoxically, because such perversion refuses shame. It is not perverse enough, then. It fails to embrace the joyous passion of a glorious, and also horrifying, potentiality that emerges at the abjected limits of divine/human selfhood—that emerges at the point where a cosmic order of bodies and subjects ever in danger of death by stagnation is sacrificed for the wild hope of eternal generation.

Chapter 3
The Desire and Pursuit of Humiliation

The justification of certain ascetic tendencies lies there: the mortifications of fasting are not only agreeable to God; they bring us closer to the situation that is the fundamental event of our being: the need for escape. . . . Shame arises each time we are unable to make others forget our basic nudity. It is related to everything we would like to hide and that we cannot bury or cover up. . . . The necessity of fleeing, in order to hide oneself, is put in check by the impossibility of fleeing oneself.

—Emmanuel Levinas, On Escape

For also when he was about to eat or sleep or to attend to the other bodily necessities, he was ashamed (āischuneto) as he thought about the intellectual part of the soul. Frequently when he was about to eat with many other monks, recalling the spiritual food, he would excuse himself and go some distance from them, thinking he would blush (eruthrian) if he were seen eating by others. He ate by himself, of course, according to his body's need, yet often with the brothers as well, feeling embarrassed (aidoumenos) because of them and yet speaking boldly because of the help his words brought them. . . . Neither did anyone ever see him undressed— indeed, no one saw the body of Antony naked, except when he died and was buried.

—Athanasius, Life of Antony 45, 47

Ancient Christians understood that the divine Logos submitted to the humiliation of flesh in order to redeem humanity. It might seem, then, that the corresponding path laid out for humans was one of sheer ascent to glory. Yet the practices of ascetics, as well as the examples of martyrs, suggest otherwise. A plunge into the abyss of abjection was necessarily undertaken by those who aspired to transcendence. In imitation of Christ, holy men and women of late antiquity engaged in elaborate rituals of self-humiliation through which they might hope to escape the unbearable weight of selfhood registered in the relentless drag of bodily existence. Paradoxically, that which was the source of shame could only be exited along a path that detoured, seemingly endlessly, through the depths of shame. Salvation never seemed nearer than when the attempt to hide oneself from oneself forced confrontation with the naked exposure of human need—or, in more visceral terms, when the stench of one's own putrification gave rise to the nauseous revolt of flesh against flesh.

Modern interpreters have frequently, and understandably, recoiled from such horrors, seemingly repressing their own nausea by forcefully pathologizing its sources. Eighteenth-century Roman historian Edward Gibbon wrote with famous distaste of "the swarms of monks, who arose from the Nile, overspread and darkened the face of the Christian world."[1] Almost as famous by now is E. R. Dodds's question: "Where did all this madness come from?"[2] The "madness" that he has in mind is manifested in the "continuous physical self-torture" of which the literature of ancient Christian asceticism provides "numerous and repulsive examples," as he puts it: "several [of the Desert Fathers] live for years on top of pillars, another immures himself in a packing-case where he cannot stand upright, others remain perpetually in a standing position; others again load themselves with heavy chains . . . ; others pride themselves on such feats of endurance as total abstinence from food throughout Lent."[3] Dodds's diagnosis? "I incline to see the whole development less as an infection from an extraneous source than as an endogenous neurosis, an index of intense and widespread guilt-feelings."[4]

A more promising approach to interpreting the "endogenous" penchant for self-humiliation may be opened by those philosophers who have discerned in the affects of shame, nausea, and anxiety a revolt against "being" itself. In an early work entitled "On Escape," Emmanuel Levinas argues that shame is a response less to human finitude (as is often imagined) than to "a plenitude of being," what he elsewhere names the "totality of being."[5] It arises from the experienced thwarting of a need that "is not oriented toward the complete fulfillment of a limited being, toward satisfaction, but toward release and escape."[6] Need cannot be oriented toward fulfillment because being is not finite any more than it is infinite: requiring no fulfillment and allowing no expansion, it simply *is*. Shame, then, for Levinas registers the inescapability of being's asserted totality, even as it likewise registers the need for escape.[7]

"Under the poignant form of modesty, shame is primarily connected to our body," Levinas further observes. Far exceeding mere awareness of moral transgression, it arises from "the very fact of having a body, of being there."[8] Being, "being there" (Martin Heidegger's *Dasein*) or the "there-is-ness" (*il y a*) of existence is "what appears in shame" through its nakedly intimate exposure—"the fact of being riveted to oneself, the radical impossibility of fleeing oneself to hide from oneself, the unalterably binding presence of the I to itself."[9] For Levinas, the weight of being experienced in the shame of embodiment manifests the bind of a subjectivity riveted to ontology by the force of a stifling assertion of self-sufficiency that simultaneously gives rise, like a gag reflex, to a need for escape. He concludes: "It is a matter of getting out of being by a new path, at the risk of overturning certain notions that to common sense and the wisdom of the nations seemed the most evident."[10]

Is the path of escape not the path of shame itself, defying the wisdom of the nations and revealing (perhaps) a plenitude that is both more and less than a "totality"? Levinas does not quite say this, yet the performative effect of a work that is most compelling where it exposes the reader to the unbearable shame of existence is arguably to hint at just that. Shame is, at the very least, coextensive with the experienced need to flee the confinements of a subjectivity construed in terms of its own inevitability and autonomy. In his later writings, Levinas seems to have found his path of escape; at any rate, he no longer finds it necessary to speak of the need for escape. By shifting weight from the self-justifying existence of the subject to the presenting "face" of the inherently unknowable "other," whose "justified existence is the primary fact," he seeks to displace the ominous totality of being with the promising infinitude of ethical responsibility. Shame, which attends "the commencement of moral consciousness, which calls in question my freedom," is crucial to a conversion at once existential and philosophical—in the latter case, the conversion of philosophy (potentially of theology as well) from ontology to an ethically based metaphysics.[11] Now "I" only exist "because I myself can feel myself to be the other of the other," he suggests. Paradoxically, perhaps, it is through accepting the burden of shame conveyed by the inescapability of the infinite responsibility of relationality that the heaviness of being's self-sufficiency is shed, in Levinas's view. "This way of measuring oneself against the perfection of infinity is not a theoretical consideration; it is accomplished as shame, where freedom discovers itself murderous in its very exercise. It is accomplished in shame where freedom at the same time is *discovered* in the consciousness of shame and is *concealed* in the shame itself."[12] Returning elsewhere to the critical discussion of a freedom that inheres not in the autonomy of the self but in the self-sacrifice entailed in unlimited responsiveness, he refers to the "anarchical passivity" of a subject created *ex nihilo* and thus unlinked from the substantiality of being. Here the language of shame shifts to that of remorse: "Its recurrence is the contracting of an ego, going to the hither side of identity, gnawing away at this very identity—identity gnawing away at itself—in a remorse. . . . It is to hold onto oneself while gnawing away at oneself."[13]

Like the early Levinas, but subtly differing from the later Levinas, ancient Christian ascetics do not move immediately or directly to resolve shame within the frame of the ethical, though the discourse of ethics, frequently displayed under the banner of *agape* or *caritas*, is by no means absent from their reflections.[14] Rather, they seem to linger within shame, as if engaged in a wager that the unrelenting drag of existence-as-we-know-it can thereby be overcome. Thus a desert abbot encapsulates his own life's learning as follows: "To blame and reproach myself without ceasing." To this his interlocutor responds: "There is no other road to follow, only this" (*Sayings of the Fathers* 15.19). Taking on the weight of their own humiliation, indeed taking it to the point of excess and thus already beginning their escape, ancient Christians pursue a humility experienced most acutely in the "face" of the infinite otherness of God. If God's judgment is the source of shame's gravity, God's grace converts an unbearable weight into the unbearable lightness of a being that is always "gnawing away at itself." Nor can judgment ever be separated from grace, from the perspective of ancient Christian asceticism: judgment itself arrives and is received as a gift. It is the gift of transcendence—not, however, a transcendence of flesh so much as a transcendence uncovered within the mutability of both flesh and spirit, less an ascent to the dizzying peaks of final or total perfection than a descent into the nauseating depths of ever unfolding possibility.

Iterating Humiliation: Palladius on the Lives of Ascetics

Palladius's *Lausiac History*, composed in the early fifth century, takes its readers on a virtual pilgrimage to the ascetic settlements of the Mediterranean where the destinations are not places but persons.[15] It thus takes the form of a collection of mini-hagiographies that derive their power, as Patricia Cox Miller argues, from the principles of repetition and condensation also evidenced in contemporary practices of visual representation. "The discrete parts of these collections are not full biographies but ekphrastic sketches that picture a 'way of life'. . . . Representational integrity, in other words, is carried by the fragment."[16] Of interest here is the play of similarity and difference mobilized across iterative representations of ascetic humility in Palladius's text. Vainglory and pride hold a privileged place in his treatment of the demonic impulses that tempt pious Christians, notes David Brakke; humility, their antidote, looms correspondingly large.[17]

Let us take as our first stopping point on Palladius's tour of saints the striking portrait of one Benjamin, a desert ascetic "who had lived eighty years and attained the height of ascetic perfection," confirmed by his gift for healing "all sickness." Palladius does not choose to relate examples of Benjamin's healing powers, as we might initially expect. Instead, he goes on immediately to inform his readers of Benjamin's own descent into sickness: "this man, so greatly honored by the gift of healing, contracted dropsy about eight months before he died." Benjamin's body is represented as so alarmingly swollen that "another person's fingers could not reach around one of his." Unable any longer to lie down, he is accommodated by a "very wide seat" on which he spends the remaining months of his life. After he dies, the door and jambs of his house have to be dismantled in order for his body to be removed. In another context, such a scene might seem at once embarrassing, poignant, and humorous (as viewers of the film *What's Eating Gilbert Grape?* can attest). Palladius, however, views and thus imbues it with a sense of awe.

Significantly, this is not the only swollen body encountered in Palladius's *History*, but it *is* one of the oddest. How is Benjamin's grotesque flesh to be interpreted? Why should it inspire our awe? Palladius himself seems somewhat uncertain, for he finds it necessary to justify his decision to narrate this story: "I felt that I must tell about this sickness so that we might not be too surprised when some accident befalls just men." This justification is not fully satisfying, not least because it sits uneasily within the context of Palladius's strong emphasis on a divine providence that does not usually seem to leave much room for accidents. More illumining are the words placed in the mouth of Bishop Dioscorus, instructing Palladius and his mentor Evagrius on what to see when they gaze at Benjamin: "Come here, see a new Job who possesses boundless gratitude while in a state of great bodily swelling and incurable sickness." The boundlessness of Benjamin's gratitude, marked by his continued gift for curing others while remaining himself without cure, is thus rhetorically matched by the apparent boundlessness of his swollen flesh. Palladius and the other visitors, unable to bear the disturbing sight of this Job-like apparition, are forced to avert their eyes. Benjamin, for his part, remains indifferent to his own suffering, praying only that "the inner man not contract dropsy." The asserted contrast between Benjamin's inner and outer states stands in subtle tension with the bishop's hint that the two are also powerfully linked. The culmination of a life of ascetic perfection is an excess of spiritual grace coinciding with an excess of fleshly humiliation—or simply an excess of flesh (*Lausiac History* 12).

Palladius makes it clear that humility is a crucial virtue for ascetics, whose very strivings for perfection constantly expose them to the temptation of pride. To be *humble* is, moreover, conceptually and linguistically indistinguishable from being *humiliated*: humility is not a static quality but an open and ongoing process. Pride in achieved virtue is cured when ascetics are "given over either to shameless conduct or to shameful experiences": thus, the monk Paphnutius, as cited approvingly by Palladius. "Because of the resultant humiliation and shame they slowly rid themselves of the pride they have in their pretended virtue. For when a person is swollen with pride . . . God removes the Angel of Providence from him" (47.8). Benjamin is a particularly revealing if also somewhat anomalous figure in Palladius's text, in large part because his perfection is not said to result in pride and his humiliation thus lacks the sting of chastisement. Rather it seems to be presented as an opportunity, even a perverse kind of reward. As his virtue increases, he swells with humility and charity. The image of his oversized corpse being carried through the burst doorway of his house conveys not only painful vulnerability but also an almost palpable dignity.

Other swollen bodies in the *Lausiac History* betray more ambivalence. Thus John, beset with avarice, "came down with elephantiasis; you could not put a finger on a single part of his body without its being contaminated" (17.4). It is not clear whether the contagious humiliation of John's flesh finally converts him to charity, but it does effectively confront him with his own greed. Macarius of Alexandria, who perceives in himself the impulse of revenge when he kills a gnat that has stung his foot, "condemned himself to sit naked in the marsh of Scete out in the great desert for a period of six months." Devoured by mosquitoes, "he became so swollen that some thought he had elephantiasis" and is recognizable only by his voice (18.4). In this case, the grotesque swelling of the flesh, manifesting a self-chastisement itself grossly in excess of the sin committed, is clearly productive of virtue. The productivity of induced excess is echoed in the account of a demon-possessed boy brought for healing to that same Macarius. Suspended in the air by the power of Macarius's prayer, he "swelled up like a wineskin and became so inflamed that he became afflicted with erysipelas."

Swollen almost to the point of bursting, he gushes water "through all his sense organs," and is thus "returned once more to his former size" (18.22). Sometimes excess is the starting point for healing. Another demon-possessed young man eats and drinks to excess and vomits compulsively, consuming even his own excrement and urine in his insatiability, until Macarius of Egypt quite sensibly puts him on a restricted diet and a regime of physical exercise (17.11–13).

Still other bodies are observed not swelling beyond bounds but falling to pieces. As in the cases of swollen bodies, these range from instances of involuntary but productive chastisement, to apparently undeserved affliction borne with dignity, to self-inflicted injury. Heron, for example, is beset by such extreme arrogance in his ascetic practice that he becomes vulnerable to the most vulgar of temptations. Attending the theater and horse races and frequenting taverns, he is abandoned to gluttony and lust. Apparently contracting a sexually transmitted disease, "for half a year he was so ill that his genitals putrefied and fell off." The emasculating disease, together with the shame of having succumbed so thoroughly to "womanish" desires of the flesh, finally cures him of his pride and restores him to grace shortly before his death (26.4). Stephen the Libyan, for his part, suffers, from no obvious fault of his own, from "the terrible ulcerous condition know as cancer." Like Benjamin, he displays uncanny serenity in his suffering, weaving palm leaves and chatting with his visitors during a surgical procedure in which "his members were being cut away like locks of hair" (24.2). Ammonius, having "attained the heights of piety," takes matters into his own hands by slicing his left ear off in order to evade ordination. When the bishop who seeks to ordain him insists that his mutilation does not disqualify him from the priesthood, declaring that he will accept even a priest with his nose cut off, Ammonius swears, "If you compel me, I will cut out my tongue." (This threat is evidently an effective deterrant.) Faced with the still graver danger presented by his own persistent desire, Ammonius "heated an iron in the fire and applied it to his limbs, so that he became ulcerated all over" (11.1–4). Of Elpidius, it is said, "He reached such a high degree of mortification and so wasted away his body that the sun shone through his bones" (48.3)

All these cases of physical fragmentation and excess seem to derive their signifying power from the blurring of the categories of self-willed and involuntary affliction and of chastisement that is apparently deserved and that which is seemingly arbitrary or accidental yet thereby no less part of God's providential plan. Within ascetic practice, such distinctions are rendered very nearly irrelevant: every humiliation is potentially productive of humility. Self-induced affliction actively courts humility; by definition, it exceeds the perceived infraction that initially motivates it. It thereby interpretively mediates involuntary suffering, which strengthens and confirms humility to the very extent that it exceeds the sufferer's sin. Indeed, the sheer undeserved givenness of physical existence may itself be rendered a source of humiliation, as reflected in Palladius's memory of his master Isidore: "I often knew him to weep at table, and upon asking the reason for the tears, I received this reply: 'I am ashamed to partake of irrational food; I am a rational being and I ought to be in a paradise of pleasure because of the power given to us by Christ'" (1.3). Isidore appears to feel inescapably bound by bodily needs that hold him back from the paradise of pleasure; his shame registers both "the radical impossibility of fleeing oneself to hide from oneself" and the desire to do precisely that, as Levinas puts it. Yet images of swelling and disintegrating flesh present bodies that are already in the process of escaping the weight of their ineluctible givenness. By revealing physical existence as always both more and less than "whole,"does Palladius not hint that flesh is ever the site and source of the humiliation of being's presumed self-sufficiency? In shame, the "I" grotesquely exceeds itself; alternately, and equally grotesquely, it falls to pieces. Palladius's ascetics discover in the body's nauseating lack of stability and wholeness a path of escape toward transcendence.

The productivity of shame is even more explicitly in evidence in tales from the *Lausiac History* that emphasize less the manifest humiliation of the body than the performative chastening of the spirit. Here demons frequently take on a role analogous to the role of pain and disease in stories of fleshly humiliation: relentlessly exposing ascetics to their shameful vulnerability to temptation, the demons inadvertently aid them in the cultivation of humility, which partly accounts for the intimacy, even near-identity, that characterizes the relation of ascetics to demons.[18] Thus the Ethiopian Moses, a former bandit, struggles mightily against the demons who are "trying to draw him back into his old ways of intemperance and impurity" (19.5). He pursues the most extreme disciplines yet still continues to be troubled by fantasies and dreams of shameful pleasures. His strenuous battles with the demons bring him almost to the point of death. Finally his mentor Isidore says to him: "Stop contending with demons and do not bother them, for there are limits in bravery as well as in ascetic practice." Isidore announces that Moses will no longer be troubled by tempting dreams, adding: "You were subjected to this for your own good, so that you might not boast of overcoming passion" (19.10). It is, then, through experiencing humiliation in his struggles with demonic temptations that the man of violence learns how to relinquish his desire to triumph.

A monk named Pachon is similarly plagued by demonic temptations, to the point that he despairs. Feeling utterly abandoned by God, he abandons himself to certain death: "I came across a hyena's cave. Here I placed myself naked one day in hopes that the wild beasts would devour me" (23.3). The hyenas, however, refuse to consume him. Instead, as Pachon tells it, "The beasts, both male and female came out. They smelled me and licked me all over from head to foot." Despite the ancient association of hyenas with an excessive and polymorphic sexuality,[19] Pachon misinterprets this scene of sensuous self-abandonment, thinking that he has been spared temptation as well as death. It is a divinely diabolical set-up: lulled into a false sense of security, Pachon is now tortured still more exquisitely by the demon of lust: "The demon took on the form of an Ethiopian maiden whom I had once seen in my youth gathering papyrus, and sat on my knees" (23.5). The demon/girl excites him physically to the point that he fantasizes that he is having intercourse with her. A box on the ear from the monk causes the image to disappear, but leaves him with an "evil smell" on his hand that endures for two full years. (We might wonder whether his hand touched more than the girl's ear. Or simply: more than the girl.)[20] Again he despairs and seeks death, this time in the sting of an asp placed on his genitals; again the deadly creature fails to bite him and thus refuses to release him from his shame. Finally a divine voice addresses him, announcing a turning point in his internal struggles: "It was for this reason that I let you be depressed, so that you might not become haughty as a strong person, but rather might know your own weakness, and that you might not trust too much in your own way of life, but rather come running to God for help" (23.6). Having felt utterly abandoned by God, Pachon has learned to abandon himself utterly to God, even as he formerly attempted to abandon himself to the sting of death. Like Moses, he has been tutored by demons in the painful virtue of humility.

Yet the desert includes more than demons and wild beasts; it is also a place of encounters between ascetics in which shame likewise paves the path of salvation. Indeed, shame arguably lines the border between the interior and the exterior, the intensely private and unavoidably social dimensions of ascetic practice. Typical is the story of Macarius of Alexandria, whose excessive humility humiliates others. Disguising himself as a common laborer, the aged ascetic humbles himself by applying for membership in Pachomius's monastery without laying claim to his own well-established reputation for virtue. Pachomius initially refuses him, declaring, "The brethren are ascetics and you cannot bear their labors; you will be embarrassed and leave, and will revile them" (18.13). Macarius, however, persists, and finally he is allowed to enter on the condition that he be expelled if he proves unsuited to the rigors of monastic life. During Lent, however, his discipline so far exceeds that of the others that they are embarrassed, threaten to leave, and revile Macarius, in a nearly exact reversal of Pachomius's prediction. Now Macarius's true identity is revealed to Pachomius in an answer to prayer. The monastic leader then addresses Macarius affectionately before politely requesting that he leave the monastery, thanking him "for having made my children knuckle down so that they might not become haughty about their own ascetic practices" (18.16).

The tale of an unnamed nun similarly features concealed identity, the courting of humiliation by others, and a revelation that results in the humbling of the very sisters who have formerly despised her. This Cinderella-like story has a sharper edge than that of Macarius, however. The woman's disguise is more elaborate than Macarius's and her humiliation more extreme: she pretends madness and demon-possession, with the result that she is both verbally and physically abused, treated like the most lowly of servants by the sisters in the monastery where she dwells for many years. "She was never angry at anyone, nor did she grumble or talk, either little or much, although she was maltreated, insulted, cursed, and loathed" (34.2). Her cover is blown by the holy anchorite Piteroum, to whom an angel appears, seeking to humble his pride by asking him, "Why do you think so much of yourself . . . ? Do you want to see someone more pious than yourself, a woman?" Journeying in search of this icon of piety, he falls down at her feet and asks for her blessing when he finally discovers her in the kitchen of the monastery where she lives. The sisters of the monastery are at first astonished and then mortified when Piteroum identifies the woman as "spiritual mother . . . to both you and me" (34.6). Their shamed confessions and abject apologies erupt in an excessive overflow. Thus deprived of the humiliation that was at the center of her own ascetic practice, the now-revered "mother" is forced to leave: admiration is apparently one form of temptation she cannot endure. "Where she went and where she disappeared to, and how she died, nobody knows," concludes Palladius (34.7). Is this tragedy or triumph? Surely the latter, from Palladius's perspective. Even the woman's disappearing is invisible, her death unwitnessed. Her dissolution within humility is absolute. Indeed, in this story, everyone is humbled in the end. The zero-sum logic of competition is exceeded: there is plenty of humiliation to go around.

Achieving such productive excess of humility is no small trick. As Palladius remarks in his prologue, inferior ascetics represent a threat to the one in pursuit of holiness not only because their laxity might prove contagious but also because it might tempt pride: "you will be puffed up and proud and will ridicule them—that much will harm you too" (prol. 15). Within a communal context, the humiliation of one would seem, then, always in danger of being achieved at the cost of the pride of another. Indeed, this is a danger that threatens Palladius himself precisely when he records the cautionary tales of ascetics who fall through pride (e.g., 25, 27, 28, 53). Pride, when viewed as a vice, is as infectious as shame, if the pride of others tempts ascetics to feel proud of their own comparative humility.

Oddly, and disturbingly, Palladius's *History* nonetheless includes at least two relatively extended tales that involve the *deliberate* shaming of one ascetic by another without demonstrating any overt criticism of the shamer. The first concerns a wealthy Alexandrian virgin whose greed is uncovered by yet another monk with the name of Macarius, who tricks her into investing some of her riches in gemstones. Accepting the virgin's money, he spends it on the hospital that he oversees, saying nothing of this to the woman. When the virgin finally overcomes her embarrassment and asks him what has come of the jewels she has purchased, he brings her to the hospital and shows her the diseased and crippled women housed there, exclaiming, "Look, here are your hyacinths!" Leading her to the men's quarters, he pronounces, "Behold your emeralds! If they do not please you, take your money back!" Subsequently, the woman falls ill from grief at her own exposed sin, and the niece to whom she had hoped to pass on her wealth dies childless (6).

If one might wonder at Palladius's apparent lack of concern for Macarius's dangerous brush with pride, not to mention the virgin's fall into despair, the second tale of an unnamed virgin's deliberate humiliation by an ascetic trickster is still more disturbing. This story, in contrast to the first, involves a woman whose piety appears exemplary, as manifested in her observance of absolute seclusion. Learning of the virtue of this Roman virgin, the wandering ascetic Serapion, clad in nothing but a loincloth, insists on seeing her, already implicitly challenging her chosen discipline. Their dialogue unfolds in a battle of wits, as the traveling monk asks her why she keeps sitting in one place, to which she responds that she does not sit but travels to God on a journey that no one can make in the flesh. Now Serapion's challenge becomes explicit, as he demands that she prove the truth of her words by imitating his own, more literal practice: "Go out and show yourself" (37.14). Despite her considerable resistance, Serapion eventually convinces the virgin to put her modesty to the test by appearing in public. Even this does not satisfy him, however: "Disrobe yourself and place your clothing on your shoulders and go through the middle of the city with me in the lead this way," he demands. When she protests that others will think her "insane and demon-ridden," he asks why she should care. She pleads with him: "If you wish anything else, I will do it; for I do not boast that I have come to this point" (37.15). Serapion again translates her apparent modesty into a manifestation of pride, claiming that she considers herself "more pious than the others"—specifically, more pious than himself. "I will show you that I am dead to the world, for I will do this without shame and without feeling," he boasts, now indeed taking the lead. Palladius concludes his tale with apparent satisfaction: "Thus he left her humbled and broke her pride" (37.16). Like the persecutors who threaten Christian virgins with rape if they refuse to deny their faith, Serapion has presented the Roman virgin with a nearly impossible choice. Either way, she loses. Then again, either way, she gains: either way, she is humbled, her pride broken.

It is perhaps no accident that these two stories of the deliberate, punitive shaming of one ascetic by another both involve the humiliation of a woman by a man, no accident either that the more extreme of the two stories of concealed identity as a laudable strategy of self-humiliation also involves a woman. As we also saw in Chapter 1, women seem to be ambivalently privileged in many ancient Christian texts due to their perceived greater vulnerability to shame. Men, conversely, can be shamed by being rendered womanish. In contexts where a sensitivity to shame is cultivated, misogyny is potentially intensified, as evidenced not only in the disturbing complacency that haunts accounts of humiliated virgins but also in the blame-the-victim strategy that taints anecdotes like that of Pachon, in which, as we have seen, a darkly exoticized female figure summoned from the depths of a monk's memory conveys the shame of a disavowed desire that clings to the monk's flesh like an "evil smell." At the same time, misogyny is very nearly imploded, as the lowliness of the female sex opens onto a bottomless capacity for the very humiliation that is most ardently courted by ascetic practitioners. Returning to the tale of Serapion and the Roman virgin, we might now ask: if the woman is left humbled, her pride broken, is the unacknowledged (and thus unredeemed) pride of the monk Serapion not also thereby exposed to humiliation, in the eyes of a knowing reader observing this staged contest of virtue? If so, perhaps they both win in the end. Consider too the painful story of the holy maidservant Alexandra, the recipient of a man's unwanted desire: "Rather than scandalize a soul made in the image of God," she tells her visitor Melania, "I betook myself alive to a tomb, lest I seem to cause him suffering or reject him" (5.2). Here the misogynistic objectification of woman as the cause of masculine lust is appropriated by the woman in an excessive performance of self-humiliation that discloses not only the dangers of desire but also the triumph of charity within the self-sacrifice of humility.

Elizabeth Clark has discussed the stereotypical rhetorical use of praiseworthy female figures to shame men into virtuous behavior.[21] In keeping with such convention, Palladius quite self-consciously includes in his *History* many laudatory entries on women admired for their virtue: "I must also commemorate in this book the courageous women to whom God granted struggles equal to those of men, so that no one could plead as an excuse that women are too weak to practice virtue successfully" (41.1; see also 42, 54, 55, 56, 57, 59, 61, 63, 64, 67). If the showcased examples of "courageous women" are, rather literally, class acts that serve as goads to other women (cf. foreword 1) and presumably to men as well, their very idealization nonetheless seems to distance such women from the suffering of humiliation and tempering of pride that mark the struggles of ascetic life elsewhere in Palladius's text. The most effective shaming exempla of the *Lausiac History* are the women (as well as the men) whom Palladius's narrative has most elaborately exposed to shame: in their unbearable humiliation, the reader glimpses the miracle of a humility worthy of imitation.

Narratively anchored by the patronage of virtuous urban aristocrats like Melania as well as that of the imperial chamberlain Lausus, to whom the history is dedicated, as a compiler of this hagiographic travelogue Palladius is also a self-represented desert dweller. Like others, he comes to the desert to confront what he would like to hide but cannot hide. He comes to encounter his own unavoidable shame, and in writing of that encounter he also deliberately exposes his shame to his readers. "It so happened that I was troubled by concupiscence both in my thoughts by day and in my dreams by night," he recounts. "My passions were such that I was on the point of leaving the desert, as I had not disclosed this matter to my neighboring monks or to my teacher Evagrius" (23.1). This humiliating confession introduces his narrated encounter with Pachon, who, as we have already seen, was similarly tempted by lust and despair. Palladius's visit to

Pachon was as secret as the desires that troubled him, but his text now reveals what was formerly hidden.

Subsequently he tells of a journey to see the ascetic John of Lycopolis that is also undertaken secretly, without the knowledge of his teacher or companions. Again Palladius deliberately exposes his own weakness to his readers, representing himself as pettily resentful when John breaks off their conference to converse with another visitor, the governor Alypius. "I grew tired and exhausted and I murmured against the old man for spurning me and giving the other the place of honor," he recalls (35.5). "Disgusted at this, I intended simply to ignore him and leave" (35.6). John, however, does not allow Palladius to leave but rebukes him for his embarrassingly inappropriate response. When Palladius asks John to pray for him, John slaps him playfully on the cheek and reveals his knowledge of the demon that tempts Palladius to leave the desert. Banishing the demon by thus exposing it, John next asks Palladius jokingly if he wishes to be a bishop. Palladius responds jokingly as well, presenting himself as the bishop of the kitchens, ordained by gluttony. Still smiling, John ignores Palladius's evasive answer and instructs him not to leave the desert if he wants to avoid the sufferings that would attend his episcopal ordination.

We already know that at the time of the writing of this text Palladius has been a bishop for twenty years (prol. 2): no surprise, then, when Palladius reports, "I forgot his advice" (35.11). Three years later, he falls sick with hydropsy. Palladius's is, then, yet another swollen body in this text. Sent first to Alexandria and then to Palestine for a cure, he eventually makes his way to Bithynia, where he is ordained bishop and suffers just as John has predicted he would. Palladius admits that he does not know whether to attribute his ordination to human ambition or divine providence, nor does his tale decisively resolve this ambiguity. Unlike Ammonius, he does not cut his body to pieces in order to avoid ordination; unlike Benjamin, he does not suffer his swelling submissively. Contrary to John's apparent advice, he fails to resist the temptation to leave the desert. Yet he also thereby fails to avoid suffering. When, following his ordination, Palladius is imprisoned in a dark cell for nearly a year, he remembers the words John spoke to him regarding his own forty years of voluntary solitary confinement, offered to Palladius "as a help for enduring the desert" (35.13). Palladius's place of imprisonment thus doubles back on the desert cell of the monk who once foretold that Palladius would have to flee the desert in order not to flee his tribulations. Episcopacy is Palladius's desert, the site of his testing.

Doubling back, the story does not, however, come to a close. Instead it gives rise to another patterned repetition, as Palladius abruptly digresses to relate the tale of one Poimenia. As he has done for Palladius, John "cleared up for her a number of secret things," offering advice on how to avoid temptation. "Now she either deceived him outright or else forget about that advice," reports Palladius (35.14), in words that both echo and complicate his own recorded forgetfulness. Subsequently Poimenia's servants are violently attacked by some "very desperate men. . . . After they had wounded all the other servants, they insulted and threatened her" (35.15). Palladius thus displaces and thereby also interprets his own tale with that of Poimenia. If episcopacy is for him the path that leads to a life of ascetic tribulations, the sufferings of the episcopal ascetic are like the humiliation of a woman insulted and threatened by desperate men.

Palladius's passage through humiliation finally allows him to take his place in the monastic landscape. He has begun by representing himself as a pilgrim gazing at living icons of a virtue that he himself does not yet possess: "I accepted the hardship of travel gladly in order to meet a man full of the love of God and to gain what I lacked" (prol. 5). He ends by locating himself among the lovers of God—an anonymous "brother" referred to riddlingly in the final chapter of his history as one "who has been with me from youth until this very day." The author no longer stands outside a text of his own making. Rather, the text has shaped him in conformity with its own iterative patterns: the brother, indistinguishable from so many others, no longer lusts either for food or for riches; his clothing is simple and unadorned; "he has undergone a thousand or more temptations from demons" (71.1); "he has had no traffic with a woman" (71.2). In his prologue, Palladius has announced the deliberate humility of his rhetorical style: the discerning reader, he is confident, will not scorn his "crude and unpolished manner of speech" (prol. 4). By the final chapter, he has become virtually identical with the humiliated word that writes him as a nameless monk.[22] "It is good to be dissolved and to be with Christ," as he has assured us from the start (prol. 4; cf. Phil. 1.23). If we are good enough readers, we too will find ourselves unwritten by this *History*—exceeded, fragmented, and dissolved in the ongoing processes of self-humiliation ("a thousand or more temptations from demons") in which the ascetic disovers the path of escape.

A Theory of Practice: Evagrius of Pontus and the Joy of Humility

Palladius's *Lausiac History* includes a lengthy entry on his revered teacher Evagrius of Pontus. By now it should come as no surprise that this mini-hagiography effects Evagrius's sanctification less by praising his virtue than by exposing his shame. Reenacting his prior humiliation so as to reproduce his holiness, the text re-embodies Evagrius's own ascetic progress. We should not miss the audacity—or the payoff—of a narrative that strategically discloses precisely what one might have thought best kept secret, namely, the scandalous love affair of a future monastic leader. Having acquired much honor in Constantinople as one proven "most skillful in confuting all the heresies" (38.2), Evagrius falls in love with a woman who is not only "of the highest social class" but also married to another, as Palladius tells it. "This woman also loved him in return," he adds. Wishing to break off the relationship, "he could not do so, so caught up was he in the bonds of concupiscence" (38.3). Following a terrifying angelic visitation, Evagrius vows to leave Constantinople immediately. He travels to Jerusalem, where he is received by the famous ascetic aristocrat Melania of Rome. There, however, he swiftly falls back into pleasure-loving habits. Subsequently he is stricken by a divinely induced fever that "wasted away his flesh which had been his great impediment" (38.8). Even as God gnaws away at his flesh, Evagrius finally begins to gnaw away at his own swollen pride, confessing "the whole story" to Melania, who (not unlike the angel of his prior vision) agrees to intervene on his behalf with prayer if he promises to take up a monastic life in Egypt (38.9).

It is in the desert that Evagrius is able to confront his shameful demons face to face. His self-exposure sometimes takes rather literal form. "The demon of fornication bothered him so oppressively, as he himself told us, that he stood naked throughout the night in a well. It was winter at the time and his flesh froze." When a spirit of blasphemy tortures him, he remains outside for forty days, "and his body grew welts in the same way brute animals do," Palladius relates (38.11). Evagrius's struggles with temptation are unremitting: "He was beaten by demons and sorely tempted by them times without number" (38.12). Close to death, he is finally able to say that he has been free of carnal desires for three years. "This after a life of such toil and labor and continual prayer!" exclaims Palladius (38.13). And so might he exclaim, given that some eighteen years of strenuous ascetic practice have rendered a mere three years of respite from sexual yearnings.[23] If the fruits of such mighty striving may seem surprisingly modest, the faithfulness of the monk's discipline thereby humbles the reader all the more. Evagrius's virtue is disclosed less in his triumph over temptation than in the power of his humility, as he fearlessly faces the shame of his ongoing vulnerability to passion. As a saying attributed to Evagrius elsewhere puts it: "Take away temptations and no one will be saved" (*Alphabetical Sayings*, Evagrius 5).

Consistent with Palladius's portrait are Evagrius's own influential writings, which consist largely of collections of condensed gnomic sayings offering guidelines for perseverance in ascetic life. In the letter that introduces his *Chapters on Prayer*, Evagrius thanks his addressee for writing him "just at a time when I was aflame with the hot urgings of my own impure passions and my spirit was afflicted by all kinds of vile thoughts." Such shameless self-exposure is not atypical of ascetic writers, as we have already seen, but it is striking nonetheless. Nor is it merely the effect of unguarded spontaneity: Evagrius, like Palladius, is well aware that self-humiliation is crucial to salvation. Or rather—to invoke more characteristically Evagrian terms—it is crucial to the approach toward the "place of prayer" where the soul free of passion communes nakedly with God. "Prayer is a continual intercourse of the spirit with God," writes Evagrius (3). Paradoxically, the humiliation of "impure passions" produces a focused intensity of erotic joy in a soul that has submitted utterly to God in prayer.[24]

Evagrius instructs the monk to "pray with tears" (6). Such tears should not tempt pride but rather should be offered as tokens of humility: "Though fountains of tears flow during your prayer, do not begin to consider yourself better than others. For your prayers have merely obtained the help you need to confess your sins with readiness and to conciliate the favor of the Lord" (7). Indeed, prayer is ever accompanied by a sense of remorse: "The specific quality of prayer is that it is a respectful gravity which is colored by compunction. It has something of a deepfelt sorrow about it, the kind one feels when, amid silent groans, he really admits his sins" (42). Tears announce "the distance that separates you from God, when you ought to be with him constantly" (78). He continues: "Surely when you take your own measure you will know a sweet sorrow" (79). If the sorrow of prayer is sweet, it is because it gives rise to a joy "above every other joy (*chara*)" (153).

It is a joy of which the demons would deprive the monk, not least by slyly endangering his humility. The demon of vainglory tempts a praying monk to believe that the absence of "impure disturbances of his flesh" allows him to perceive God in an image, giving "a form to the divine and essential knowledge," when in truth any image of God is an effect of demonic trickery (73). Similarly, the demons may trick a monk into thinking that he has conquered his thoughts and has "cast fear into the demons" (134). Such a threat of complacency must itself be banished by strategic recitation of a psalm that, Evagrius assures his readers, will arm ascetics against their adversary "with humility" (135). "Strive to cultivate a deep humility," he urges, "and the malice of the demons shall not touch your soul" (96). Even one who has achieved perfection must sustain this by psychic practices of self-humiliation: "A wise man is one who does not cease to recall the painful memory of his own sins before he has been perfectly converted—and the eternal punishment by fire that they merit as well" (144). "Do not seek to avoid those who would give you a good drubbing," he advises with characteristic masochistic fervor (140). In particular, the lashes of the demon of fornication must be endured "with constancy": "He shall attack you like a wild beast and buffet your entire body" (91). As David Brakke remarks, Evagrius's writings depict "violent, punishing demons that rival any found in the *Life of Antony*."[25] "Happy is the one who thinks himself no better than dirt," the monk proclaims succinctly (121).

But just as sorrow is lined with joy, so too is self-abjection lined with love: "Happy is the monk who views the welfare and progress of all men with as much joy as if it were his own. Happy is the monk who considers all men as god—after God" (122, 123). The self-dissolution discovered within humility is the source of a deep sense of solidarity with all others: "A monk is one who is separated from all and who is in harmony with all. A monk is one who considers himself one with all because he seems constantly to see himself in everyone" (124, 125).

Evagrius's widely disseminated *Praktikos* lays out somewhat more systematically the theory of ascetic practice that also underlies his *Chapters on Prayer*. The dedicatory letter that introduces the treatise foregrounds humility as the antidote to "that long-standing evil which is pride and which caused Lucifer, who rose like the day-star in the morning, to be cast down to the earth." Closely related to pride is the threat of vainglory: "ever searching out praise from men, it banishes faith." In the chapters that follow, Evagrius initially outlines the eight "thoughts" (*logismoi*) that tempt the monk—"gluttony, impurity, avarice, sadness, anger, *acedia*, vainglory, and, last of all, pride" (6). Vainglory and pride receive special attention here, as in the dedicatory letter.[26] "The spirit of vainglory is most subtle and it readily grows up in the souls of those who practice virtue," asserts Evagrius. "It leads them to desire to make their struggles known publicly, to hunt after the praise of men" (13). If the spirit of vainglory is the most subtle, "the demon of pride is the cause of the most damaging fall for the soul. For it induces the monk to deny that God is his helper and to consider that he himself is the cause of virtuous acts" (14). Evagrius, like Palladius, is well aware that the very ambition entailed in the pursuit of ascetic perfection constantly exposes the monk both to the admiring eyes of others and to the temptation of self-congratulation.

Shaming is implicit in Evagrius's exposure of each of the tempting "thoughts," and the particular relevance of shame or humiliation to the chastening of vainglory and pride is so obvious as scarcely to need naming. Yet it is in relation to avarice that explicit language of shame surfaces poignantly in the opening chapters of the treatise: "Avarice suggests to the mind a lengthy old age, inability to perform manual labor (at some future date), famines that are sure to come, sickness that will visit us, the pinch of poverty, the great shame that comes from accepting the necessities of life from others" (9). Shame thus clings to the vulnerability of flesh and the consequent dependence of humans on others, in Evagrius's account. It appears to attend "the very fact of having a body," as Levinas puts it.[27] Avaricious thoughts tempt one to imagine, falsely, that it is both possible and desirable to avoid such shame. A similar poignancy attends Evagrius's initial description of sadness, which he links closely with humiliation. In sadness, as he describes it, a sense of deprivation leads to fantasies of pleasures followed by a renewed experience of loss: "so the miserable soul is now shriveled up in her humiliation to the degree that she poured herself out upon these thoughts of hers" (10). As for Levinas, so too for Evagrius, pleasure is "an escape that fails. . . . And, at the moment of its disappointment, which should have been that of its triumph, the meaning of its failure is underscored by shame."[28]

Where avarice defends vainly against the shame of unmet bodily need, sadness seeks solace from the humiliation of unmet desire for pleasure, equally vainly. Here Evagrius unfolds a subtle psychology in which shame and humiliation are viewed through a lens of compassionate detachment that reveals not only the inevitability of shame but also the peace that ensues when humans cease to defend against shame, by embracing the humility of ascetic practice. Later he observes that "there are two peaceful states of the soul." The first "arises from the natural basic energies of the soul" and is attended by "humility together with compunction and tears, longing for the Infinite God, and a boundless eagerness for toil." He adds that the one who preserves this first, internal state of peace "will perceive with greater sensitivity the raids made upon it by the demons." It is the withdrawal of the demons that produces the second of the soul's two "peaceful states" (57).

Evagrius can refer interchangeably to "demons" or "thoughts."[29] In general, he does not appear interested in drawing sharp distinctions between internal and external sources of temptation so much as in observing the ways that temptation traverses the boundaries of the self. Nonetheless, vainglory and pride are typically presented in the externalized terms of "raiding" demons (57). If vainglory in particular presents a frontal attack on humility, the intimately interior insinuation of shameful thoughts humiliates the soul. In an intriguingly complex bit of psychological analysis, Evagrius suggests that the ascetic "drive out a nail with a nail," that is, that he expel vainglory by invoking the shame of dishonorable thoughts or, alternately, combat shameful desires by invoking the desire for honor. "Whichever of these two draws near to harass you, feign that the thought of the other antagonist is present within you." He adds: "Beyond any doubt, the ability to drive away the thought of vainglory through humility, or the power to repel the demon of impurity through temperance is a most profound proof of *apatheia*"—that is, freedom from the passions aroused by tempting thoughts (58).

As in the *Chapters on Prayer*, so also in the *Praktikos*, Evagrius associates ascetic practice with an on-going humiliation of self that gives birth to a capacity for love. In his dedicatory letter he writes that "*apatheia* has a child called *agape* who keeps the door to deep knowledge of the created universe." Later he echoes this notion: "*Agape* is the progeny of *apatheia*. *Apatheia* is the very flower of *ascesis*" (81). "The goal of the ascetic life is *agape*" (84). He acknowledges that "it is not possible to love all the brethren to the same degree," adding: "But it is possible to associate with all in a manner that is above passion, that is to say, free of resentment and hatred" (100). Free of all "passions," the Evagrian soul has begun to make its escape from the constraints of selfhood, dissolving into a divine communion of love wherein is disclosed a joy "above every other joy."

The Nauseating Stench of Sanctity: The *Life of Syncletica*

The anonymously authored fifth-century *Life of Syncletica* brings together the traditions of hagiographical and "sayings" literatures. To be sure, other ancient Lives of Saints also record lengthy speeches of instruction delivered by the holy one to his or her followers: this is the case, for example, with the *Life of Antony*, which appears to haunt the Syncletican text at various points. Nonetheless, the *Life of Syncletica* strikes a distinctive balance, or rather sustains a distinctive imbalance, in comparison with its precursors. Although longer than any of the mini-hagiographies included in Palladius's *Lausiac History*, the biographical portions of Syncletica's *Life* are more formulaic and condensed, and in some respects therefore more vivid, than is typical of hagiographies devoted to a single figure, while the "teachings of the holy and all-virtuous Syncletica" very nearly overwhelm the text. The author may assert that this ascetic woman taught "rather more by actions than by words" (103), but it is her words that hold the reader's attention for 81 of the *Life*'s 113 chapters. Moreover, Syncletica's teachings are presented less in the manner of a well-rounded speech than as a loosely jointed string of wise "sayings," as is characteristic not only of the collections of *Sayings of the Fathers* but also, as we have seen, of Evagrius's "chapters"; indeed, Evagrius's writings would seem to have exercised a direct influence on this text.[30] As Elizabeth Castelli notes, "The teachings themselves are not edited for coherence nor to assure lack of contradiction. . . . [T]he author of the text piles language upon what is already there, compiling a rich (if occasionally confounding) compendium of advice for the initiate."[31]

Regardless what kind of authorial or editorial process led historically to such a "piling on" of language, the cumulative effect is of an embarrassment of riches—an overflow of wisdom that is only very imperfectly contained by the biographical framing. As Derek Krueger puts it, "If the *Life of Syncletica* demonstrates her humility by portraying her reluctance at first to speak, her teaching then flows in a steady stream until the source dries up."[32] I would add that, however "steady" the "stream" of Syncletica's words, both their excessive length and the disjointed incoherence noted by Castelli disrupt any easy flow of narrative temporality in the *Life*. Time is interrupted, even exploded. So too is the space of subjectivity. It is Syncletica who speaks, yet her speech is curiously polyglossal, at once fractured and multiple in its very disregard for consistency or unified structure. As Castelli points out by way of example, "the reader is informed variously at different moments: 'the worst evil is love of money,' 'the three worst evils are desire, pleasure, and grief,' and 'the last and most important of evils is arrogance.'"[33]

The fracturing or multiplication of the speaking subject that results is all the more striking because it is not performed explicitly as a multitude of voices in the manner of either collective hagiographies like Palladius's or sayings collections; nor does Syncletica emerge as an author as Evagrius

does. Moreover, the narration of Syncletica's death, as much as the record-
ing of her teachings, stages Syncletica's ultimate fragmentation, as we shall
see. As Krueger points out, what remains after the dissolution of her body
is the materiality of the hagiographical text. He adds: "Textuality is no
longer an object of shame because materiality is no longer problematic in
quite the same way. . . . This is the difference incarnation makes, not only
for its explicit revaluing of the body but also for framing the subsequent
production of the logos. For the author of the *Life of Syncletica*, . . . writing
is no longer debased: it is a licensed, saintly mode, an imitation of God."[34]
This may be so, particularly in comparison with prior Platonic tradition.
Yet it must also be acknowledged that the materiality of the text, like the
materiality of Syncletica's body and indeed also of her "logos" or speech, is
neither stable, unified, nor whole. Moreover, if textuality is no longer an
object of shame, writing itself no longer debased, it may nonetheless become a site for the encounter with shame.

As I have noted, the initial framing of Syncletica's biography is relatively formulaic, consisting of a pastiche of narrative tropes and metaphorical figures familiar from other hagiographical literature. Syncletica is both
well-born and beautiful, attracting many suitors yet possessing "the inclination for the divine Bridegroom alone" (7). Like other late ancient women
saints,[35] she is identified with Thecla: "For no one was ignorant of the mar-
tyrdoms of the blessed Thecla, as she struggled bravely through fire and
wild beasts; and I think that many people will not escape noticing the virtuous and sweaty sufferings of this one [Syncletica]." The comparison with
Thecla as martyr allows the author both to introduce the agonistic meta-
phors that pervade the *Life* and to translate the site of martyrial combat
to the interior arena of the ascetic's psyche: "And I understand the gentler
sufferings to be Thecla's, for the evil of the enemy attacked her from the
outside. But with Syncletica he displays his more piercing evil, moving from
the inside by means of opposing and destructive thoughts" (8). The invocation of masculinizing athletic and military images to depict feminine virtue
is striking, if not unusual, as we have seen in Chapter 1.[36] "Being trained
sufficiently in sufferings, and having been led to the very height of the stadium, she made progress in virtues," we are told (13). Or again: "When the
adversary continued to wage war, she used as her weapons prayer . . . ; and
her helmet was composed out of faith and hope and charity" (18).

In the *Life of Syncletica*, the language of athleticism and militarism is
more distinctly metaphorical—or perhaps more distinctly "Evagrian"—in
its intense interorization than is the case, for example, in the *Life of Antony*,

as Brakke notes.[37] Yet, at the same time, the somatization of Syncletica's ascetic practice is also peculiarly intense. Fasting lies at the center of this practice and, as Krueger points out, it links Syncletica's asceticism to a complex web of food images that convey the broader conversions of materiality performed in this text.[38] From the start, her fasting is, rather literally, metabolically transformative. When she breaks her fast by eating more or at different times than usual, it depletes rather than renews her. "For her face was a pallor, and the weight of her body collapsed; for when one is disgusted by an action, the action itself is changed" (10). Her disgust is strategic, her dietary ascesis a weapon deployed with precision when she is faced with particular temptation, the author also insists (19). Abstaining from one kind of food enables Syncletica to receive nurturance from the very body of her Lord: "From his breasts we are fed with milk, the Old and New Testaments," she declares, weeping in her humility before her own students "as though a newborn at the breast." Thus transformed through her own food practices, which at once chasten her body and humble her soul, Syncletica (like Jesus) becomes food for others, despite her reluctance to take on the audacious role of teacher. Her students receive her word "gladly as if tasting honey and honeycomb" (21). Her teachings are compared to "chalices of wisdom." For her disciples, "the blessed Syncletica was . . . like the pouring out of divine drink and liquid" (30). As Syncletica's humility is converted into a sign of virtue and a source of teaching authority, her teaching itself becomes a vehicle of further humiliation as she pours herself out in an act of voluntary self-emptying that matches the kenosis of Christ.

Humiliation and humility frequently surface in the outpouring of Syncletica's words. Continuous progress from lesser to greater virtue requires that the ascetics always view themselves as "unworthy servants" (23). A "shameful thought" can itself be humiliated through the resources of the imagination: "For if a vision of seemly appearance should come into being in the regions of thought, . . . erase the eyes of the image, and extract flesh from the cheeks; cut away under the lips, and further imagine the ugly coagulated state of bare bone. . . . It is necessary on the whole to represent the body of the beloved as a wound that smells oppressive, and is inclined to putrefy, briefly put, as resembling a corpse, or to imagine oneself as a corpse." Syncletica offers this advice as an instance of the Evagrian call to "drive back a nail with a nail," but her example seems to reflect a rather more "feminine" flair for the imaginative arts of self-humiliation than Evagrius's suggestion that the ascetic counter impure thoughts with a feigning of vainglory's love of honor (29). She urges the necessity "to take every care in order to have our spiritual benefit escape notice," observing that those who are most virtuous "narrate out their small faults with the addition of what they have not done, eschewing human opinion" (38). "Useful grief," she declares, "includes moaning over our own sins and over our ignorance of things pertaining to our neighbor and toward the completion of our purpose and the achievement of the perfection of goodness" (40).

Pride is nonetheless always poised to attack precisely the most virtuous, as the evil one "increases the soul's magnitude by indecently elevating it against its sisters" (49). To counter such temptation, one should meditate on such scriptural words as the following: "I am a worm and not a human being" (Ps. 21.7, LXX); "I am earth and ashes" (Gen. 18.27), "All human justice is like the rag of one who menstruates" (Is. 64.6). Here again, Syncletica reveals a penchant for graphic images of self-humiliation. Concerning the ascetic tempted by pride, she recommends harsh medicine: "Let her be punished by women of like age, and let her be rebuked, and let her be greatly censured, as if she has achieved nothing great" (50). Not only the saints but also the demons can be invoked as shaming exempla for the chastening of arrogance: "For demons have done and do more than you do; for they neither eat, nor drink, nor marry, nor sleep; but they live in the desert, even inhabiting a cave, if you think doing that is a great thing" (53). "It is clear that arrogance is the greatest among the evils," Syncletica opines. "And from this its opposite, humility, shows itself. It is difficult to acquire humility." "The most beautiful of all virtues" (56), humility nonetheless often presents an ugly face: "Humility corrects by means of reproaches, by means of violence, by means of blows." Syncletica reminds her audience that the Lord "spoke to the Samaritan himself and to the one who had a demon. He took the form of a slave, he was beaten, he was tortured with blows" (58). These are the "acts of humility" that must be imitated (59). God providentially provides many occasions for humiliation: "For toward the salvation of the soul and the education of the body are there famines and droughts, illnesses and sufferings, and all other various accidents" (84).

Syncletica is well aware of the particular humiliations suffered by women: "In general for women the hatred in the world is great." Their bodies are burdened with the pain and danger of childbirth, the responsibility "of nourishing babies with milk" and of tending sick children and sharing their illnesses, receiving little enough reward for their labors. Ascetics thus should not be tempted to envy their worldly sisters: "For when they give birth, they perish from sufferings; when they don't bear children, they waste away sterile and childless under reproaches" (42). However traditional this rhetoric, at once unavoidably misogynistic and potentially subversive of misogyny, it nonetheless takes on ringing tones when represented as feminine speech. Ascetic women, in contrast to matrons, escape the humiliations of motherhood precisely by taking on the humbleness of infants, as Syncletica imagines it. Not even quite infants: dwelling like unborn children in a "second maternal womb" (90), they are "fetuses inside their mother" preparing through baptism and good works for their ultimate birth into glory (91). They are also brides "betrothed to the heavenly Bridegroom," adorned not with jewels but with humility (92).

Syncletica does finally fall silent, but only when her flesh begins to disintegrate before our eyes, in an uncanny replay of her own fantasy of a beloved body represented "as a wound that smells oppressive, and is inclined to putrefy, briefly put, as resembling a corpse" (29).[39] The account of her final illness, which lasts three and a half years, effectively confounds the distinction between living body and putrefying corpse. It also produces an intensely carnalized interiority that, paradoxically, brings what is hidden within to the surfaces of sensation while at the same time dissolving the distinctions between soul and flesh.[40] Whereas the initial comparison of Syncletica's asceticism with Thecla's martyrdom highlights the arena of psychological combat where the enemy moves "from the inside by means of opposing and destructive thoughts" (8), the closing narration of Syncletica's illness shows the devil "grasping her internal organs" (104) and introduces a comparison not only with the tortures endured by the ancient martyrs but also with the sufferings of Job: "On Job the devil made the beginnings of wounds on the outside; on her he added punishments from the inside" (106).

The "inside" is, then, no longer a space of tempting "thoughts" but one of corrupting flesh. The self is not invaded at its boundaries but dissolved at its core. Thus the devil "first smites the most necessary organ in life, the lung. . . . For breaking up the lung into small pieces by means of spittle that brought them up, he cast it out" (105). Even the distinction between inside and outside is here transgressed and reversed. Still, Syncletica, like Palladius's Benjamin—another Joblike figure—continues to teach and to heal others, while remaining without healing herself. Next, then, her frustrated enemy "struck her speech organ, to cut off the spoken word." No longer audible, Syncletica continues to thwart the devil by becoming all the more intensely visible: "perceiving her with their eyes," her followers are strengthened, and the very sight of her wounds "cured stricken souls" (110).

Continuing to gnaw away not only at Syncletica's flesh but also at the realm of sensation by which she might be perceived, the devil now transforms the saint into a grotesque spectacle. Corruption proceeds visibly from a tooth to the gums until it seems to have overtaken her entire body. "And the bone fell out; the spreading passed into the whole jaw, and became decay of the body pressing on the neighboring parts; and in forty days the bone was worm-eaten." The surface of Syncletica's body is now a blackened hole into which sight disappears, in another reversal of interiority and exteriority. The holy woman cannot be heard, nor is she any longer recognizable to the eyes. Indeed, her visitors, like the visitors of the grotesquely swollen Benjamin of Palladius's *History*, may find themselves averting their eyes. But the final and most potent attack of the devil is through the sense of smell—a peculiarly feminine sense, perhaps, and also a sense peculiarly vulnerable to shame. "Putrefaction and the heaviest stench governed her whole body so that the ones who served her suffered more than she did." Her followers and caregivers are forced to withdraw, "not bearing the inhuman odor"; even when armed with burning incense, they withdraw "because of the inhuman stench" (111). The one whose glorious sufferings were formerly described as giving off a "sweet fragrance" (21) is now rendered other than human by her nauseating smell. If she passes beyond our perception, it is not by evading but by overloading our senses with disgust.[41]

We may recall Julia Kristeva's words; "Refuse and corpses show me what I permanently thrust aside in order to live. These body fluids, this defilement, this shit are what life withstands, hardly and with difficulty, on the part of death. There, I am at the border of my condition as a living being. My body extricates itself, as being alive, from that border."[42] Syncletica appears to be suspended at just the border that Kristeva here describes. Her movement, however, is in the opposite direction, as she begins to extricate herself from the body—to find her path of escape. She remains thus suspended for three full months, continuing to contend with the devil. As the saint's final round of combat is narrated, we discover that the sensory register is not, after all, quite exhausted. In the depths of her abjection, Syncletica tastes triumph, and so do her readers. Like Gregory of Nyssa's Christ, she is said to be "offered as bait." Perceiving a mere woman, the enemy fails to recognize Syncletica's "virility"; "seeking a feast," he becomes "food." He does so by swallowing the bait—or perhaps by gnawing away at it, bit by bit. The enemy, thus hooked, becomes God's prey, then, and also Syncletica's source of nourishment. Through the very sufferings inflicted by the devil, "her whole body was strengthened by divine power."

Nourished, she is also, however, still fasting: "for how was she able to take meals, when she was ruled by such putrefaction and stench?" (112). Syncletica's nausea—revealing "the impotence of pure being, in all its nakedness," as Levinas puts it[43]—seems finally to propel her beyond the bounds of her own "being." Broken into small pieces, she casts herself out of herself.

Casting herself from herself toward a death that is also a resurrection, Syncletica sees visions of angels, holy virgins, light, "and the land of paradise." Just as she has become one with the image of her prior fantasy of putrefaction, so too now "with the vision of these she became as if one herself" (113). The distinction between imagination and reality gently dissolves as the boundary of life and death is traversed. The distinction between the putrid and the paradisal seems likewise to blur, as corruption is revealed as release. "It is to hold onto oneself while gnawing away at oneself," writes Levinas, regarding the freedom both discovered and concealed in shame. Where Levinas's image opens a split within remorse that destabilizes subjectivity in the face of the demands of the Other, the *Life of Syncletica* presents the salvific dissolution of the humiliated subject as simultaneously the work of God, of the devil, and of the saint herself. The Other is thus no longer exterior, for the boundaries of interiority and exteriority do not hold. To the extent that the reader of this *Life* is overwhelmed not only by the sound of Syncletica's excessive outpouring of words but also by the nauseating sight, stench, and even taste of her corrupting flesh—to the extent that the reader is touched by the saint's shame—the boundaries of interiority and exteriority do not hold in relation to the text, either. The imagination is the site of sensation, and we ourselves "become as if one" with what we are made capable of imagining.

Conclusions

"I wear my skin only as thin as I have to, armor myself only as much as seems absolutely necessary," writes novelist Dorothy Allison. "I try to live naked in the world, unashamed even under attack, unafraid even though I know how much there is to fear. . . . I tell myself that . . . I have to try constantly to understand more, love more fully, go more naked in order to make others as safe as I myself want to be. I want to live past my own death."[44] Admittedly a decidedly queer addition to the company of ancient Christian ascetics whose voices are here assembled, Allison nonetheless captures important yearnings and insights shared by those ascetics. "When I am writing I sink down into myself, my memory, dreams, shames, terrors," she confesses. The best in us, she avers, "comes from the place where the terror hides, the edge of our worst stuff." With the fierce challenge of an ascetic mentor, she advises: "Use any trick. I want to know what it was that you looked at unflinchingly, even if you did not know what you were seeing at the time."[45]

In the face of their own fears and hopes, ancient ascetics both expose themselves boldly and armor themselves diligently—precisely as much as they deem absolutely necessary. The imaginative worlds they construct are sites of aggressive combat, yet their weapons of discipline and virtue are turned neither against others nor simply against themselves, as they understand it. Rather, they are turned against the complex temptations that arise from both within and outside the borders of the psyche. To arm oneself against temptation is, however, already an ambivalent act, entailing the exposure of one's shameful vulnerability to temptation, entailing even the courting and intensification of temptation. As Geoffrey Harpham has noted, asceticism always walks the fine line between resistance and trangression—walks the line of temptation, in other words: "Resistance to temptation is *both* imperative and impossible."[46] Indeed, confrontation with the shame encountered in an always nearly irresistible temptation—including the temptation to defend against shame—is arguably at the heart of ascetic practice. To confront one's own shame requires enormous resourcefulness: one must be prepared to use any trick.

To resist temptation is to triumph, but it is to triumph in a most peculiar way. It is to triumph *against* oneself, and thus it is crucially not a triumph *of* the self. The encounter with temptation produces a splitting within the subject that continues, in theory, *ad infinitum*, ever approaching (but never quite reaching) a state of utter dissolution. To triumph is also, then, to submit extravagantly—to submit to the devil in the very exposure to temptation, to submit to the God who turns temptation toward a salvific purpose, to submit, again and again, to one's own humiliation. Yet the possibilities for self-humiliation are, paradoxically, also the possibilities for self-transcendence. The flip side of the ascetic's cultivation of a humility that is seemingly bottomless is a soaring ambition to achieve a "perfection" beyond what is yet imaginable—a perfection that lies beyond "being," in Levinas's terms. This desired perfection is no more static than is humility; it is not construed in terms of "completeness" any more than humility is construed in terms of an incompleteness desiring completion. At work is an infinite (ever unfinished) process of self-humiliation that is also an infinite (ever unfinished) process of self-exceeding. Where the shame of temptation reveals the porosity and instability of the subject, the hope of perfection manifests the possibilities for transformation in and through shame, occurring at and beyond the borders of subjectivity. Ultimately, the sense of nakedness that initially announces the presence of all we would hide but cannot hide becomes the baring of a soul that willfully destroys its own defenses. Paradoxically, it is by continuously splitting itself from itself that the soul strips itself of the veils that separate it from God or (other) others. In this utter nakedness, in this radical submission of the self, a safety—a "salvation"—is discovered. In this exposure to the other, in this othering of the self, something that precedes and exceeds both self and other is surfaced. Where ontology gives way to soteriology, soteriology also becomes *hontologie*—"shame-ology"—as Lacan's punning French has it.

Here soul is no longer separable from body. If it is in relation to the needs and desires of the body that ascetics (among others) experience shame most viscerally, the humiliated flesh also reveals the radical transience and and thus the radical convertibility of all human subjects. In Palladius's text, as we have seen, flesh is the site of excess and fragmentation, as bodies subjected to ascetic discipline both expand beyond imaginable limits and fall to pieces, a process that is parallelled on the psychological plane. Whereas Evagrius understands the body as a site of passionate temptation that will ultimately be transcended by the soul that finds its path of escape in *apatheia*, the *Life of Syncletica* refocuses the senses on the flesh in its intimate corruptibility. The flesh disintegrates; it is ingested by worms; it vomits, casting itself from itself. It assaults our eyes with sights that refuse to resolve into clear images, our ears with incomprehensible sounds, our tongues and noses with the tastes and smells of putrefaction. It touches us with the taint of our own unbearable mortality. Yet it thereby brings us to the threshold of immortality. The transience of embodiment is both the image and the condition of the infinite convertibility of the soul. In all of the texts here considered, gender partly conveys the malleability of subjectivity, albeit differently in each case. In the context of the deliberate inclusivism of Palladius's collective biography, the masculine body most readily displays the grotesque disfigurability of flesh while the feminine psyche proves most susceptible to the chastening power of shame. For Evagrius, gender is elided in the straining toward the dissolution of all difference through the humbling of the self. For the *Life of Syncletica*, both the feminized soul and the feminine body most powerfully convey the link between humiliating corruptibility and joyous transformability.

Chapter 4
Shameful Confessions

As everybody knows, Christianity is a confession. This means that Christianity belongs to a very special type of religion—those which impose obligations of truth on the practitioners. . . . Everyone in Christianity has the duty to explore who he is, what is happening within himself, the faults he may have committed, the temptations to which he is exposed. Moreover, everyone is obliged to tell these things to other people, and thus to bear witness against himself.
—Michel Foucault, "Sexuality and Solitude"

For there to be a confessional declaration or avowal, it is necessary, indissociably, that I recognize that I am guilty in a mode of recognition that is not of the order of cognition, and also that, at least implicitly, I begin to accuse myself—and thus to excuse myself or to present my apologies, or even to ask forgiveness. There is doubtless an irreducible element of "truth" in this process but this truth, precisely, is not a truth to be known or . . . revealed.
—Jacques Derrida, "Typewriter Ribbon: Limited Ink (2)"

For behold, "you have loved truth" [Ps. 50.8], since "the one who makes truth comes to the light" [John 3.21]. I want to make truth in my heart before you in confession, and in my book before many witnesses.
—Augustine, Confessions 10.1

In the spectacle of martyrdom, words are reduced to a bare minimum: "I am Christian!" The broken body itself becomes the book shamelessly splayed and displayed before many witnesses, and the truth that it inscribes, or *makes*, is split, doubled—testimony both to the coercive power of the torturer and to the defiant resistance of the one tortured, to the overwhelming greatness of God and to the abysmal abjection of humanity. This palpably Christlike confession of flesh, at once exacted and volunteered, is echoed by the confession of words in other arenas of ancient

Christian performance, not least Augustine's famous text. Indeed, as Michel Foucault argues, however intensely incarnated it may be, confession seems to remain crucially a verbal act—or, perhaps better, a verbal*izing* act. Seen, touched and tasted, even smelled—as we have learned—shame must still make itself *heard*.

In particular, the pragmatic theorizing of Augustine's contemporary (and sometime rival) John Cassian suggests to Foucault that the willed submission of thoughts to the power of words is indispensible for the process of conversion toward which confession always aims. This is the case first because verbalization allows for discernment: evil thoughts—that is, the kinds of thoughts that *need* confessing—can be conveniently identified by their resistance to linguistic expression. Yet that formulation is already somewhat misleading, for confessional language does not simply represent pre-existing thoughts but collaborates continuously, and indeed vigilantly, in their strategically reluctant production. In so doing, it generates the very psychological depths that it likewise attempts, vainly, to plumb: the thoughts that are articulated in confession are credited with "an inapparent origin, obscure roots, secret parts, and the role of verbalisation is to excavate these origins and these secret parts."[1] It is finally by bringing to light what is construed as hidden or secret that confession effects conversion. Paradoxically, perhaps, this conversion is marked as much by loss as by gain. The truth about the self that is produced in confession is also renounced in confession, as if one discovers who one is—a "sinner"—only in order recklessly to relinquish an identity that is less illusory than all too real. As Foucault remarks, "Truth and sacrifice, the truth about ourselves and the sacrifice of ourselves, are deeply and closely connected."[2]

The act of confession is, then, at once assertive and yielding, a willful appropriation of the (divine) power of judgment that is at the same time a deliberately mortifying submission of will and self to judgment, and thus also—*perhaps*—to mercy. It is neither simply coerced nor simply voluntary but rather sits necessarily on the border of what is coerced and what is offered freely. This is why it continues to make trouble for legal systems committed to distinguishing between forced and voluntary confession.[3] One must want, at least a little, to be broken, to be exposed, or the confession is sterile: it makes no truth; worse still, it forces stillborn lies. One must also resist, at least a little, being overcome by this desire, or the confession, rendered glib by the promise of cheap grace, is equally fruitless: as Jacques Derrida notes, "mechanical, machinelike, automatic forgiveness and excuse self-destruct without delay—and lose their meaning, even their memory."[4]

Thus confession does not merely expose the dividedness of the subject: it actively produces such a fracturing. The self turns back on itself—eagerly, reluctantly—in a first splitting. "When one confesses, one always confesses the other."[5] It splits again (and again) along the faultlines of its performative ambivalence: I accuse myself; and in the same breath, I excuse myself, I beg pardon, I court forgiveness. As J. M. Coetzee observes, "in the economy of confession . . . the only appetites that constitute confessable currency are shameful appetites."[6] The subject is fragmented, then, in and by shame. If the self who is confessed and thereby alienated is necessarily marked by shame, so too is the self who confesses—marked not only by the shame of the temptation to hide but also by the shame of the desire shamelessly to tell all. Indeed, it may be that "one is more ashamed of the exposure of the desire to expose oneself" than of the shameful desires exposed, as Paul de Man argues, adding that "shame is primarily exhibitionistic."[7] The self-exposure of confession is desirable, and thus shameful, largely because the act of confessing is entangled with the act of excusing oneself, of laying claim to absolution: it is as if the very suffering of shame audaciously promises to atone for the shameful thoughts or acts exposed. The desire to be absolved in this way may even become so compelling as to motivate the production of shame. "Excuses generate the very guilt they exonerate," notes de Man ominously. Confession may thus take on the character of a deadening compulsion, cut off from any referential—and thus, any ethical—efficacy.

Yet the coproduction of guilt and exoneration is strategically out of balance in any given instance. If excuses can never hope to "catch up" with the guilt they proliferate, it is also the case that "there can never be enough guilt around to match the text-machine's infinite power to excuse," as de Man puts it.[8] This wobbling imbalance, however predictable in itself, may nonetheless create space for the possible arrival of the unexpected—for the novel inbreaking of a transformative event. "An event is traumatic or it does not happen, does not arrive," insists Derrida, seeming to reach for a wrench to with which to disrupt the works of de Manian pessimism.[9] Confession, when it *happens*, takes one by surprise, *arriving* in and as a cut against the desiring subject, at once fueled by and profoundly interruptive of the relentless mechanics of excuse and forgiveness. Confession, when it happens, breaks (upon) us, disrupting the very certainty of our yearnings. (So too does forgiveness.) Its aim may be framed as the nostalgic recovery of a fantasized wholeness yet it manifests as an abysmal and salvific brokenness. It opens onto a shame from which there is no escape but that may, as Levinas intuits, itself provide a path of escape that remains necessarily uncharted.

To whom is the confession offered? To everyone, and to no one. Augustine, for his part, addresses God yet frequently pauses to puzzle over the utility of confessing his "inmost thoughts" to the very one who (he imagines) already knows him better than he knows himself: "For the heart may shut itself away, but it cannot hide from your sight," he acknowledges; "whatever good you may hear in my heart, you have first spoken to me yourself" (*Confessions* 5.1, 10.2). Perhaps, then, Augustine is really talking to himself, re-membering for the first time the story that God—his offstage interrogator—already knows. "Whose story is it?" queries Peter Brooks with regard to the confessional narrative. He goes on to note: "Most confessions by criminal suspects traditionally take the form of a statement written by the interrogators and signed by the suspect."[10] Yet Augustine is also well aware that by inscribing his divinely provoked (if not even divinely dictated) account he is simultaneously addressing other ears. Confession is the secret shame, arriving from elsewhere, that is not only spoken and heard but also *overheard*. "I do not tell all this to you, my God, but in your presence I tell it to my own kind, to humankind, however few of them as may chance upon these writings of mine" (2.3); later in his text, as we have seen above, the "few" have swelled to "many witnesses." Confession thus exposes and exploits the permeability of private and public arenas of self-performance, traversing the ever-betraying border between the realm of the flawed heart and its (equally but differently) flawed published word. Indeed, it would seem that the more interior the secrets, the more prolific must be the words produced, produced for an ear, for some other to hear—perhaps for *any* other ear to hear. The indeterminacy of its address is itself a source of further shameful culpability in confession, as Derrida observes. "As soon as I write this, as I sign it and leave a trace, it becomes available for everyone, if not for everyone, at least for others. And I'm already in a position to confess that I sinned, because I was guilty of leaving a trace, which is not distinct or accessible only to the unique one, be it to God or anyone, a person, a man or a woman, even any living being, even what one calls an animal."[11]

What is confessed? Everything, and nothing—famously, in Augustine's text, the youthful and inconsequential theft of some tasteless pears. Confession may try to contain culpability by itemizing sins committed and expiable, but in so doing it encounters the inexhaustibility of such a process: the list of sins, whether trivial or great, multiplies with every effort to bring it to conclusion. Derrida suggests that the literary confession "capitalizes a sort of interest . . . of *guilt*," that it "overproduces this *shame*, it archives it instead of effacing it."[12] Here as elsewhere, the wavering of terminology is telling. Confession, it seems, reveals the continuity of guilt with shame, exposing the extent to which guilt is always overflowing into the uncontainable depths of shame. For we do not merely confess our sins: we confess our sinfulness. We do not merely confess our acts: we confess our thoughts, as Foucault emphasizes. We do not merely confess what we have done or thought: we confess "the thoughts we may have committed," what we *may* have imagined or done, including "both the evils I committed voluntarily and those which, led by you, I did not commit" (*Confessions* 2.7). God only knows what we might be capable of.

Here we touch upon the problematic relation of confession to truth—to the "order of cognition," as Derrida puts it. "When they hear me speak about myself, how do they know whether I am telling the truth?" wonders Augustine. To receive a confession and thus to claim to know another—to risk *acknowledging* an other—is a hopeful extension of love in the face of the unverifiability of *veritas*: "charity believes all things" (10.3). Yet the point is not just that others have no way of verifying the actual state of one's heart or the true nature of one's intentions; one cannot know this with certainty oneself. As Augustine puts it: "I will confess both what I know of myself and what I do not know of myself" (10.5). Pressing the limits of what he imagines he can know, he trusts he will be led to further discoveries. The process of confession is endless: one never gets to the bottom of it all. As Coetzee notes, "behind each true, final position lurks another position truer and more final."[13] Yet in confession one is perhaps not so much pushing back the borders of ignorance as always teetering on the ever-shifting boundary of knowing and not knowing. To echo Foucault, truth and sacrifice go hand in hand: a more profound knowing is also a more profound unknowing, as kataphasis and apophasis continually fold into one another. Thus, in the process of uncovering knowledge, Augustine becomes not an answer but a question to himself, as he phrases it (4.4, 10.33). The question multiplies and increases as his words accumulate. He discovers in himself the depths of a mystery—divine depths. Only God knows him truly, and no human mind can encompass God. Summoning God is itself a grand wager: "Grant me, Lord, to know and understand whether a person . . . must know you before he can call you to his aid" (1.1).

Our abysmal inability to know ourselves is also directly and reciprocally related to our abysmal inability to take the measure of our implicated ness in the lives of others. To both may be attributed a certain innate shame—a notion that may far better capture the logic of the Augustinian doctrine of original sin than does the controversial concept of inherited guilt. Where, after all, would one begin the account of human complicity? With the violence of desire that leads, as if by accident, to the conception of life? With the violence of birth, which does not spare the m/other? With the violence of infant hungers so closely observed by Augustine (1.7)? Where, if anywhere, would one place the limit on complicity? With the grief that leaves its trace on others, as the effect of our having risked living and loving in the face of our inescapable mortality? We are ever exceeding the circumscribed space of our notional innocence, our pridefully fantasized autonomy. We are ever exceeding our own memories. Unaddressable responsibility is incurred with every gesture: we cannot shrink small enough to evade it. "It is always as if one were treading on the other's toes," as Derrida puts it.[14] Transgression occurs with the very advent of speech, no matter how trivial. "As soon as I leave a trace, I have to ask for forgiveness, because I imply, I assume, that it is interesting. . . . And then of course, there is guilt and I'm ashamed."[15]

What does confession effect? Not an eradication of shame but a continuous turning within shame—a sustained state of contrition, repentence, conversion. Not a catharsis but an ongoing responsiveness—a painfully unrelieved openness. Confession performatively constitutes the matrix of the infinite responsibility of which Levinas writes. It does not produce independently verifiable truth but offers testimony to the desire to *make truth*, as Augustine's gravely scriptural line inscribes the impossible ambition. As Foucault intuits, we make truth "in the heart" and also by submitting ourselves to the authority of an other.[16] To risk making truth is thus also to risk perjury—not least (if also most subtly) to risk having lied to ourselves and thereby having inadvertently harmed another. "We are always already in the process of excusing ourselves, or even asking forgiveness, precisely in this ambiguous and perjuring mode," notes Derrida.[17] To risk responsibility is, then, to incur the inevitable if also unknowable possibility of failure: the shame of confession arises not least at the point of the undecidability of veracity with regard to intentionality, where intention always exceeds our consciousness; it points, then, to the unresolvable hauntings of intentionality as such. Guilt in the face of specifiable injury may most effectively announce responsibility yet shame bears the awareness of the mysterious and uncontainable depths of our culpability. Guilt may appropriately pursue exoneration along the path of expiation yet it is in shame that we beg a forgiveness that exceeds all possible expectation of receiving the very forgiveness that seems to be sought. "If confession is guided by a teleology, it is not confession."[18]

Traditionally, the doctrine of original sin marks a momentous fracture within Christian thought, measured by the distance between the eschatological mappings of Augustine and Cassian. Yet the fracture may seem more internal to both, the distance narrower, as we pursue the traces of shame's confessional disclosures. This exploration of both Augustine's and Cassian's texts will be triangulated by a brief consideration of a slightly later eastern hagiographical work that gained great popularity in the early medieval west—the *Life of Mary of Egypt*. If Cassian's monastic writings allow us to consider confession from the point of view of the confessor as well as the confessant, the *Life of Mary of Egypt* provides an opportunity to explore more fully the desire of the confessor. Here we encounter the ambivalent productivity not only of speaking but also of giving witness to speech by offering a shamelessly, even a greedily, charitable ear to the confession of a nearly unspeakable shame.

Ridicule and Tears: Augustine's *Confessions*

Augustine opens Book 1 of his *Confessions* with a lengthy and impressive performance of rhetorical self-abasement, one of the first of many to come. "Dust and ashes though I am, let me speak before your mercy (*apud misericordiam tuam*)," he pleads; "let me speak, because it is your mercy—not the human, my mocker (*inrisor meus*)—to whom I speak." Having thus appealed to an abstract personification of divine *misericordia* in order to dodge the all-too-concrete laughter of humanity, he allows his address to God to become momentarily more direct: "Perhaps you too mock me (*inrides me*), but you will be converted to have mercy on me (*conversus misereberis mei*)." These lines convey several interesting assumptions that will be carried through the text. First, Augustine expects to be laughed at and shamed by other humans. Second, he is nonetheless able to speak his confession freely because of his confidence in God's forthcoming mercy. Third, he anticipates a merciful response from God only because he assumes—with no little audacity!—that God's mocking laughter (unlike humanity's?) *will* be transformed. Augustine thus aligns God with fallen humanity in so far as God may mock Augustine. At the same time, Augustine's confession of his lowly status enacts not only his own "turning" but also God's "turning": his verbal self-humiliation—"me, dust and ashes!"—provokes the conversion of divine ridicule to compassion; indeed, it can be relied upon to do so. As he searches his memory for signs of this compassion, he discovers it first in the "comforts of human milk" that he knows himself to have received as a newborn babe—milk human but also holy, for only God (opines Augustine) could have filled the breasts of his mother and nurses with nourishment so perfectly suited to his infancy. Yet still he imagines God laughing at him for his incessant questioning regarding his own ever-receding origins, itself reminiscent of a toddler's prattling: how did I behave as a baby? what was it like in my mother's womb? where was I before that? The blush of shame thus gently tints both his earliest reconstructed memories and his adult desire to uncover those memories in the presence of his divine auditor (1.6).

Quickly, however, shame begins to burn more darkly in Augustine's text. He perceives in children not innocence but sinful impulses indulged by others only to the extent that they can be trusted to disappear in a process of maturation that is linked closely with stern discipline. Proof is that adults would be rightly ashamed—rightly *made* to feel shame—were they to exhibit even a modified version of the behavior of babies: "For if I should now weep as I did then, not for the breast but for food more suited to my years, I would justly be laughed at and reproved" (1.7). Ridicule thus plays a salutary role in the chastening of errant souls yet strikingly Augustine's earliest (and never convincingly repudiated) prayers are that he might be spared both the pain and the shame. Not for the last time, God turns a strategically deaf ear on his pleas, and insult is added to injury as Augustine is not only beaten mercilessly for his disobedience by his teachers—an experience that he compares melodramatically to a martyr's tortures—but also laughed at heartlessly for his fearfulness by his elders, "including even my parents, who in no way desired that anything evil befall me." He wonders aloud that his own well-wishing mother and father could have "laughed at our torments," and he scoffs at the hypocrisy of the teachers who administered them (1.9). Yet he nonetheless hints that God is at work in such chastisement, even professing extravagantly: "Lord my God, I sinned by acting contrary to the commandments of my parents and of those teachers" (1.10). Though he is sure that one learns best in a spirit of free curiosity, he is also convinced that the "flow" of curiosity requires the constraint of divine laws, whether enforced via the schoolmaster's rod or the persecutor's torturings (1.14). As Leo Ferrari remarks, "The irate schoolmaster of Augustine's infancy therefore becomes the scourging God who purifies his soul through the many punishments of life."[19] Sometimes heavenly mercy is indistinguishable from worldly mockery, it would seem: divine love is tough love indeed. Augustine's ambivalence is already tautly stretched.

Shame assaults him from many directions, and ambivalence only intensifies as the complexity of his account increases. The question is not only how to submit oneself to mockery that is paradoxically at once malicious and inhibiting, on the one hand, and providential and transformative, on the other. The question is also how to resist being lured too far down the path of shame itself—not least the shame of the desire to confess. In Book 2, Augustine recounts the misadventures of his sixteenth year: "I was hurled and spilled out, and I flowed and boiled over in the midst of my fornications, and you were silent" (2.2). God, then, colludes tacitly in Augustine's dissipation, even as his earthly father brags loudly (and embarrassingly) to his mother upon first seeing the physical stirrings of his son's sexual maturity exposed in the public baths. For his part, Augustine confesses unabashedly that he was seduced repeatedly for the simple reason that he was so very *seducible*; he would have blushed to follow his mother's womanish admonitions to preserve his chastity. Titillated by such rhetorical insinuations, we may fail to note the surprisingly vague and oddly metaphorical character of his report of his sexual exploits—he spilled out, he overflowed, he was scattered, and so on. We may even miss a possibly important hermeneutical clue—namely, his bold disclosure that when shameful acts failed him, he simply made them up in order to impress his friends. "Afraid of being reviled I grew viler, and when I had no ruinous act to admit that could put me on a level with these abandoned youths, I pretended that I had done what I had not done"(2.3). It would have been too embarrassing to have nothing to brag about, too disappointing to have nothing to confess.

The shame that Augustine does finally expose to his readers in Book 2 is an adolescent theft—a petty theft at that, as he himself emphasizes, involving a group of restless boys and some worthless pears that were discarded and thrown to pigs almost as soon as they were stolen (2.4). We may feel robbed of the juicier repast that he initially appears to promise—a full disclosure of the entanglements of love and lust that had captured his youth. Then again, we may not pause to register disappointment, for somehow Augustine manages to make the boring event interesting: his bait-and-switch tactic works surprisingly well, in other words. Indeed, the theft of the pears, as he recalls it, seems to bring pleasure as sharp and disturbing as a teenager's sexual encounters might be imagined to be.

It is disturbing in part because it appears senseless. Augustine is not hungry, and the pears are not tasty. The pleasure of the crime, he emphasizes repeatedly, cannot therefore lie in possession or consumption. What, then? It is the act of disobedience that thrills him—that is, the simple, shameful fact of having done something he should not have done. His sin is to take pleasure in sin, his shame—as de Man might have predicted—to take pleasure in shame. Initially he proposes that such a gratuitous crime lies beyond perversion: it lacks "even that sham and shadowy beauty with which vices deceive us." However, he subsequently discovers in his disobedience a vicious and perverse imitation of virtue, after all: "Was I, being a captive, mimicking a maimed freedom through the dim likeness of omnipotence by getting away with something forbidden?" he wonders aloud (2.6). The point is not that to play God is a sin but rather that to sin is to play God—a much more interesting proposition. Even when he rebels, his very perversions imitate and thus confess the goodness of his creator. Or . . . *especially* when he rebels?

But there is still more at stake in this theft than the pleasure of disobedience, the joy arising from the mimicry of divine freedom. As Augustine searches his memories, he avows regarding "that at which, now remembering, I blush" that "I would not have done it alone; I most certainly would not have done it alone." What delighted him was "the crime as committed in the company of others who shared in the sin" (2.8). He acknowledges that "the theft gave us a thrill" and repeats: "I would not have done that deed alone; in no way would I have done it alone. . . . To do it alone would have aroused no desire whatever in me, nor would I have done it." He seems sure of himself on this point! "Let the others only say, 'Come on, let's go and do it!' and I am ashamed to hold back from the shameless act," he confesses. He concludes that it is friendship—albeit "an exceedingly unfriendly friendship"—that seduces his mind and draws him to behave shamelessly (2.9).

Given the mutual exposure already entailed in a sin committed in the company of friends, confession might here seem redundant. It does, however, have the effect of both prolonging the pleasure and extending the circle of intimacy. Later, he will wonder less at the sharpness of various sensual pleasures he experiences than at his "pleasure in discussing these topics, shameful as they were, with my friends" (6.16). In this case, confession also explicitly inscribes itself in a book that many others may *take and read*.

Confession does not efface but archives shame, as Derrida notes. Augustine begs that his readers not laugh at him (2.7), for his theft is now archived for all humanity, and so is his confession. It is deliberately made part of a memory and a history of confessions: this is the first point in his book at which he acknowledges the presence of his human readers (2.3). But his confession of theft also enfolds its own memory and history, since Augustine is not, of course, the first to have tasted forbidden fruit.

If the episode of the pears is not only consciously archived but also archivally produced—produced, above all, from the archives of scripture—how are we to judge its claims to veracity? Augustine has already confessed that he invented accounts of sexual transgression in order to be able to confess them to his friends. This confession of a lie, occurring in the midst of his confessions of fornication, complicates our assessment of the latter, which we may begin to suspect are so many empty boasts—especially since all we get, when we search for plausible details, is a story about stealing pears. Is even the theft a fiction, or at least a quasi-fiction, a nearly mechanical archival production that will repeat itself down the centuries?[20]

Yet the repetition is crucially inexact: there is genuine creativity at work in this confessional making of truth that is at once archival and archived. Unlike the Adam of Genesis 3, Augustine claims not to remember whether he actually tasted the flesh of the forbidden fruit. "Perhaps we ate some of them," he initially admits (2.4). Later, he insists that "of them I ate only my own transgression, in which I delighted and rejoiced; for even if some part of those pears entered my mouth, its sauce was the crime" (2.6). Has he departed from the script of Genesis or is he rewriting that script? He confesses unambiguously that he tasted the thrill of freedom. He tasted the pleasures of friendship. Indeed he "loved" them both. But the flesh of the pears may or may not have passed his lips—he is not sure, he cannot recall, but the main point, it seems, is that *it does not matter*. The pears *could* have been the objects of his love but in fact they were not: interestingly, it is love (*amor*) as well as acquisitive desire (*cupiditas*) that he here invokes so as to deny both (2.8). His text will not quite appropriate the scriptural event of the consumption of the flesh of the fruit, nor will it quite refuse it. It equivocates, it covers over clarity—just as his confessions more generally equivocate regarding the sensual pleasures of sexual acts, which remain secreted in his text, at once repeatedly avowed and ever undisclosed. Untouchable, out of our reach, refusing pornographic representation (refusing to be written as fornications, after all)—and thereby continuing to seduce, perhaps.[21]

Augustine prefers to confess the pleasures of relationality. He prefers to convert lust into love, to promise shameful fornications while in fact delivering friendships charged with the excitement of confessed or otherwise exposed shame. Yet the translation of lust into love—the effective switching of the bait—only serves to erode the distinction between lust and love, thereby reminding us of the lust secreted *within* love. We may imagine that we catch him with a bit of pear in his mouth—or a beautiful body in his bed. But he has already caught himself lusting for friendship, for sociality. He has already confessed his desire. This, as much as his disobedience, is the original sin revealed in the theft of the pears in Book 2 but also exposed with particular clarity in two other passages—the extended account of his intense grief at the death of an unnamed (male) friend in Book 4 (4.4–8) and the brief but vivid description in Book 6 of his grief at the forced departure of the unnamed woman with whom he lived for many years and with whom he had a son (6.15). If only *either* of these relationships had been merely "a bargain struck for lust" (4.2) instead of the "madness" of "loving one who was mortal as though that one were never to die" (4.7, 8). Then their grip on his soul would not have been so relentlessly tight; the pain of loss would not have been so unbearable; and Augustine would not have found himself looking so desperately for the comfort of substitute loves— other friends, another mistress. It is in the theft of the pears, related just after he has told of his father's report of seeing the stirrings of desire in his adolescent body, that Augustine detects the beginnings of the lust for love that will lead him astray repeatedly.

If the confession of the theft of the pears inscribes misguided, and thus willfully disobedient, love as the original sin, it also hints that the perversion of sin is the path of salvation, a path down which Augustine is driven by the goads of shame. He is not promiscuous *enough*, not scattered *enough*: monogamy is his great temptation![22] His loves and friendships are not carnal *enough*: he is prone to imagine them sublimely immortal! His shame is that he does not have more shameful acts to confess. He should perhaps just make them up, for acts of imagination count too: indeed, what we are capable of imagining may make all the difference. *All* things are good, and *all* things are transient—the "things" that are concrete, like fruit, and those that are not, like freedom or friendship. He himself both notes and erases the distinction—the beloved theft is "itself nothing"—as if he is impatient with the grammar of objectification, as if he is trying to test its limits (2.8). *All* things are to be enjoyed and none are to be possessed. *All* things are lovable. The beauty of even a markedly inferior pear, its taste on the tongue.

The thrill of spontaneity. The joys of companionship. The wondrous abundance, indeed the rotting excess, of divine creation. So many more pears than anyone could possibly want, so many more friends. So much more piggish desire than any pears—or lovers—could possibly satisfy. At this point, the avowal of sin and the praise of God—the shame and the shamelessness—may become truly indistinguishable in the performance of confession. Which is also to say, in the provocation of conversion, if the momentum of confession's repetition has not become merely mechanical, like a bad habit. And conversion is queerly continuous with perversion: to turn around is also to twist.

"I was in torment, reproaching myself more bitterly than ever as I twisted and turned in my chains," writes Augustine, approaching and also already suspending the narration of his famous moment of conversion. "And you, O Lord, never ceased to watch over my secret heart. In your stern mercy you lashed me with the twin scourge of fear and shame. . . . In my heart I kept saying 'Let it be now, let it be now!', and merely by saying this I was on the point of making the resolution. I was on the point of making it, but I did not succeed. . . . I stood on the brink of resolution, waiting to take fresh breath. I tried again and came a little nearer to my goal, and then a little nearer still, so that I could almost reach out and grasp it. But I did not reach it. I could not reach out to it or grasp it. . . . But this did not drive me back or turn me from my purpose: it merely left me hanging in suspense" (8.11). Augustine's agonies refuse easy release, but the suspense does not last forever. It cannot. Shortly after he has staged his deliciously sadomasochistic performance, which takes place not incidentally in a garden, "a great storm" breaks within him, "bringing with it a great deluge of tears." He withdraws from the company of his dear friend Alypius "to avoid being embarrassed even by his presence" (8.12). After the flood, the scourge of shame is no longer pleasurable, it would seem.

Or is it? As it turns out, Augustine has not reached any climax; he has merely shifted his tactics of deferral. Sitting alone under not a pear but a fig tree, he still imagines himself in chains. Sin turns him against himself. So too does the act of confession. He is split, fragmented, as he plays both the dominant and the submissive in his own erotic drama. "Why not now?" he cries out. The suspense is killing him. How long will he be able to keep this up? Long enough to provoke the address of others—first the androgynous voice of an unseen child whose novel (almost but not quite citational) incantations urge him not to "take and eat" but to "take and read," then the archived memory of other readers and other books consumed and transforming, and finally the lash of the apostolic whip that his friend Alypius is still holding for him patiently. Rendered obedient at last, Augustine takes the text of Paul's letter to the Romans and reads. In an instant, he is released from the bonds of sexual desire. Yet the interior event is not quite real until it has been verbalized, spilled out, confessed—until it has been addressed to another and the address has been returned. "My looks were quite calm as I told Alypius what had happened to me. He too told me what he had been feeling, which of course I didn't know" (8.12). Following his companion's lead, Alypius picks up the text that Augustine has helpfully marked and takes the next verse for himself: "Find room among you for a man of over-delicate conscience." Augustine notes that "it very well suited his moral character, which had long been far, far better than my own" (8.12).

This is an interesting statement. On the one hand, it is not at all surprising: Alypius is, after all, arguably a stand-in for Augustine's true love, Lady Continence, at once role model and salvific seducer. Unlike Augustine, he is not tempted by marriage, having failed to derive pleasure from the one sexual experience he had as a teenager: his chastity seems to come naturally, at least where women are concerned. Moreover, he has been undermining Monica's misguided arrangements for her son's marriage ever since Book 6. "It was Alypius who prevented me from marrying," claims Augustine at that point, "because he insisted that if I did so, we could not possibly live together in uninterrupted leisure, devoted to the pursuit of wisdom, as we had long desired to do" (6.12). Yet there are other sides to Alypius's "moral character" as Augustine has chosen to present it. He is dangerously impressionable, for starters. He is also persistently lured by spectacles of violence—lured too, it would seem, by the desire to have his own resistance to desire violently overcome. Carried off to the gladiatorial shows by a group of friends, he indulges in his own bit of melodrama: "You may drag me there bodily, but do you imagine that you can make me watch the show and give my mind to it?" This is a taunt that has the desired effect of encouraging his friends to test his resolve. He shuts his eyes on the alluring scene but at a roar from the crowd he cannot resist peeking. From that point on, he is lost. "His soul was stabbed with a wound more deadly than any which the gladiator, whom he was so anxious to see, had received in his body," laments Augustine. Alypius grows "hot with excitement"; his eyes cannot get enough; his curiosity is insatiable (6.8). Later, even the sight of Augustine's submission to his desire for women tempts Alypius to entertain thoughts of marriage: "He was amazed at my state of bondage, and amazement led to the desire to test it for himself" (6.12). Alypius likes to look. He submits himself to visual impressions—especially to visual impressions of domination and submission.

Indeed, it begins to seem that it is more his capacity for submission than his lack of heterosexual drive that makes Alypius superior to his former teacher. He is far, far better at submitting than Augustine. Or is he? At times (such as the scene of shared conversion in Book 8), Alypius seems to give way too easily; his submission is too passive; there is no resistance to be overcome, thus no suspense. To the extent that Augustine's resistance is higher, he may be far, far better at submitting after all. Which is also to say, he may be far better at dominating, more able to top his own resistance— for the erotic play of domination and resistance is always staged interiorly as well as in relation to another: Augustine plays both the dominator and the submissive in his own inner drama. But the interior is also externalized: he must still be mastered by another. Which is to say, he must be able to sustain his faith that he is in safely expert hands, no matter what happens. When the master is both omnipotent and omniscient (when the master is believed to be such), all forms of bondage become good and all shame may give way to shamelessness.

God is, then, omnipotent and omniscient—also beneficent—to the extent that Augustine avows God to be such. And it is crucial that other responses are imaginable. Indeed, a nearly silent undercurrent of reproach runs through *Confessions*. God abandons him to sin—says no word, is silent. God ties him up and leaves—and God only knows when God will return to set him free. God is everywhere and nowhere in this text that is constantly addressing and being addressed by God, seducing and being seduced by God. God is the effect of Augustine's seduction of the world, of his submission to the need to resist its temptations, if joy and excitement are to be sustained.[23] Sometimes the tables may even be turned: Augustine may very nearly play at dominating God.

Yet not before more tears of shame are shed. Augustine's conversion will be indelibly marked as incomplete in Book 10, where he continues, post-conversion, to confess his sins. Prior to that, its finality has already been subtly undercut by the addition, in Book 9, of another culminating event that both repeats and dissolves the clarities of a divine encounter. In the company of his mother Monica, Augustine's conversion in the garden now receives the supplement of a shimmeringly mystical moment: "while we spoke of the eternal Wisdom, longing for it and straining for it with all the strength of our hearts, for one fleeting instant we reached out and touched it" (9.10). Less than two weeks later, Monica has departed from life, and Augustine is left to struggle with his living grief. His very sorrow becomes a source of shameful self-exposure: despite the Wisdom that he has so recently reached out and touched, he continues (it seems) to desire that mortal creatures might extend their lives forever, as if in crude mimicry of divinity; he cannot quite submit to a transience that is always already melting into eternity, cannot quite accept the knowledge that every finite human love is sustained only by its participation in the infinite love of God.

As he struggles to suppress the all-too-revealing grief that "would have overflowed in tears if I had not made a strong effort of will and stemmed the flow," Augustine both exploits and resists his own fear of human ridicule. This fear hardens the surface of his stoic repression while he confesses nonetheless: "I knew well enough what I was stifling in my heart" (9.12). His shame, split ambivalently between earthly and heavenly realms of anticipated mockery, finally gives way to a shameless flow of tears that prove to be both transformative and themselves transformed. "It was a comfort to weep for her and for myself and to offer my tears to you for her sake and for mine." Freeing the flow of tears, Augustine makes of them a pillow for his heart, as he puts it. Once again, it is the expectation of divine mercy that enables the confessional release: "for your ears were there, not the ears of a human who might have interpreted my weeping scornfully." His professions now flow with an assertive shamelessness, as he opens himself to a broader audience: "I confess to you in writing. Let any one read it who will and interpret it as he or she will; and if that one should find that I sinned in weeping for my mother, even if only for a fraction of an hour, . . . let him not laugh at me (*non inrideat*)." His mother has wept for him and now Augustine returns the gift of tears, by both receiving and offering his own tears as a gift. In so doing, he not only effects the conversion of divine mockery to mercy but also courts the conversion of his reader. "Let him not laugh at me but weep himself, if his charity is great" (9.12). Confession, the confession born of tears—borne *on* tears—*arrives* in a flood of shame that also washes away shame: or rather, it converts the inescapable vulnerability of shame into the source of a shameless compassion.

Beyond Shame: Augustine's *City of God*

In the initial books of his magisterial *City of God*, Augustine attempts nothing less (if also something considerably more) than the conversion of Roman history. This process can be observed in miniature in his treatment of an already ancient tale of shame suffered and honor restored. Rereading Livy's account of the rape of Lucretia, Augustine makes a sinner of a renowned heroine whose sacrificial death was said to have provoked Rome's legendary liberation from the chains of tyranny. Rewriting Lucretia, he strikes "not only at perceived misconceptions about sexual purity, but at the most basic forces behind Roman social relations, the prickly goads of honor and shame," as Dennis Trout puts it. "The cumulative impact of such revisionary discourse," Trout concludes, "is a measure of cultural transformation."[24] Yet how do we best describe that momentous transformation? Trout's image of striking at goads is both odd and revealing, suggesting something like fighting fire with fire—or shame with shame. Indeed, Augustine does not merely hollow out the space of an interiority that can make secrets of the possibly shameful desires of even a famously chaste and forthright woman. He also forcefully reinscribes humiliation by publicly performing a mock trial in which judgment is passed precisely by being deferred. Deprived of her innocence, Lucretia remains suspended in her shame.

Livy's story begins with a drinking party in a soldier's tent, during which the men fall to bragging about their wives. One of them, Collatinus, makes a fateful proposal—namely, that they visit their spouses unannounced, to see which of them (if any) are actually living up to their husbands' boasts. In all cases but one, the women are discovered to be comporting themselves ignominiously. The exception is Collatinus's wife Lucretia, who is busy with her wool into the late hours, paragon of feminine virtue—indeed, almost too good to be true. Both her beauty and her chastity excite the desires of the king's son, Sextus Tarquinius, who secretly returns alone to Collatinus's home. Hospitably received, he steals into Lucretia's bedroom at night, threatening to kill her if she will not submit to his lust. Predictably, she refuses. "If death will not move you," Sextus insists, raising the stakes, "dishonor shall. I will kill you first, then cut the throat of a slave and lay his naked body by your side. Will they not believe that you have been caught in adultery with a servant—and paid the price?" Faced with the horrifying prospect of being thought guilty of indulging in sexual relations with her slave, the proud Lucretia yields to her aristocratic ravisher.

As soon as Sextus has left, Lucretia summons her father and husband, requesting that each bring a trusted friend as witness, and when they arrive she tells all. At her urging, the men promise to avenge her by killing Sextus—a mission that eventually leads to the overthrow of the Tarquin kings and the establishment of the Roman Republic. In the meantime, Lucretia vows to take her own life. The men try to dissuade her, assuring her that she is not at fault: "It is the mind that does wrong, not the body; without intention there is no guilt." She responds: "Though I acquit myself of the wrong, I do not absolve myself from punishment; in the future no unchaste woman shall live by invoking the example of Lucretia." Just as she has chosen rape over the false appearance of voluntary adultery, so now she choses death over the false appearance of shameless guilt. Her innocent intention, which she herself does not question, will not efface the taint of shame that clings so tenaciously to a woman's sexual reputation. Observing the dictates of Rome's patriarchal code, she may also expose its cruelty, as she pulls a knife from under her robe and plunges it into her heart. She thereby shifts the burden of shame to her shamer, or such is her wager: henceforth she will be remembered not for her disgrace but for the excessive sacrifice she is willing to make in order to reclaim her exceeding virtue (Livy, *History of Rome* 1.59).

Or so she will be remembered until Augustine's eye probes the depths that lie (as he imagines it) beneath the surface of this history. One always confesses the other: here he confesses the other, (as) woman. "What are we to say of her? Is she to be judged adulterous or chaste?" A shocking question with regard to one whose reputation has stood unquestioned for at least four centuries. Undeterred by the force of tradition, Augustine does not merely call upon Lucretia to give testimony against herself; he explicitly makes her both confessor and confessant, at once judger and judged, in her original self-trial. Without claiming to know the truth himself, he nonetheless skillfully manoeuvers her so that she hangs suspended between equally shameful possibilities. On trial once again, Lucretia is either guilty of "having put to death a woman not only uncondemned but chaste and innocent" or innocent of that crime but guilty of another, namely, unchastity. It is the second possibility that clearly draws him. "For suppose (a thing which only she herself could know) that, although the young man attacked her violently, she was so enticed by her own desire that she consented to the act and that when she came to punish herself she was so grieved that she thought death the only expiation" (*City of God* 1.19). Making his own truth, a voyeuristic Augustine here adeptly exposes the faultlines in Livy's story. Agency is not altogether absent from Lucretia's choice to submit to Sextus, after all; moreover, even her father and husband protest that her death is unnecessary if her intentions are pure. Only Lucretia could know whether they are pure, and Augustine can only imagine that they might not be. Perhaps even Lucretia couldn't know: in the face of such relentless scrutiny of the heart's secrets, the line between rape and seduction may become nearly impossible to detect. How could she be absolutely sure that no part of her will, however small, submitted to the mastery of lust (his, hers), however briefly? Even as he revoices the comforting assurances of Lucretia's father and husband—"without intention there could never be guilt"—Augustine virtually eradicates the possibility of affirming innocence by placing intention beyond the reach of certainty while also requiring that it always be pure.

In so doing, he very nearly puts into question not only longstanding traditions of noble death but even Christian practices of martyrdom that are continuous with those traditions. Lucretia, after all, is viewed as a proto-martyr by prior Christian writers,[25] and Augustine lives in an asceticizing age that favors similar stories of virgin martyrs—"brides of Christ"—who submit willingly to death in order to preserve their faith *and* their chastity.[26] Crucially, he also writes at a moment when a new kind of martyrdom is being both made and contested on the battleground of rape during the Visigothic invasion of Rome in 410. The rhetorical context of his retelling of Lucretia's story is shaped by the fact that some non-Christians are attributing shame to the Christian God due to that God's apparent failure to protect Christian women, even sanctified ascetic women, from sexual violation (1.16). Among those women are some who have survived rape, some who have killed themselves subsequent to rape, and some who have killed themselves to avoid it (1.17–18). Stemming the flood of both the reported taunts of pagans and the anticipated tendency of Christians to defend their faith by discovering martyrs in those who have evaded defilement by their self-chosen deaths, Augustine insists that, where the mind is pure, physical violation "involves no blame to the sufferer." Neither God nor God's church is ultimately dishonored by a crime committed by another. Nor, therefore, does killing oneself to evade or counteract rape accrue particular glory. In fact, "anyone who kills him- or herself is a murderer," he asserts boldly (1.17). He acknowledges, however, that rape "does still engender a sense of shame, because it may be believed that an act, which perhaps could not have taken place without some physical pleasure, was accompanied also by a consent of the mind" (1.16). By the time he has put Lucretia on the witness stand, the implications of this statement are chillingly clear. Far from restoring a public reputation for honor, a woman's self-killing betrays the possibility, even the probability, of her secret shame. Augustine's strong rhetorical spin thus turns not only Lucretia but also her late ancient sisters into suspected sinners, transforming them from shameless witnesses into confessional subjects. As shame spreads, grace *may* abound. In the meantime, there seems to be precious little charity in Augustine's reception of the testimony that he himself has inscribed on behalf of women who can no longer speak for themselves.

Intriguingly, Trout suggests that Augustine's "discomfort with Lucretia" may have been "prompted in part by an eschatological vision of the body that, if it would only emerge in the final book of *City of God*, was already intimated by the work's preface."[27] For Augustine does not merely rewrite Roman history in *City of God*. His broader ambition is the revising of salvation history, from the dawn of creation to the end of time itself, if not also before and beyond. In so doing, he very nearly (but not quite) writes the human body out of history. A work of immense audacity, from start to finish *City of God* manifests a tension between the will to know and control all and the reach for a truth that exceeds the limits not only of knowing but even of credibility. That tension, as Trout hints, both strains and sustains the linear flow of the text. Repeatedly, Augustine must go back to beginnings that themselves prove unknowable, though not unimaginable, in order to approach ends that defy imagination.

The eschatological vision of the resurrected body that will be unveiled in the final, twenty-second book of *City of God* is already being sought after in the account of creation launched with Book 11. In the creation of humanity, there is visible "something like the beginning, in the human race, of the two cities; their beginnings, that is, in the foreknowledge of God, though not in observable fact" (12.28). Graced with a measure of hindsight, Augustine apparently participates partly, though only partly, in the clear sight of divine foreknowledge, as he follows the traces of this split history. His eyes readily expose the onset of shame that attends the fall of the first human couple: having disobeyed God, "immediately they were embarrassed by the nakedness of their bodies." He continues: "They even used fig leaves . . . to cover their *pudenda*, the 'organs of shame' [Gen. 3.7ff]. These organs were the same as they were before, but previously there was no shame attaching to them." The organs are the same, and also not the same, for now Adam and Eve feel "a novel disturbance in their disobedient flesh, as a punishment which answered to their own disobedience" (13.13). The stirring of bodily desire is, then, the punishment that fits the original crime of rebellion. The shame that arises concurrently with this disturbing movement is the trace of a memory of lost innocence. It is what at once separates and joins pre- and post-lapsarian humanity. It may be the only sign that remains that we were once otherwise and thus someday may become other than we are—if still also not quite the same as we were before.

It is through the veil of shame that Augustine must peer in order to perceive the state of humanity before the fall, but he does so in order to follow the trajectory of a salvation that is more than a restoration. He is pressing through multiple veils, then—passing behind the origins of shame in order to arrive at an as yet undiscovered shamelessness. The resurrected body, he asserts, will submit with "an obedience so wonderfully complete that the body will fulfill the will of the spirit in such a way as to bring perfect assurance of indissoluble immortality, free from any feeling of distress, and relieved of any possibility of corruption, any trace of reluctance." This body, melting into perfect obedience, "will not even be such as it was in the first human beings before their sin" (13.20). It will be even better! The submission that will arrive through the overcoming of reluctance will be more perfect than the merely natural obedience of the innocent. To fall into perdition, it would seem, is to take the first step on the path to greater perfection.

Further explication of this insight requires, for Augustine, further meditation on the nature of sin. Disobedience is the effect of pride, and pride, like the Devil, lies (14.3). It lies by insinuating that humans are autonomous. Here we may fold back on the lie that haunts all confessional discourse: any account that we give of ourselves says both too much and too little, in so far as it insinuates our containability as *selves*. That humans are not autonomous is indicated first and foremost by the fact that they are the creatures of God, but also secondarily by the fact that they are innately sociable creatures—ever treading on each others' toes. The genesis of all of humanity, including Adam's companion Eve, from a single individual was divinely designed so that "the unity of human society and the bonds of human sympathy be more emphatically brought home to humanity" (12.22). Indeed, "the human race is, more than any other species, at once social by nature and quarrelsome by perversion" (12.28). Even before quarrels begin, sociability itself is the source of perversion: if Adam was led astray by Eve, it was because "they were so closely bound in partnership," while Eve for her part seems to have been lured by a charitable desire to accept the serpent's words as truth (14.11).

Desire or love remains at the troubled heart of things, and indeed it lies at the heart of human sociability. Still gazing through the veil of shame, Augustine reaches for a time in which there was no distinction between *amor* and *caritas*, for the scriptures do not distinguish between these two terms, as he points out.[28] The split that fractures history opens not between the longing of *amor* and the generosity of *caritas*, he insists, but between a will rightly directed and one that is wrongly directed; it is will or desire wrongly directed that is conventionally referred to as lust—*cupiditas* or *concupiscentia* (14.7). What would the relations of the first human couple have been like, had lust not intervened? They would still have been sexual relations, he famously insists. But the body and will would have been as one, because the will itself would not have been fractured by ambivalence. Sexual relations would have been without shame, even as nakedness was without shame: "nakedness was not yet disgraceful, because lust did not yet arouse those members independently of their decision" (14.17). That shame attends fallen desire is to him self-evident: intercourse between marital couples— far more illicit sex—seeks privacy: "it blushes to be seen" (14.18). "A man would be less put out by a crowd of spectators watching him visiting his anger unjustly upon another than by one person observing him when he is having lawful intercourse with his wife" (14.19). Even the famously shameless Cynic Diogenes, he suspects, "merely went through the motions of lying together before the eyes of others who had no means of knowing what was really going on under the philosopher's cloak" (14.20). If Augustine can easily see through Lucretia's sham innocence, he can also see through the Cynic's false shamelessness. Pushing through the veils of falsehood, he continues to pursue, in the ambitious reach of his imagination, a sexuality without shame—the kind that Adam and Eve *might* have had, but did not.

"If there had been no sin, marriage would have been worthy of the happiness of paradise, and would have given birth to children to be loved, and yet would not have given rise to any lust to be ashamed of; but, as it is, we have no example to show how this could come about. Yet that does not mean that it should seem incredible that the one part of the body could have been subject to the will, without the familiar lust, seeing that so many other parts are now in subjection to it" (14.23). Here Augustine, making heavy use of the subjunctive mood, writes of a past that *would* have been, had sin not intervened. He writes of a past that never was, then, a past that he wills into being, masterfully—a willed past that embodies fantasies of the will's absolute mastery. Augustine is playing God; indeed he is topping God's act of creation in order to anticipate God's act of redemption. With every member rendered fully obedient—even that one unruly "part"— there would have been no cause for shame in Eden, as *he* imagines it. Sexual intercourse would have been conducted under conditions of strictest self-control. "Then the instrument created for the task would have sown the

seed on 'the field of generation' as the hand now sows seed on the earth,"
he suggests (14.23). He repeats the point, now including reference to the
female partner: "The man would have sowed the seed and the woman
would have conceived the child when their sexual organs had been aroused
by the will, at the appropriate time and in the necessary degree, and had
not been excited by lust" (14.24).

In the absence of concrete examples, the argument proceeds by anal-
ogy. Perceiving possible problems with his prior comparison of penis to
hand, Augustine cites the mouth, face, and lungs as examples of bodily organs that lack skeletal structure yet can still be controlled by voluntary mus-
cles. So why not the penis? Or for that matter the vagina? "The male seed
could have been dispatched into the womb, with no loss of the wife's integrity, just as the menstrual flux can now be produced from the womb of a
virgin without loss of maidenhead," he intones. "For the seed could be injected through the same passage by which the flux is ejected" (14.26).

This is sex so plainly vanilla that one wonders why Adam and Eve
would have bothered. It is sex as Alypius might have liked it, perhaps—but
then Alypius did not much like to bother with sex. But what about sex in
heaven? For it is to a heaven that has not yet arrived that Augustine is really
trying to take us, and himself, via this narrative detour into a past that never
was. And heavenly bodies, as he has told us earlier, will be even better than
prelapsarian bodies; so too, presumably will heavenly sex top sex as it would
have been before the fall. Resurrected flesh "will submit to the spirit with a
ready obedience," he enthuses (13.20).

If this sounds suspiciously (and disappointingly) like Edenic sex, it is
nonetheless necessarily different in at least one crucial respect: heavenly
bodies perform a submission that has overcome resistance, a shamelessness
that has passed through shame. As we have seen, Augustine detects embarrassment arising in the first humans from the sight of genitals in which are
now felt the movements of sexual arousal. We are back, then, with him in
the public baths, blushing: shame is an appropriate response to the involuntary stirring that arises from prideful disobedience. Indeed, the blush of
shame is itself no source of shame, for it is a trace of the goodness of created
nature that perdures beyond the fall—an acknowledgement that humans
are neither autonomous nor invulnerable, nor, therefore, are they ever innocent. That they once *were* innocent is perceived only by a scripturally
enhanced projection of imagination beyond what memory can contain. Augustine foregrounds the ambivalence of a subjectivity shadowed with the
awareness of its own destructive tendency toward pride—an awareness that

itself cuts against pride and thus almost (but only almost) doubles back to the moment when nakedness is not yet attended by shame because humanity is yet untouched by sin. There was no pride or disobedience then, as he imagines it; but perhaps there was also no humility or obedience. If his eschatology does not simply loop back to the beginning (as he insists it does not) this is in part because it must make place for humility and obedience. But how can we begin to imagine the eschaton? What will heavenly sex be like?

"Sadism is the seduction of control," writes Karmen MacKendrick.[29] The Augustine of *City of God* may *really* start to seduce us (as he already has in his *Confessions*) when he begins to fantasize a control that is over the top—unnatural, perverse. He finally discovers such heavenly possibilities not in the fictive past but in present realities more bizarre than any fiction. Previously he has insisted on the plausibility of his willful reconstructions of what *might have been*, forcefully denying our right to incredulity. Now he admits that what he is going to describe—what *is*—will seem unbelievable. Oddly, the more incredible his reports become, the more we may want to submit to the seduction of his control—which is also to say, to submit to the seduction of his tales of hyperbolic control. There are some people, he relates, who "can do things with their body which are for others utterly impossible and well nigh incredible when they are reported." Like what? Well, for instance, they can wiggle their ears or move their scalps; swallow improbable items and regurgitate them on command; make uncannily inhuman sounds such as bird calls; create music by passing odorless gas through the anus; sweat or cry at will (14.24). His examples may not seem erotically compelling, to say the least. But we must remember: these are analogies, the best Augustine can do as he tries to imagine the unimaginable. Sex in heaven will be a perversion of nature as we know it—and then some. It will extend the perversions that nature already miraculously proliferates. Bodies and souls will achieve control beyond control and submission beyond submission: as the difference between control and submission disappears, they will discover a freedom beyond freedom. They will perform acts of lust now deemed shameful with shameless abandon. Bodies and souls will do things that we would not believe even if he could tell us about them. But he cannot, quite. To press the imagination beyond shame is to press beyond the limits of the imagination. It is to reach for the heaven that arrives with, but cannot be compelled by, a confession in which the sublime heights of divine praise and the abject depths of human desire meet.

The Discipline of Discernment: John Cassian's *Conferences*

Discernment of the heart's innermost secrets is at the center of John Cassian's monastic discipline. "All corners of our heart must . . . be examined thoroughly and the marks of all that rise up into them must be investigated with the utmost wisdom" (Conference 1.22). To expose one's thoughts to scrutiny is already to begin to discipline them, in an ongoing process of self-alienation: if one always confesses the other, then one can hope to disown the self who is confessed. Yet the practice of self-examination cannot be confined to the privacy of the monk's prayerful devotions, for it would be dangerously prideful for the monk to rely on his own judgment. Are we not always facing the temptation to lie to ourselves, not least when trying to make truth? One confesses the (self as) other, but one must do so by confessing to an other, submitting to the authority of a brother. Whether the confessor deserves the authority granted him as "elder" remains to be seen. Yet there is already benefit for the confessant in the very act of humiliating submission. Cassian, apparently too humble to speak for himself, records Abba Moses's words: "True discernment is obtained only when one is really humble. The first evidence of this humility is when everything done or thought is submitted to the scrutiny of our elders. This is to ensure that one trusts one's own judgment in nothing, that one yields to their authority in everything" (2.10). *Everything? Nothing?* Cassian's call to confession presses ambitiously against the limits of the absolute. Does it thereby also exceed all limits, dissolving into the abysmal infinitude that Augustine seems to have discovered in his own confessions? This is a question to which we must return.

Abba Moses, as Cassian tells it, goes on to relate an instructive story told to him by Abba Serapion. In his youth, when he was living with Abba Theo, Serapion developed a bad habit. "After a meal shared by me with the old man at the ninth hour each day I would conceal on my person a bit of bread which I secretly devoured later, unknown to him." He extends this meticulous confession of what *might* be deemed a relatively minor infraction: "I continued to be guilty of this hidden act. My will cooperated and there was no restraint at all on my urges." Eating may have satisfied his gluttony, but it also produced "guilty torment that was much worse than any gratification I had experienced while eating," he avows. "Each day my heart suffered the torment of this compulsion and yet I was unable to break free of this most cruel tyranny and I was too ashamed to reveal my thieving to the old man." If the sense of being tyrannized by habit is reminiscent of

Augustine twisting in his chains, the heavy emphasis on the problematic character of a shame that inhibits the exposure of confession is distinctly Cassian's. (Augustine, in contrast, finds confession all too tempting.) For it is less Serapion's unbridled gluttony—his crumbs of bread being no more impressive in themselves than Augustine's barely tasted pears—than his compulsive secrecy that is devouring his soul, as becomes clear.

But perhaps we should linger a bit longer with the relation of gluttony to secrecy in Serapion's theft of a bit of bread, for secrecy may here be itself the secret ingredient that converts hunger to sin. In an intriguing interpretation of Jean Jacques Rousseau's confessional account of the shame that he feels when he walks into a shop to make a simple purchase of food, Coetzee suggests that Rousseau is "offended by the openness and legitimacy of monetary transactions" that threaten to commodify and thus efface the singularity, and the singular force, of his desires. "To Rousseau, his own desires are *resources* as long as they remain unique, hidden—in other words, as long as they are potentially confessable." Coetzee continues: "A shameful desire is a valuable desire. Conversely, for a desire to have value it must have a secret, shameful component." Similarly, Serapion's desire for the bread that has been freely offered only has value in the monastic economy of confession once it has been converted into a secret shame by an act of theft. As Coetzee puts it, "*Stealing* . . . has its compensations in replacing the revealed, and no longer shameful, desire with a crime—itself confessable currency."[30] The shameful desire to steal is currency that will continue to circulate, once archived. Each subsequent narration will yield fresh profit.

Serapion's initial confessional payoff is enabled by the arrival of some visiting monks, in whose company the elder Theo begins to speak "about the sin of greed and about the way secret thoughts take a grip on someone." Listening to his master's discourse, Serapion can only imagine that God has revealed his secrets to Theo, so that a deep sadness is now added to the other hidden emotions that fill his heart to the point that it can no longer contain its burdens: "Then my heart grew ever more scalded until I broke openly into sobs and tears. I pulled out the piece of bread which in my sinful habit I had taken away to be eaten secretly. I pulled it out from my breast which had shared the knowledge of my furtiveness and which had gone along with it. I put it out in front of everyone and, prostrate on the ground, I begged for pardon and I confessed how each day I was eating secretly. I poured out a rich flood of tears and I implored them to ask of God that I be delivered of my captivity."

Serapion's tears, like Augustine's, bring him both the relief and the release of self-exposure. Yet while Augustine continues to shed "tears of another sort" (*Confessions* 9.13)—namely, tears that acknowledge the indelibility, thus the ongoing shamefulness, of even sins confessed—Theo marks the moment of Serapion's confessional conversion with an air of finality: "Without me saying anything, your confession has set you free from this captivity." He assures Serapion that "this most loathsome serpent will not take up a hiding place within you, for he has been pulled out into the light from your shadowed heart by this saving confession of yours." Serapion himself affirms that the "diabolical tyranny was wiped out and forever laid to rest." He never again feels "moved by the wish to engage in stealing of this kind." The moral of the story is hammered home. The path of the elders must be followed; novelty is to be avoided; monks should "not presume to decide anything on the basis of our private judgment." The traditions and the authority embodied by the monastic teachers "must always be followed with the utmost care and every thought in our hearts must be submitted to them, stripped of the cover of false modesty" (Conference 2.11).

However decisively triumphal and rigidly authoritarian—and in this respect, non-Augustinian—Cassian's perspective here might seem, the illumining practice of confession in fact (in practice) remains shadowed by a productive doubt. The *Conferences* accumulate and archive the wisdom of the elders, yet even the cited dicta and instructive anecdotes of such a plenitude of venerable abbas as are here textually gathered surely remain incomplete, just as the act of submitting to the examination of one's own heart is never finished. Vigilance must always be sustained: even modesty may prove to be a false cover. As the monk Germanus remarks after hearing Moses's account of Serapion's tale, the fault for duplicity or hiding may often lie as much with the confessor as with the confessant: "We knew someone in Syria who was deemed the most outstanding of the elders, but when a brother came to him to confess openly the thoughts that were troubling him he was moved to rage and he very sternly upbraided him. As a result, we bury our thoughts and we blush to tell our elders about them, so that we find ourselves unable to acquire the remedy for these problems" (2.12). The twin scourge of fear and shame is as present, and as ambivalent, in the monastery as in the wider world, it would seem.

Germanus's comment inspires Moses to tell another story that expands on the same basic plot line. It involves an earnest young monk who approaches an elder for help with the sexual desires that trouble him. (Tactfully, Moses does not reveal either of their names.) The elder responds by berating the young man "in the bitterest terms, calling him an unworthy wretch, exclaiming that he had no right to bear the name of monk in view of the fact that he was stirred by this kind of sin and concupiscence." Such a shaming tactic brings only hurt and a deadly despondence that leave the confessant more than ever at the mercy of his sexual desires. At this point, however, he encounters "Apollo, the holiest of all the old monks." Reading the despair evident on the young monk's face, Apollo inquires regarding its cause. The monk is, not surprisingly, tongue-tied. As struck by what is being "veiled in silence" as by what is plain on the young man's face, Apollo inquires more persistently regarding "the causes of such hidden grief." Finally, the unhappy monk tells his story, announcing his intention of leaving the monastery and getting married. The elder responds gently, "claiming that he too was moved each day by the same urges and tossed by the same storms." (It is unclear whether this is a true confession or a strategically compassionate lie.) He assures him that the ferocity of such temptations is no cause for surprise, nor should one expect to be able to prevail against them by one's own efforts but rather one must hope to do so by the grace of God. Requesting that the younger man wait one more day before acting on his decision, Apollo races off to the dwelling place of the other elder.

Stretching out his hands and weeping, he prays that God will transfer the young monk's desires to the heart of the old man who has judged him so harshly, so as to teach him kindness and sympathy for the frailty of the young. The effect of this prayer is immediate. As soon as he finishes, Apollo sees "a loathsome Ethiopian standing by that man's cell and hurling fiery javelins at him."[31] Stricken by the darts of desire, the old man rushes off madly "along the same road taken by the young man." When the virtuous abba confronts him regarding his frenzied behavior, the tormented elder fears "that his heart's passion had been detected and that the deep secret of his soul had been uncovered by the old man," and he finds himself, like the young monk before him, unable to speak. The tables have been neatly turned, and now Apollo can bring his point home: no true monk, the old man cannot fend off, much less endure, even the temptations that typically beset youth. God is teaching him not only "to have sympathy for the weakness of others" but also to recognize that temptation comes to those whose strength, unlike that of the old man, is great enough to arouse the envy of the enemy. Finally, Apollo prays that the temptation be withdrawn from the old man, who has now been effectively shamed and humbled, and once again God complies immediately. Interestingly, Moses's own conclusions seem to exceed those drawn by Apollo, as he turns our attention back to the young confessant: "Our enemy, who is very cunning, uses the white hair of age to fool the young. Let there be no falsely modest veil. Everything must be told openly to our elders" (2.13). Like Augustine, Abba Moses suggests that even sinful mockery can convey a divinely salutary chastisement. No monk should give way to despair.

Where Augustine gives explicit voice to his own ambivalence in the face of the unplumbable mysteries arising from confession made in the face of mockery at once worldy and divine, Cassian's authoritative abba seems to cover over the contradictions that remain nonetheless exposed by his own narrative. Indeed, the surface of this tale, like the young monk's face, will continue to betray the existence of hidden depths. Any confessor, however white his hair, may be discovered to be a false monk—which is to say, an instrument of the enemy yet still also one that is turned to the purposes of divine discernment. At the same time, no confessant, however humble and obedient, can possibly tell *everything* to his elders, and any truth made in confession will be haunted by the possibility of an undetected and even unintended lie—the possibility that *something* has been left out. Does the young monk's reluctantly confessed despair at his own unchaste thoughts validate or invalidate the old man's challenge (no matter what motivates it) that his vocation is false? How can one know for sure whether modesty— for example, the initial choice not to pass judgment by telling tales on the old man or, similarly, the decision to accept his own unworthiness—is true or false? There are always more veils to be stripped away, not least because modesty is ever in danger of becoming a matter of pride. Behind Cassian is Moses, behind Moses Apollo, and behind Apollo ambiguities proliferate. If there are always more veils to be stripped away, there are also always more stories to be told. We do not know what becomes of the young man, what confessional truths he continues to make and unmake. Nor do we know what becomes of the old man who has been subjected to the mockery of an attack of youthful lust—whose confession has, moreover, been entirely scripted by his interrogator Apollo's self-certainties. The unraveling of such certainties may here take place in a reading that runs slightly against the grain of Cassian's text. Yet it is also continuous with the very process of examining the heart's secrets in which Cassian clearly intends to school his readers.

A subtle debate runs through scholarly assessments of the place of sexual temptations in Cassian's hierarchy of troubling passions, which builds on but does not simply repeat the thought of his teacher Evagrius.[32] Peter Brown acknowledges that sexual desires not only serve to inculcate humility, according to Cassian, but also constitute a privileged indicator of the state of the monk's soul. "Sexual fantasies were like signals on a screen. They registered processes that lay out of sight, in the depths of the self." Closely linked to "the more faceless drives of egotism and rage," the stubborn persistence of sexual desires warned the monk "that these drives still lingered, unconsciously, within his soul." Nonetheless, for Cassian, "sexuality was a mere epiphenomenon," insists Brown. "Augustine, by contrast, had placed sexuality immovably at the center of the human person."[33]

Yet Foucault, in an essay lauded by Brown as "brilliant,"[34] seems to find sexuality at the center of Cassian's understanding of the human person as well. He observes that in the fifth conference the first six items on Cassian's list of vices are linked to one another in a causal chain—greed or gluttony, fornication, avarice, anger, despondency, *acedia* or listlessness—in which each rests on the one before it. Vainglory and pride, in contrast, "do not form part of the causal chain of other vices" but rather "result from victory over them." It is the temptation of fornication that links pride and vainglory—but especially pride—to the prior vices. "Fornication, the most disgraceful of all the vices, the one that is most shameful, is the consequence of pride." As Brown also notes, fornication serves the function of the chastisement of pride. In Foucault's phrasing: "When the soul has only itself to combat, the wheel comes full circle, the battle begins again, and the prickings of the flesh are felt anew, showing the inevitable continuance of the struggle and the threat of a perpetual recurrence." Foucault notes, as well, that fornication possesses "an ontological particularity," since it not only straddles the boundary between the flesh and the imagination but also, unlike greed for food, the other fleshly vice, can and indeed must be "totally eradicated." He concludes: "Thus, one sees how fornication, though just one of the elements in the table of vices, has its own special position, heading the causal chain, and is the sin chiefly responsible for backsliding and battles, at one of the most difficult and decisive points in the struggle for ascetic life."[35]

From another perspective (one familiar from traditional doctrinal debates), what distinguishes Cassian from Augustine is not so much the respective weight placed by each of them on the centrality of sexual desires as the different positions taken regarding the eradicability of such desires—which brings us back to the question of the possible differences in their understandings of confession. Much rests on certain limit cases. Intriguingly, Cassian goes so far as to raise the question of whether Jesus experienced sexual desire. That he did not *submit* to this temptation, or for that matter to any other, Cassian takes for granted, but the question remains: was Jesus even *tempted* by lust? Yes and no, is the answer. Born sinless, Jesus did not experience "the fiery darts of carnal lust, which in our case rise even against our will," yet nonetheless "he took on himself something like this, by sharing in our nature." What does "something like this" mean? Cassian develops this thought through an ingenius interpretation of the biblical account of Jesus' threefold testing by the devil (Luke 4.1–3; cf. Matt. 4.1–11), in which he is able to detect a sort of abbreviated (or perhaps fast-forwarded) progression through the sequence of the eight primary passions that recalls Adam's similarly compacted (and contrastingly unsuccessful) testing.[36] Like Adam, Jesus is first tempted by gluttony, when the devil commands that he turn stones to bread. Having passed that test, unlike Adam, he cannot be subjected to the trial of lust, "which had shot up from the root of the first fault." Thus, Jesus proleptically passes the test of lust by failing to be moved by greed for food, a necessarily prior desire. For this reason, Cassian explains, the devil skips (albeit equally pointlessly) to the third passion, avarice (or perhaps to the seventh, vainglory), when he offers him all of the kingdoms of the world. Finally, in desperation, by urging Jesus to put God Godself to the test by casting himself from a mountaintop and thus forcing the divine hand of salvation, the devil passes directly to the final, fatal temptation of pride, "by which he knew that those who are perfect and have overcome all other sins, can be affected." Jesus, of course, passes this test too, and with it demonstrates conclusively his resistance to *all* of the passions (5.6).[37] If he has nothing to confess, he still knows what it is to be tempted.

But what of those who are not sinless but merely saintly? Cassian's more extended discussions of sexual desire are enfolded into his *Conferences* in two later sequences. Abba Chaeremon's discourse on chastity (12) is sandwiched between his discourses on perfection and on divine protection (11, 13), while Abba Theo's discourse on nocturnal emissions (22) occurs between his discourses on lenten observances and on sinlessness (21, 23): in both cases, sexuality is placed structurally at the center of a revered abba's concerns with the cultivation of purity of heart. The coy omission of the twelfth and twenty-second conferences from the otherwise complete nineteenth-century English translation of Cassian's work by Edgar Gibson lends the further impression that sexuality is not only central but at the center of the heart's *secrets*—an impression, however arbitrary, not dispelled by Cassian's own legible Latin.

Here the limit case is presented by nocturnal fantasies and emissions, an issue, so to speak, already surfaced in the twelfth conference and to which the twenty-second is wholly dedicated. Even when a wakeful and watchful monk has reached the point that he is able first to ignore, then to eradicate, the involuntary arousal of both his flesh and his imagination—even when he has advanced so far that he can discuss sexual intercourse without having his serenity disturbed by thoughts of pleasure—he may still be betrayed by the fantasies and bodily stirrings that arise during sleep (12.7). These fantasies can, according to Cassian, be the effect of a variety of factors—gluttony, at the most basic level; the secret persistence of daytime desires that reveal themselves under the veil of night; or an attack by the devil (22.3). The occurrence of nocturnal fantasies is, then, itself a kind of involuntary confession, witness to the hidden depths of the soul, as both Brown and Foucault suggest. Such thoughts, and the movements of the flesh that accompany them, must also be rendered the object of a voluntary act of verbalization that tests the limits not only of the confessant's shame but also of the confessor's expertise. Only the most experienced and holy elders are able to discern the causes for their arising, and such discernment is of no small import. A monk who experiences a nocturnal emission as the result of demonic attack may receive holy communion, while a monk whose fantasies erupt from the most secret places of his heart's desires is deemed impure (22.5, 6).

Such a painfully rigorous practice of confession, as David Brakke points out, has as its goal the production of "an integrated self, wholly chaste," whose spirit and flesh, inner and outer parts, are as one. Yet, as Brakke also observes, the very process of integration also requires repeated "divisions of the monastic self."[38] Cassian's confessional theory presumes, much as Augustine's does, a split between the will and movements of both thought and flesh that evade the will's control, as well as between what can be seen or known and what remains stubbornly secret. It presumes a split between the self who confesses and the self who is confessed. Moreover, contrary to what Abba Moses's tale of the monk who steals bread seems to suggest, these splits do not always follow the same fracture line: as the limit case of nocturnal fantasies reveals, what is confessed and made known is not necessarily thereby fully controlled or eradicated. The monk who progresses to ever greater heights of chastity may reach a point at which his sexual emissions—which, however obediently confessed, will still likely occur every two to four months, Cassian estimates[39]—involve so little participation of the mind or will that they are not deemed to compromise purity. If not quite mindless acts of the flesh, envious attacks of the devil, then. Some few monks may actually achieve perfect chastity, signaled by the complete cessation of wet dreams: Cassian knows of *one*—the blessed Serenus (7.2, 12.7). Having confessed themselves dry, having confessed *everything*, have these improbably perfect monks become like Jesus, with *nothing* left to confess? Here again we encounter the absolutes toward which Cassian's limit cases stretch. But perhaps (strong differences of rhetorical performance notwithstanding) these examples of perfect chastity are as fantastical, as excessive, thus finally as uncontained by limits, as are Augustine's resurrected bodies, which (as we have seen) participate in sexual relations so pure that one can no longer distinguish between the absolutes of submission and domination.[40] *Everything* and *nothing*, total self-control and total self-sacrifice, meet at their excessive extremes. Or so we are able to imagine.

As Brakke observes, "the need for senior colleagues to diagnose a chronic problem with wet dreams" implicitly problematizes the self that is split off in confession—the self that confesses and thus cannot be confessed, except by another.[41] But such a displacement simply begs another question, namely, the status of the senior colleagues who serve as confessors. Even white hair can prove but a lying sign of wisdom, we recall. The hearts of the holiest elders may harbor secrets buried deeper than those of younger monks. Thus the processes of confessional displacement and dispersion are, in theory, without end. Cassian's apparent desire to veil this inexhaustibility of confession, even as his monastic discipline depends on it, perhaps marks the distance that separates him most decisively from Augustine. The plentiful accumulation of elders merely reaches toward the plenitude of divine knowing; at its worst, it becomes a veil of false modesty—a prideful mockery of God's all-hearing ear.

Nonetheless, such significant differences in confession's institutionalization should not altogether overshadow similarities. For both Augustine and Cassian, sexual desire remains both the most trivial and the most hauntingly elusive of confessable sins. More than any other temptation, it seeks to hide its own tracks, not least by calling too much attention to itself. If the persistence of occasional wet dreams is as remarkable as the attention that Cassian devotes to it, this is only because desire always points toward something else: to say that desire is for desire is, paradoxically, to say that it always wants more than its own satisfaction. Fantasies dissolve in the light of day, and even the well-trained flesh of a monk eventually depletes its own stoked fires, if only momentarily. A theft, a rebellion, a stubbornly-kept secret—*these* betray the ambition of our human hearts not only to love other things and persons as if they were the immortal God but also to love them as if we were gods—generously, bountifully. The reach of desire (in contrast to gluttony) so far beyond the accessible pleasures of the flesh is an unnecessary excess. It is where we fall hardest and rise highest—where we begin to break down, and thus to transcend our very selves. This is because desire is the most shameful of the temptations. This is also *why* it is the most shameful of temptations.

The Desiring Ear: The *Life of Mary of Egypt*

The *Life of Mary of Egypt*, a Greek hagiographical text authored by Sophronius, patriarch of Jerusalem from 634 to 638, seems to have been translated into Latin by the end of the seventh century.[42] That this work should have received a warm reception in the confessional culture of the west is no surprise. Particularly striking is the attention that the text gives to the desire not only to confess but to hear the confession of another. Sophronius insists that it would be a sin to allow the story of Mary to remain shrouded in silence (*Life of Mary of Egypt* 1). Yet arguably the tale of transformation that he relates is more that of Mary's confessor, Zosimas, than of Mary herself. It is literally Zosimas's story, told by him to the monks of his monastery, who preserve it via a chain of oral transmission that eventually reaches the receptive ears of Sophronius himself. As far as he knows, he is the first to write it down, having attempted to record "everything, putting truth above all else" (41). The matter of truth and its possible contestation, reasserted in closing, troubles him from the outset. He fears that his narrative will seem incredible yet insists: "No one should disbelieve me when I write about what I have heard" (1). What Sophronius has heard, Zosimas heard first. Had his own ears not been so hungry to receive Mary's confession, none of us would be hearing its truth now.

Zosimas first encounters Mary as a mysterious apparition that he feels compelled to pursue, at top speed, in a bizarre foot race through the desert. He does not know at first whether what he chases is human. He is astonished to discover that "it" is a woman, and a naked woman at that (12). The sight of her is too much for his eyes to bear, but her words quickly incite his desire to know all about her. "Do not conceal anything from your servant, who you are and where you came from and when and in what way you came to dwell in this desert," he begs—after lending her his cloak. "Do not conceal from me any detail of your life, but tell me everything. . . . Tell me everything, in the name of the Lord" (16). Zosimas's insatiable curiosity recalls less the relentless will to knowledge that animates Cassian's monastic inquisitors (though that too) than Augustine's eager probing of the mysterious depths of his own soul.

The woman, who has already pronounced herself shamed by her physical exposure, declares herself now also ashamed to speak of her life. Yet she concedes: "Since you have seen my bare body, I shall lay bare to you also my deeds. . . . And I know that when I start telling you the story of my life, you will avoid me, as one avoids a snake" (17). Not so: Zosimas's ear will prove a most greedily charitable receptor for Mary's shameful confessions. At first speaking freely, she pauses in the narration of her extraordinary sexual shamelessness: "I told you, Abba Zosimas, not to force me to tell you of my disgrace. God is my witness, I am afraid of defiling you and the very air with my words." Weeping, Zosimas pleads with her not to stop. "Speak, my mother; in God's name, speak and do not interrupt the flow of such a beneficial narrative" (19–20). She complies—more, it would seem, for *his* benefit than for *hers*—eventually bringing her story of sin and conversion to its logical end in the desert, where she now pursues an ascetic life (26).

Still, Zosimas is not satisfied. His questions seem inexhaustible. How many years have you been living in the desert? What have you found to eat? How have you avoided illness, how have you endured such radical change? He presses: "Do not hide anything from me: speak to me without concealing anything" (27). She continues to answer; he continues to ask. Have you not required food and clothing? Have you read the scriptures?

Ultimately, Mary sends him back to his monastery, promising that they will meet again. They do, but by then Zosimas has begun to learn that verbal confession will never reach a satisfying end. At her request, he shares with her the taste of holy communion. He shares too his desire: "I only wish it would be possible for me to follow you from now on, and look always upon your holy face" (36). Having started by seeing her naked body, he now desires to immerse himself in a different kind of specula(riza)tion. The next time he gazes upon her, however, she is already a corpse. He dares touch only her feet with his tears (37). But there is more to see: bending time, Mary has inscribed on the shifting sands of the desert the account of her own death, as well as her desire to be buried by Zosimas (38). The senses converge, and confession becomes incarnate as text even as the flesh of the body mingles with the sand on which it is written. Not yet satisfied, but rather already overflowing, Zosimas converts the searching for knowledge into the making of new truth: "He told the monks everything, without holding back anything of what he had heard and seen" (40). His confessing of Mary flows from tongue to ear, from ear to tongue. Finally it is archived by Sophronius, translated by others, to be read by an indeterminate multitude of witnesses. Sophronius begins by continuing Mary's act of self-inscription. Her confession is Zosimas's confession but it is also his own. It awaits reappropriation by each new reader: from the depths of the archives, confession ever arrives again; it breaks upon the ears of our desiring hearts.

Conclusions

Confession, as an act of verbalization, takes the form of narrative—takes a fabulous, even fictional form, then. "My narrative begins *in media res*, when many things have already taken place to make me and my story possible in language," notes Judith Butler. "I am always recuperating, reconstructing, and I am left to fictionalize and fabulate origins I cannot know." She adds, "My account of myself is partial, haunted by that for which I can devise no definitive story." Nonetheless, as Butler also insists, we must continue to give accounts of ourselves, again and again, and thus to render ourselves accountable to the innumerable others in whose lives we are always already implicated. In so doing, we open ourselves onto "an ethics based on our shared, invariable, and partial blindness about ourselves."[43] The abyssal depth of the ever emerging self—the fertile groundlessness of subjectivity—thus becomes an ethical resource more valuable than that which any moral certitude could possibly offer. A truth bound by the stasis of certainty tilts toward violence, wrapping itself in a veil of false nostalgia for a mastery that never was, while ethical accountability, in the sense that Butler intends, seeks out a path that might lead us away from violence precisely by acknowledging the limitlessness of our shared vulnerability.

That the truth made in confession is fabulous and fictional, both exceeding verifiability and eluding finality, may itself seem a source of shame. Surely it is, at the very least, cause for humility. It is also the reason why we cannot stop confessing, must not refuse the shame of our own inevitable failure ever to get the account of our shameful culpability quite right. While holding this insight close, the confessional practices of ancient Christians may nonetheless seem all too focused on the salvation of the self, all too little concerned with relations to others, because all too overwhelmed by the demands of *the Other*—God. Augustine's prayer closet, in particular, does not appear at first glance to leave room for anyone else. At the same time, even *his* confessions, perhaps *especially* his confessions, in opening onto God also open on to all of the other others of God's creation that draw human love—that indeed draw it so powerfully that love turns to an acquisitive lust. In confessing both his love for God and his lust for God's creatures, Augustine seeks to take lust around another turn, to convert it, and thus to achieve an "integrity" of love that is, as MacKendrick argues, not less but more intense that ever:[44] even as God's love overflows in creation, so too Augustine's love of God yearns to overflow toward created things in a convergence of longing with receptivity—of *eros* with *agape*, *amor* with *caritas*—at the point where earthly transience and heavenly eternity meet.

Cassian's monastic confessional culture, in turn, explores with almost painful rigor the extent to which confession must always be not only confession of the self *as* other, a split-subject at best, but also confession *to* another—indeed, to innumerable others. To cite Butler again: "I begin my story of myself only in the face of a 'you' who asks me to give an account."[45] In Cassian's texts, the mutuality of accountability at work in confession—the mutuality of vulnerability at play—is both revealed and partly covered over by his emphasis on the authority of the elders. So too is the extent to which the inexhaustibility of the secrets to be confessed is mirrored by the inexhaustibility of potential others to whom one must confess. He seems finally to teeter at the brink of an insight that is also partly Augustine's: the infinitude of divinity is approached simultaneously in the ever-receding depths of the soul *and* in the ever expanding reach of intersubjective accountability. Even an errant nocturnal fantasy speaks both of the limits of what we can know or control with respect to ourselves and of the ways in which our most private thoughts are still entangled in webs of desire that do not leave others untouched.

Finally, the *Life of Mary of Egypt* reveals with particular intensity the implicatedness of love and desire in the very act of confession, as well as the volatile reversibility that characterizes the relations of hearing and telling that are shaped by confession. Augustine ardently spills his words of confession into the divinely receptive ear of God, hoping both that God will be converted to mercy and that others will listen in. Cassian's monks reluctantly share their secrets with their brethren, in the faith that God will act through those brethren to purify their hearts. Mary, however, seems to confess out of charity, because Zosimas *needs* her to, though in the end it is no longer clear who is confessing (to) whom. If Mary is a seducer who becomes an ascetic without ceasing to seduce, Zosimus is an ascetic who becomes a seducer without ceasing to be an ascetic. Perhaps God, who is invoked most often in this doubly confessional Life in passionate ejaculatory address, inheres in the very power of confession to draw, or seduce, transformation at the very point where what is verbalized becomes incarnated, even as flesh is simultaneously converted to the materiality of a text that we too are urged to "take and read."

Confession draws confession. It draws subjects toward one another at the limits of shared vulnerability, converting mockery to mercy, violence to humility, shame to the shameless joying of a divine-human communion that exceeds the limits of both belief and imagination.

Afterword: Shame, Politics, Love

What I am calling for, in effect, is something that I do not expect we shall ever fully achieve: a society that acknowledges its own humanity, and neither hides us from it nor it from us; a society of citizens who admit that they are needy and vulnerable, and who discard the grandiose demands for omnipotence and completeness that have been at the heart of so much human misery, both public and private.

—Martha Nussbaum, Hiding from Humanity

In the face of an alarming increase of public appeals to shame and disgust, Martha Nussbaum yearns for something that she also does not imagine to be fully realizable—namely, an eschatological community of citizens who do not hide from their humanity, as she puts it, but are able to acknowledge their finitude and need for one another. A society without shame? Not quite. Rather, a society in which shame—or perhaps more accurately the temptation to *deny* shame by projecting it onto others—is disciplined by rationality. Shame, argues Nussbaum, not unlike disgust, is a complex emotional gesture in which humans recoil from the painful awareness of their own frailty. It need not be pathological, but often it is, and never more so than when directed outwards. Stigmatizing others, we attempt, however vainly, to protect ourselves from the taint of shared vulnerability. The result is "so much human misery."[1]

Nussbaum's views have met with strong critique in some quarters. Roger Kimball, for one, directly challenges her claim that we are experiencing a "remarkable revival" of shame: "One thing indisputably missing in our society is anything like a traditional sense of shame or disgust."[2] Witness all those flamboyantly exposed, pierced, and otherwise shameless bodies! he urges. Whereas Nussbaum argues that humiliation and stigmatization have no place in political discourse or legal practice, Kimball protests that we must actively cultivate a lost sense of shame if we are to recover our collective capacity for virtue. Their positions align with the poles of a larger political debate about shame. As Christina Tarnopolsky characterizes it, "Shame is either considered an outdated, irrational, or painful emotion that we need to avoid and recourses to it are then considered naive or prudish, or shame is considered to be an infallible guide to morality and civic order."[3]

Tarnopolsky's description aptly captures the tendency of participants in this debate to caricature their opponents' positions and even, at times, their own positions. Yet closer examination suggests, not surprisingly, that few if any theorists are simply for or against shame, as she also points out. When Kimball charges Nussbaum with advocating a "shameless life,"[4] this is not quite fair. Nussbaum herself explicitly affirms the constructive role of shame in inciting moral responsibility; she notes further that "the vulnerability to shame is part of the exposure of self that is involved in intimacy."[5] Nonetheless, Nussbaum's analysis of shame remains primarily focused on the dangers of stigmatization that arise from what she calls "primitive" or "narcissistic" shame, manifesting psychologically in the tendency to disavow one's own imperfections by projecting them onto others. Indeed, she discovers therein no less than "a threat to all possibility of morality and community, and indeed to a creative inner life."[6] Kimball, in contrast, seems to regard the destructive effects of shame and social stigmatization that so preoccupy Nussbaum as no more than necessary evils. Is moral judgment itself not inherently shaming? he asks. Nussbaum herself is not shy about passing moral judgment in the form of judgments about morality: she confidently distinguishes between destructive and constructive kinds of shame, characterizing constructive shame by its attunement to apparently self-evidently "morally good norms."[7] Her utopianism may feel stretched, even very nearly inconsistent, at the points where she seems to imagine a society purified of shame (or at least of the bad variety): as Kimball notes, one cannot simply eliminate shame by legislative or rational fiat, nor should one want to do so. Yet, as Nussbaum argues, the impulse to stigmatize others does not in itself produce justice—on the contrary. Reading slightly against the grain of her own rhetoric, we may also hear Nussbaum calling us to live more effectively *with* our own shame—to cease *hiding from shame*, in other words. But what might that mean?

Returning to Carlin Barton's analysis of the Roman Empire, we find hints for understanding what is at work in the American Empire that take us beyond the impasse of oppositional rhetoric. (Do we have too much or too little shame? Is shame politically productive or destructive?) Now as in the Roman imperial era, sources of shame are all too numerous. U.S. imperialism, jarring troublingly with traditional democratic and anti-imperialistic ideals, is a cause of shame, as are U.S. failures at imperialism, most momentously in the wake of the September 11, 2001, attack on New York City's Twin Towers. Poverty, disease, ineffective educational institutions, drug addition, and violence on city streets and in homes are all further sources of shame for those burdened with them, as is the national inability to address such enormous problems. What is "missing in our society" is not shame or disgust (pace Kimball) but rather a cultural mechanism for dealing effectively with an excess of shame and disgust in a world that has, like that of the Romans, grown far too large and complex to be managed effectively by the subtle give-and-take of communal appeals to a shared sense of honor. Now as in the Roman imperial era, absolutizing invocations of transcendent authority reflect a desire to displace such traditional processes of social regulation. Tellingly, when the American president speaks for God, he does not have to answer to anyone else: laying claim to honor without subjecting himself to the vulnerability of a shame that has become overwhelming, he confidently shifts the blame to others. Many citizens find in this promise of a "self-respect without shame" (as Barton puts it)[8] a source of restored comfort while others discover cause for rising alarm. In the face of such a crisis, the question is not whether we are for or against shame but what we do when confronted with *so much* of it.

Nussbaum focuses sharply on the problem of shame as stigma, reminding us repeatedly that the term referred in antiquity to the brutal practice of tattooing or branding criminals,[9] while Kimball cites as evidence of shamelessness "the nose rings, the tongue or eyebrow or nipple studs that are so popular with the young and not-so-young today."[10] Despite their differences, each assumes that the stigma, whether involuntary and shameful or voluntary and shameless, is simply a bad thing. Indeed, its harmfulness cannot be denied any more than can its current prevalence. Yet ancient Christian texts—martyrological, christological, ascetic, confessional—offer a more complicated and ambivalent understanding of stigmatization and of shame more generally.[11] Their ambivalence may also be our own.

When a mark of shame, whether physical or verbal, is shamelessly embraced, the stigma is transformed in the process—a gesture graphically exemplified, and also partly displaced, within the contemporary aesthetics of body piercing or tattooing. Far from representing a simple absence of shame, shamelessness here manifests as a turning or conversion *within* shame, whereby the subject performs his or her fragile dignity apart from, and even in resistance to, the social privilege signified by hegemonic codes of honor. He or she performs, perhaps, the fragility of dignity as well as the dignity of fragility, in so doing. The defiant appropriation of the stigma thus both contests shaming—*shames shame*—and renders it unexpectedly productive, for the stigma opens the site of a yet-to-be-defined identity. As Judith Butler notes with reference to hate speech, "If to be addressed is to be interpellated, then the offensive call runs the risk of inaugurating a subject in speech who comes to use language to counter the offensive call."[12] That is to say, wounding words make a place, paradoxically, from which hitherto unheard voices may talk back. At its worst, the politics of identity hardens defensively in a refusal to negotiate that matches the absolutizing of the stigmatizers. At its best, however, it allows a complex, fluid, and heterogeneous society not only to subject itself continuously to internal critique but also to expose itself to unpredictable metamorphoses precisely at its sites of greatest vulnerability. Monolithic and universalizing definitions of moral value thus give way (at least partly) to responsive exchanges across unstable differences. Like the ancient Christians, we live in a volatile age in which the extremity of difference and the violence of stigmatization are matched (at least sometimes) by a capacity for creative transformation.

The common coupling of anti-shame stances with identity politics, and conversely of pro-shame stances with opposition to identity politics, obscures this deeper linking of shame, stigma, and identity. As a result, it becomes difficult to appreciate the extent to which *all* marks of particularity or difference—marks that become sharply visible in contexts of immense cultural pluralism—share in the character of a stigma. We are vulnerable—we are easily shamed—precisely in the ineluctability of our particularity. The stigma both rivets this particularity and fails to disclose it satisfactorily, a failure that is also a subtle source of shame. Our identities cannot quite be shrugged off yet also never quite suit us. Curiously, both opponents and supporters of the invocation of shame in public discourse agree that such vulnerability exists and also maintain that it must be minimized at all costs. Nussbaum insists that feelings of shame intensify vulnerability intolerably: thus she seeks to legislate against irrational acts of stigmatization that produce and police prejudicially defined social norms. "A decent society will not permit the desire to stigmatize to hijack the legal process and will insist on giving all citizens the equal protection of the laws, no matter how unpopular they, and their practices, are."[13] Jean Bethke Elshtain, in contrast, argues that a sense of shame is what safeguards the bodily privacy necessary to civility, and she chastises identity politics for its breaching of this boundary. "When one's intimate life is put on display on television or the streets or in other public spaces, one not only invites but actively seeks the exploitation of one's body to a variety of ends not fully under one's control."[14] Despite the dramatic differences in their positions, Elshtain and Nussbaum seem to agree that the vulnerable particularity of the gendered, sexualized, racialized, dis/abled, and otherwise *marked*—stigmatized—flesh should remain veiled protectively in the realm of political life. In order to see clearly, justice must be blind to difference, "no matter how unpopular."

But is it safe to be rendered secure against shame? (Should we desire to become so, even if we could?) One who seeks, however vainly, the impenetrable cloak of total privacy cannot be known any more than he or she can be shamed, nor can one who seeks, however vainly, the non-negotiable transparency of full exposure—Barton's unblushingly "honest" man or woman, lacking not only a sense of shame but also a sense of humor and the ability to forgive.[15] It is in the encounter with others—in the never-quite-perfect mutuality of *acknowledgment*—that identity is effectively constituted and reconstituted, remaining thereby not only contingent and provisional but also partial, since "the identity we say we are cannot possibly capture us and marks immediately an excess and opacity that falls outside the categories of identity," as Butler puts it.[16] Perhaps justice is neither blind nor all-seeing, after all. Arising at the borders of our visibility and our invisibility—of what is knowable and what eludes knowledge—justice may present a more modest face than expected, peeking at us from under the lids of half-shut eyes. "Modesty presupposes the disclosure of the hidden as concurrently hidden and disclosed," suggests Elliot Wolfson.[17] It is in this play of hiddenness and exposure mobilized in transformative encounters with others that our sense of self is ever emerging and withdrawing.

By now it is clear that shame does not merely guard the boundary between the public and the private, the political and the personal, the inter- and intrasubjective, but also constantly traverses those boundaries—even very nearly dissolves them. This traversal—this near-dissolution—binds shame tightly to the erotic. If the embrace of the stigma of identity represents a conversion that takes place within shame, so too does the plunge into the abjection of flesh-and-soul that undoes identity, giving rise to both wild joy and abysmal humility—courting the arrival of grace. The stigma itself turns out to be both the inscription and the erasure of identity, at once the face of difference and its effacement. We are marked by countless others, by our responsiveness to others—our abysmal responsibility. Stigmata arrive like a gift, then, in the paradox of a granted receptivity that is also an unexpected overflow. Like so many Saint Sebastians, we may seem finally to exceed identity—to escape the inescapability of our "being"?—by being riveted to it many times over. In the ecstatic excesses of shameful vulnerability, ethics draws close to erotics.

Indeed, what is at stake in the politics of shame is nothing less than our capacity for love. It is, moreover, no accident that the problematics of love and desire, like those of shame, announce their urgency in historical moments of swift change and in social contexts of intense heterogeneity and imbalance of power. In such times and from such places we pause to ask ourselves what it means to love, whether and how love is possible. In such times and from such places we may also begin to feel our own shame—the shame of our fleshly and psychic exposure, our naked yearnings, our hidden fears and secret hopes, our sense of connection and dread of transgression. The question is what we do with it.

Notes

Introduction

Epigraph. Bernard Williams, *Shame and Necessity* (Berkeley: University of California Press, 1993), 19–20.

1. Silvan S. Tomkins, *Affect, Imagery, Consciousness*, vol. 2, *The Negative Affects* (New York: Springer, 1963), 123.

2. Joseph Adamson and Hilary Clark, "Introduction: Shame, Affect, Writing," in *Scenes of Shame: Psychoanalysis, Shame, and Writing*, ed. Joseph Adamson and Hilary Clark (Albany: State University of New York Press, 1999), 15.

3. Donald L. Nathanson, "Foreword," in *Scenes of Shame*, ed. Adamson and Clark, vii. See also his "Preface," in *The Many Faces of Shame*, ed. Donald L. Nathanson (New York: Guilford Press, 1987), viii: "The nearly simultaneous appearance of these writings and the astonishing regularity with which they have been ignored signified to me the sort of ferment (attended by cultural denial) that usually precedes a major shift in cultural understanding." Nathanson is obviously addressing specific cultural and disciplinary contexts when arguing for the novelty of interest in shame. Among Continental theorists, shame is arguably a significant (though not a foregrounded) concern for Jacques Lacan, for example, and philosophers working in the early twentieth century—notably, Heidegger, Sartres, and Levinas—were centrally preoccupied with the nexus of anxiety, nausea, and shame.

4. Donald L. Nathanson, "A Timetable for Shame," in *The Many Faces of Shame*, ed. Nathanson, 9.

5. Tomkins, *Negative Affects*, 137.

6. Eve Kosofsky Sedgwick and Adam Frank, "Shame in the Cybernetic Fold: Reading Silvan Tomkins," in *Shame and Its Sisters: A Silvan Tomkins Reader*, ed. Eve Kosofsky Sedgwick and Adam Frank (Durham, N.C.: Duke University Press, 1995), 22–23.

7. Ibid., 7.

8. Helen Block Lewis notes: "Shame, which appears to be other connected, is actually one's own vicarious experience of the other's scorn. Guilt, which seems self-initiated and self-propelled, is actually often initiated by the behavior of another person in relation to the self." She also, however, emphasizes the necessary relational context of shame, as well as its global effects: "Shame is about the whole self. . . . Guilt is more specific." Lewis's comparative phenomenology of shame and guilt is summarized conveniently in table form. "Introduction: Shame—The 'Sleeper' in Psychopathology," in *The Role of Shame in Symptom Formation*, ed. Helen Block Lewis (Hillsdale, N.J.: Lawrence Erlbaum, 1987), 15, 18, 22.

9. Tomkins, *Negative Affects*, 118.

10. Lewis speculates that "the neglect of shame in both psychiatry and psychoanalysis reflects prevailing sexist thinking." She goes on to note: "In any case, shame in men of the Western civilized world is usually reserved only for Friday, Saturday, or Sunday religious services. For women, it is their silent lot on these and all other days" ("Shame—The 'Sleeper,'" 4). Anthropologists, for their part, have argued that Mediterranean cultures characteristically privilege the relation of female sexuality to shame: a woman's chastity secures the honor of her kinsmen while threats to her chastity endanger the honor of her male relatives. See David G. Gilmore, "Introduction: The Shame of Dishonor," in *Honor and Shame and the Unity of the Mediterranean*, ed. David G. Gilmore (Washington, D.C.: American Anthropological Association, 1987), 2–21. As Carol Delaney puts it: "Women . . . are, by their created nature, already ashamed. . . . Shame is an inevitable part of being female; a woman is honorable if she remains cognizant of this fact and its implications for behavior, and she is shameless if she forgets it." "Seeds of Honor, Fields of Shame," in *Honor and Shame*, ed. Gilmore, 40.

11. Tomkins, *Negative Affects*, 133.

12. Eve Kosofsky Sedgwick, *Touching Feeling: Affect, Pedagogy, Performativity* (Durham, N.C.: Duke University Press, 2003), 37.

13. According to the Oxford English Dictionary, the word *shame* has Teutonic origins, and many scholars hold that behind the Teutonic root *skam- is the pre-Teutonic *skem-, which means "covering."

14. Sedgwick and Frank, "Shame in the Cybernetic Fold," 22.

15. Tomkins, *Negative Affects*, 118.

16. Leon Wurmser, *The Mask of Shame* (Baltimore: Johns Hopkins University Press, 1981), 17.

17. Leon Wurmser, "Shame: The Veiled Companion of Narcissism," in *The Many Faces of Shame*, ed. Nathanson, 67–68.

18. Leon Wurmser, "'Man of the Most Dangerous Curiosity': Nietszche's 'Fruitful and Frightful Vision' and His War Against Shame," in *Scenes of Shame*, ed. Adamson and Clark, 121.

19. Tomkins, *Negative Affects*, 157, argues that "intimacy is in fact greater in interocular experience than in sexual intercourse *per se*."

20. Williams, *Shame and Necessity*, 92.

21. Adamson and Clark, "Introduction," 28.

22. Ibid., 1. See also the essays collected in that volume.

23. Georges Bataille, *Erotism: Death and Sensuality*, 1957, trans. Mary Dalwood (San Francisco: City Lights Books, 1986), 11–25. Language of shame appears only infrequently in this work, yet the concept, I would argue, is pervasive. Anguish, a term to which Bataille resorts repeatedly, is closely linked in his thought with shame as the feeling that attends the transgression of a taboo (133). Shamelessness, in contrast, he equates with "the indifference that puts the most sacred on the same footing as the profane" (135); this is not, of course, the way I am using the term. Bataille sharply critiques the notion that "sexual taboos are nothing but prejudice and it is high time we are rid of them" or that "the embarrassment and shame that go hand in hand with strong feelings of pleasure are supposed to be simply proofs of stupid-

ity" (266). The overcoming of shame, for him, would be the annihilation of the sacred. Horror is also a term that, for Bataille, seems closely aligned with anguish and shame: "In order to reach the limits of the ecstasy in which we lose ourselves in bliss we must always set an immediate boundary to it: horror" (267).

24. Nathanson, "A Timetable for Shame," 5, 9. The close linking of shame to relatedness has been particularly emphasized by Lewis, who notes that shame is "a means by which people try to preserve their loving relationships to others" ("Shame—The 'Sleeper,'" 2). Sedgwick writes: "Blazons of shame, the 'fallen face' with eyes down and head averted—and, to a lesser extent, the blush—are semaphores of trouble and at the same time of a desire to reconstitute the interpersonal bridge" (*Touching Feeling*, 36).

25. Sedgwick and Frank, "Shame in the Cybernetic Fold," 23.

26. Ruth Benedict, *The Chrysanthemum and the Sword: Patterns of Japanese Culture* (Boston: Houghton Mifflin, 1946), esp. 222–27.

27. Note that E. R. Dodds was inclined to date the moment of conversion considerably earlier, in the late archaic and early classical periods of Greek history. *The Greeks and the Irrational* (Berkeley: University of California Press, 1951), 28–63. Williams, *Shame and Necessity*, nuances and complicates Dodds's account, finding in Plato a pivotal shift toward an ethically centered account of agency and responsibility that anticipates modern, Kantian understandings of guilt, while also arguing for significant overlaps and continuities between "shame" and "guilt" cultures.

28. J. G. Peristiany and Julian Pitt-Rivers, "Introduction," in *Honor and Grace in Anthropology*, ed. J. G. Peristiany and Julian Pitt-Rivers (Cambridge: Cambridge University Press, 1992), 7–8. Note that Peristiany and Pitt-Rivers also reflect a broader tendency in studies of the Mediterranean to mark a distinction between "official" Christian doctrine and popular opinion: "The Church has always claimed to annex it [honor] to doctrinal issues by making it equivalent to 'moral conscience' but it clearly is not that in the view of most laymen" (3).

29. The literature here is extensive. Representative works by key contributors to the conversation among New Testament scholars include Bruce Malina, *The New Testament World: Insights from Cultural Anthropology* (Louisville, Ky.: Westminster/ John Knox Press, 1993); Halvor Moxnes, "Honor and Shame," in *The Social Sciences and New Testament Interpretation*, ed. Richard L. Rohrbaugh (Peabody, Mass.: Hendrickson, 1996), 19–40; Jerome H. Neyrey, *Honor and Shame in the Gospel of Matthew* (Louisville, Ky.: Westminster/John Knox Press, 1998); and David A. deSilva, *Honor, Patronage, Kinship, and Purity: Unlocking New Testament Culture* (Downers Grove, Ill.: InterVarsity Press, 2000). The body of anthropological literature drawn on includes prominently J. G. Peristainy, ed., *Honour and Shame: The Values of Mediterranean Society* (London: Weidenfeld and Nicholson, 1966), Gilmore, ed., *Honor and Shame*; Peristiany and Pitt-Rivers, eds., *Honor and Grace*. This social scientific trajectory in New Testament studies has tended to take a fairly uncritical attitude toward anthropological models constructed on the assumption that it is possible to generalize, at least to an extent, about "Mediterranean culture" across vast distance of time and place.

30. Williams, *Shame and Necessity*, 102.

31. Carlin Barton, *Roman Honor: The Fire in the Bones* (Berkeley: University of California Press, 2001), 280.

32. Note that Robert A. Kaster, *Emotion, Restraint, and Community in Ancient Rome* (Oxford: Oxford University Press, 2005), 11, appears to resist the subtle account of change offered by Barton when he insists that shame and other related emotions "do not . . . undergo significant change" in the period of the late Roman Republic and early Empire. He does, however, acknowledge that "the rise of Christianity surely reflects and produces changes in cultural psychology that deserve a book to themselves," as evidenced, for example, in the shift from "regret" to "remorse" in the understanding of the sentiment of *paenitentia*.

33. Peristiany and Pitt-Rivers, "Introduction," 6, 4.

34. Sedgwick, *Touching Feeling*, 13.

35. Julian Pitt-Rivers, "Postscript: The Place of Grace in Anthropology," in *Honor and Grace*, ed. Peristiany and Pitt-Rivers, 243.

36. Ibid., 241.

Chapter 1. Shameless Witnesses

Epigraph. Eve Kosofsky Sedgwick, *Touching Feeling: Affect, Pedagogy, Performativity* (Durham, N.C.: Duke University Press, 2003), 62.

1. Relatively recent works on the spectacles of the arena include Thomas Wiedemann, *Emperors and Gladiators* (London: Routledge, 1992); Paul Plass, *The Game of Death in Ancient Rome: Arena Sport and Political Suicide* (Madison: University of Wisconsin Press, 1995); Alison Futrell, *Blood in the Arena: The Spectacle of Roman Power* (Austin: University of Texas Press, 1997); Donald G. Kyle, *Spectacles of Death in Ancient Rome* (London: Routledge, 1998); Richard C. Beacham, *Spectacle Entertainments of Early Imperial Rome* (New Haven, Conn.: Yale University Press, 1999); Rupert Matthews, *The Age of the Gladiators: Savagery and Spectacle in Ancient Rome* (Edison, N.J.: Chartwell Books, 2004). Most influential in relation to my own thinking is, however, the nuanced cultural and psychological analysis of Carlin Barton, *The Sorrows of the Ancient Romans: The Gladiator and the Monster* (Princeton, N.J.: Princeton University Press, 1993).

2. Barton, *The Sorrows of the Ancient Romans*, 31, 33.

3. Sedgwick, *Touching Feeling*, 36.

4. Ibid., 37.

5. Ibid., 38, emphasis in original.

6. Ibid., 38.

7. Ibid., 31.

8. Ibid., 30.

9. Ibid., 33.

10. Ibid., 63.

11. Ibid., 64–65.

12. Ibid., 64.

13. Tertullian here refers not to martyrs but to gladiators. On the resonance of

gladiatorial and martyrial performances, see Carlin Barton, "Savage Miracles: The Redemption of Lost Honor in Roman Society and the Sacrament of the Gladiator and the Martyr," *Representations* 45 (1994): 41–71.

14. As Harry Maier notes, "John's post-Apocalypse treats us to playful games with time. John presents us with an Apocalypse that is a first-person retrospective telling of what is and will be." *Apocalypse Recalled: The Book of Revelation After Christendom* (Minneapolis: Fortress, 2002), 136–37. The doubling or splitting of vision produced by this text is thus always also a doubling or splitting of time. See also Catherine Keller's reflections on the complex temporality of this text. *Apocalypse Now and Then: A Feminist Guide to the End of the World* (Boston: Beacon Press, 1996), 84–138.

15. Christopher A. Frilingos, *Spectacles of Empire: Monsters, Martyrs, and the Book of Revelation* (Philadelphia: University of Pennsylvania Press, 2004), 52.

16. Representative is Tina Pippin, *Death and Desire: The Rhetoric of Gender in the Apocalypse of John* (Louisville, Ky.: Westminster/John Knox Press, 1992), 57–68.

17. Frilingos, *Spectacles of Empire*, 60.

18. Ibid., 62.

19. As Maier points out, "Quotation is perhaps John's favorite means of closing temporal distance. Again, chapter 18, with its sequence of quoted laments, makes us hear what John heard and so brings a recalled transcription of what will be into the present" (*Apocalypse Recalled*, 139).

20. Ibid., 155.

21. See also K. C. Hanson's analysis of the "Alas!" lamentations in Rev. 18.10, 19 and elsewhere as forms of shameful reproach equivalent to "Shame on you!" in "How Honorable! How Shameful! A Cultural Analysis of Matthew's Makarisms and Reproaches," *Semeia* 68 (1994): 98.

22. Cf. Tertullian's citation of this final vision: "How vast a spectacle then bursts upon the eye!" (*On the Shows* 30).

23. Carlin Barton, *Roman Honor: The Fire in the Bones* (Berkeley: University of California Press, 2001), 286.

24. Maier, *Apocalypse Recalled*, 196. Chris Frilingos complicates the account, noting that "Revelation grants the Lamb a moment of manliness in Rev 14, only to replace the Lamb in successive chapters with its more aggressive colleagues." On Frilingos's reading, the return of the Lamb to a more ambiguously "feminized" position as the object of the gaze of the citizens of the New Jerusalem functions less to subvert a traditional, dominative masculinity than to continue to instruct readers in the arts of arena spectatorship and thereby to shore up their "manly spirit." "Sexing the Lamb," in *New Testament Masculinities*, ed. Stephen D. Moore and Janice Capel Anderson (Atlanta: Society of Biblical Literature, 2003), 316–17; see also Frilingos, *Spectacles of Empire*, 75–88, 111–15. Stephen D. Moore, *God's Gym: Divine Male Bodies of the Bible* (New York: Routledge, 1996) offers an even more stridently pessimistic assessment of apocalyptic masculinity.

25. As Maier suggests: "By the time John turns, in chapter 21, to depict Jerusalem as everything Babylon is not, he has prepared his audience to listen for political caricature. His portrait of life in the heavenly Jerusalem is immediately recognizable as a rehearsal of well-known imperial claims" (*Apocalypse Recalled*, 195). For Maier,

it is not only the improbable figure of the slain Lamb but also the unexpected, even narratively inconsistent, reappearance outside the gates of Jerusalem of the nations who had warred against the Lamb, that decisively destabilizes and ironizes the stereotypical and idealized representation of the heavenly city (197).

26. Pippin, *Death and Desire*, 72.

27. For an especially nuanced retrieval of her divinity, see Keller, *Apocalypse Now and Then*, 64–73, 83.

28. This is not, of course, to deny that prior Christian texts—including not only the Apocalypse but much of the rest of the New Testament—contain significant martyrological elements, as do prior Jewish and (to a lesser extent) pagan literatures. Nonetheless, something new emerges in the early second century, evidenced by texts like the Ignatian letters or 4 Maccabees, where the martyr's death is viewed as a privileged, desirable, and possibly even indispensable performative profession of religious faith and personal identity, rather than an event occasioned by particular political circumstances; see, e.g., Daniel Boyarin, *Dying for God: Martyrdom and the Making of Christianity and Judaism* (Stanford, Calif.: Stanford University Press, 1999), 93–97. The rise of a discourse of martyrdom must be correlated not only with the history of imperial spectacles but also with the broader turn to interest in suffering and passivity, as charted, e.g., by Judith Perkins, *The Suffering Self: Pain and Narrative Representation in the Early Christian Era* (London: Routledge, 1995).

29. As pointed out by Robert Seesengood, *Competing Identities: The Athlete and the Gladiator in Early Christian Literature* (London: Continuum, 2007).

30. For a more detailed treatment of Ignatius's staging of his impending martyrdom as an arena spectacle, see Alexei Khamin, "Ignatius of Antioch: Performing Authority in the Early Church," Ph.D. dissertation, Drew University.

31. Elizabeth A. Castelli, *Martyrdom and Memory: Early Christian Culture Making* (New York: Columbia University Press, 2004), 79.

32. Ibid., 80.

33. Ibid., 62. On the masculinity secured by martyrdom, see also Stephen D. Moore and Janice Capel Anderson, "Taking It like a Man: Masculinity in 4 Maccabees," *Journal of Biblical Literature* 117, 2 (1998): 249–73.

34. Sedgwick, *Touching Feeling*, 63.

35. Page duBois, *Torture and Truth* (New York: Routledge, 1991), 35–36.

36. Ibid., 69–74.

37. Ibid., 91.

38. The boundary between free and slave was rendered more fluid and problematic in the early Roman imperial period, due in part to the way political autocracy threatened to make all persons "slavish," in part to the dramatic upward social mobility of some slaves and former slaves, particularly those connected with the imperial household. Juridical practice negotiated a number of shifting social distinctions, encompassing not only slave versus free but also non-citizen versus citizen, and increasingly *humilior* versus *honestior*. All these distinctions might be performatively inscribed via practices of torture and slaves were not in this period *uniquely* subject to torture. Nonetheless, as K. R. Bradley points out, the juridical use of torture did remain distinctive in relation to slaves, given that slaves could not be threatened with any reduction in legal status: "extreme physical punishment of

the slave was thus the only avenue open to the law." *Slaves and Masters in the Roman Empire* (Oxford: Oxford University Press, 1987), 134. On the destabilization of masculinity, see especially Carlin Barton, "All Things Beseem the Victor: Paradoxes of Masculinity in Early Imperial Rome," in *Gender Rhetorics: Postures of Dominance and Submission in History* (Binghamton, N.Y.: Center for Medieval and Early Renaissance Studies, 1994), 83–92, and Maud W. Gleason, *Making Men: Sophists and Self-Presentation in Ancient Rome* (Princeton, N.J.: Princeton University Press, 1995).

39. Note that Tertullian speaks at some length about Mary's breast-feeding of Christ, without any show of embarrassment (*On the Flesh* 20). His display of medical (as well as exegetical) expertise in this passage does not occur in the context of celebrating the shame of the flesh that Christ took on (an emphasis very much in evidence elsewhere in the treatise); nor however does it clearly reflect his own experience of breast-feeding women. Both Galen and Soranus seem to assume that the elite Roman matrons whose husbands they are implicitly addressing would not personally breastfeed their children, but it is difficult to know whether this situation would apply to North African Carthage and thus whether there is anything unusual, much less shaming, about Perpetua's breastfeeding. Probably not.

40. Most recently, Castelli, *Martyrdom and Memory*, 90–92.

41. For a wonderful account of Augustine's understanding of the "spiritual theater of the mind," see Patricia Cox Miller, "Relics, Rhetoric and Mental Spectacles in Late Ancient Christianity," in *Seeing the Invisible in Late Antiquity and the Early Middle Ages*, ed. Giselle de Nie, Karl F. Morrison, and Marco Mostert (Turnhout: Brepols, 2005), 28–36.

42. Patricia Cox Miller sees in this scene the culmination of a sequential revising of a masculinity initially representative of a "discourse of mastery and domination" marked as both sinister and pathological, now refigured as "an image of maleness whose highly valued stance is a recognition of female identity" and which is itself "intensely feminized or radically eroticized in the direction of female desire." *Dreams in Late Antiquity: Studies in the Imagination of a Culture* (Princeton, N.J.: Princeton University Press, 1994), 182.

43. Sedgwick, *Touching Feeling*, 65.

44. Perkins, *The Suffering Self*, 112.

45. Barton, *The Sorrows of the Ancient Romans*, 67.

46. Nicole Loraux, *Tragic Ways of Killing a Woman* (Cambridge, Mass.: Harvard University Press, 1987).

47. Even Castelli's nuanced exploration of the gendering of the martyr vis-a-vis tropes of sacrifice (*Martyrdom and Memory*, 59–67) may not go far enough in acknowledging the ambivalent complexity of martyrial manhood and the striking prominence of women in the martyrial tradition.

48. As discussed by Seesengood, *Competing Identities*.

49. See my "Reading Agnes: The Rhetoric of Gender in Ambrose and Prudentius," *Journal of Early Christian Studies* 3, 1 (1995): 25–46.

50. E.g., Patricia Cox Miller, "Desert Asceticism and 'the Body from Nowhere,'" *Journal of Early Christian Studies* 2 (1994): 137–53, and Richard Valantasis,

"Constructions of Power in Asceticism," *Journal of the American Academy of Religion* 63, 4 (1995): 775–821.

51. Georgia Frank, *The Memory of the Eyes: Pilgrims to Living Saints in Christian Late Antiquity* (Berkeley: University of California Press, 2000).

52. David Brakke, *Demons and the Making of the Monk: Spiritual Combat in Early Christianity* (Cambridge, Mass.: Harvard University Press, 2006), 183.

53. See my *The Sex Lives of Saints: An Erotics of Ancient Hagiography*, Divinations: Rereading Late Ancient Religion (Philadelphia: University of Pennsylvania Press, 2004), 91–127.

54. Brakke, *Demons*, 183, 197.

55. Derek Krueger, *Symeon the Holy Fool: Leontius's Life and the Late Antique City*, Transformation of the Classical Heritage (Berkeley: University of California Press, 1996), 90–107.

56. Ibid., 48–49.

57. Ibid., 56.

58. As Krueger himself notes, "Leontius calls up a number of themes associated with the figure of Diogenes. Diogenes' public shamelessness was a bit of street theater which expressed a rejection of social conventions. The retelling of these anecdotes functioned as a form of cultural criticism" (96). See also Krueger's discussion of Diogenes's shamelessness as social critique in "The Bawdy and Society: The Shamelessness of Diogenes in Roman Imperial Culture," in *The Cynics: The Cynic Movement in Antiquity and Its Legacy*, ed. R. Bracht Branham and Marie-Odile Goulet-Cazé (Berkeley: University of California Press, 1996), 222–39.

59. Michael J. Bader, "The Psychodynamics of Cynicism," *Tikkun* 11 (May-June 1996).

60. Krueger, "Bawdy and Society," 238.

61. Ibid., 239.

62. Note, however, that my rhetorical insinuation of a rather simple contrast of ancient and modern "cynicisms" covers over the complexity of the Enlightenment reception of the Cynic tradition, as analyzed by Heinrich Niehues-Pröbsting. He notes, furthermore, that the attempt to distinguish between an "authentic" and a "false" Cynicism "is coextensive with the history of Cynicism itself" and depends on principles external to the fundamentally nondogmatic and nontheoretical stance of Cynicism ("The Modern Reception of Cynicism: Diogenes in the Enlightenment," in *The Cynics*, ed. Branham and Goulet-Cazé, 364–65).

63. Donald L. Nathanson, "The Shame/Pride Axis," in *The Role of Shame in Symptom Formation*, ed. Helen Block Lewis (Hillsdale, N.J.: Erlbaum, 1987), 183–205, and *Shame and Pride: Affect, Sex, and the Birth of the Self* (New York: Norton, 1992).

64. In antiquity, *dignitas* is potentially—though not ideally—out of synch with honor. As Robert Kaster puts it, shame (*pudor*) arises when one's sense of dignity or personal worthiness is discounted by others. *Emotion, Restraint, and Community in Ancient Rome* (Oxford: Oxford University Press, 2005), 29. In Barton's analysis, dignity constitutes a demand for honor deemed deserved (but which may or may not be met); for the late Roman (or contemporary American) it can also slip loose from its moorings in honor/shame, underwriting a disturbingly austere

autonomy (*Roman Honor*, 218, 271). The sense of dignity I am evoking slips loose from honor not so as to claim autonomy but so as to acknowledge the fragility that binds it to shame.

Chapter 2. An Embarrassment of Flesh

Epigraph. Julia Kristeva, *Powers of Horror: An Essay on Abjection*, trans. Leon S. Roudiez (New York: Columbia University Press, 1982), 9.

1. Helen Block Lewis, "Introduction: Shame—The 'Sleeper' in Psychopathology," in *The Role of Shame in Symptom Formation*, ed. Helen Block Lewis (Hillsdale, N.J.: Lawrence Erlbaum, 1987), 16–17.

2. See the nuanced analysis of touch in Karmen MacKendrick, *Word Made Skin: Figuring Language at the Surface of Flesh* (New York: Fordham University Press, 2004), 49–70.

3. Silvan S. Tomkins, *Affect Imagery Consciousness*, vol. 2, *The Negative Affects* (New York: Springer, 1963), 194.

4. Tomkins, *Negative Affects*, 201.

5. Kristeva, *Powers of Horror*, 1.

6. Lynda Hart, *Between the Body and the Flesh: Performing Sadomasochism*, Between Men—Between Women: Lesbian and Gay Studies (New York: Columbia University Press, 1998), 10.

7. Kristeva, *Powers of Horror*, 3.

8. Ibid., 11.

9. Ibid., 15.

10. For an extended theological unpacking of the implications of the "darkness" of Genesis 1.2, see Catherine Keller, *The Face of the Deep: A Theology of Becoming* (London: Routledge, 2003).

11. See Daniel Boyarin, *Border Lines: The Partition of Judaeo-Christianity*, Divinations: Rereading Late Ancient Religion (Philadelphia: University of Pennsylvania Press, 2004), 98.

12. See Boyarin, *Border Lines*, 99: "The 'darkness' of the Genesis midrash has now become the cosmos, which, although made by the light, does not recognize or receive it."

13. Luce Irigaray, *An Ethics of Sexual Difference*, trans. Carolyn Burke and Gillian C. Gill (Ithaca, N.Y.: Cornell University Press, 1993), 197.

14. Ibid., 191.

15. A thorough study of tropes of consumption is provided by Jane S. Webster, *Ingesting Jesus: Eating and Drinking in the Gospel of John* (Atlanta: Society of Biblical Literature, 2003).

16. See the nuanced interpretation of this exchange in Stephen D. Moore, *Poststructuralism and the New Testament: Derrida and Foucault at the Foot of the Cross* (Minneapolis: Fortress, 1994), 43–64. Moore suggests that the Samaritan woman "has insisted, in effect, that earthly and heavenly, flesh and Spirit, figurative and literal, are symbiotically related categories: each drinks endlessly of the other, and so each is endlessly contaminated by the other" (62).

17. Kristeva, *Powers of Horror*, 119.

18. Ibid., 4.

19. Ibid., 12.

20. Ibid., 9.

21. On the homoerotic or, more precisely, pederastic dimensions of this relationship, see Sjef van Tilborg, *Imaginative Love in John* (Leiden: E.J. Brill, 1993), 59–110, and Theodore W. Jennings, *The Man Jesus Loved: Homoerotic Narratives from the New Testament* (Cleveland: Pilgrim Press, 2003), 19–74.

22. MacKendrick, *Word Made Skin*, 40.

23. Is it significant that Jesus' "mother is never named in this Gospel," as pointed out by Turid Karlsen Seim, "Descent and Divine Paternity in the Gospel of John: Does the Mother Matter?" *New Testament Studies* 51 (2005): 366? She is "the mother of Jesus"—or "woman." Seim goes on to make the argument that ultimately for John "the mother does not matter because matter is what she provides" (375). Without denying the truth of her position, I would suggest that it is *also* the case that for John the mother matters because matter is what she provides.

24. Julia Kristeva, "Stabat Mater," trans. León S. Roudiez, in *The Kristeva Reader*, ed. Toril Moi (Oxford: Basil Blackwell, 1986), 177, 184–85.

25. As Seim, "Descent and Divine Paternity," 367, puts it: "The mother must give way to the Father (cf. 6.42); the Son's unity is with his Father, and it is the Father's will that governs the will and the acts of the Son."

26. MacKendrick, *Word Made Skin*, 34, emphasizes the signficance of this porosity: "The resurrected body seems to be not less, but more, material, more marked by its encounters with other matter, with the spear and nails that have torn it open."

27. T. P. O'Malley, *Tertullian and the Bible: Language, Imagery, Exegesis* (Utrecht: Dekker & Van de Vegt, 1967), 173.

28. See, e.g., Eric Osborn's somewhat scholastic framing of the debates surrounding the rhetoric of paradox that pervades Tertullian's treatise *On the Flesh of Christ. Tertullian, First Theologian of the West* (Cambridge: Cambridge University Press, 1997), 48–64.

29. Tertullian opts for a version of this Johannine passage that makes it a singular christological statement, rather than a plural, inclusive statement about those who receive the word. See John F. Jansen, "Tertullian and the New Testament," *Second Century: A Journal of Early Christian Studies* 2, 4 (1982): 197.

30. This is a move anticipated by Irenaeus, *Against Heresies* 5.19.1, 5.21.1.

31. Kristeva, "Stabat Mater," 178–80.

32. Robert Sider points out the parallels to Tertullian's argument in the rhetorical handbooks of Cicero and Quintillian that provide similar instances of the argument "from the necessary sign"; e.g., if a woman gives birth to a child, this is a sign that she has had intercourse with a man. *Ancient Rhetoric and the Art of Tertullian* (Oxford: Oxford University Press, 1971), 66. Obviously, Tertullian is working somewhat innovatively within this tradition.

33. As Willemien Otten points out, Tertullian "makes the law of the opened body one which even the divine Word chooses to heed" and thereby also opens his own discourse to an expressiveness that transcends mere paradox. "Christ's Birth

of a Virgin Who Became a Wife: Flesh and Speech in Tertullian's *De Carne Christi*," *Vigiliae Christianae* 51 (1997): 257.

34. Kristeva, "Stabat Mater," 179.

35. See David Satran's subtle reading of a passage from the treatise *On the Resurrection*, on the basis of which he argues that Tertullian's vision of the resurrection clearly entails "a release not from the body but from bodily change and corruption." "Fingernails and Hair: Anatomy and Exegesis in Tertullian," *Journal of Theological Studies* n.s. 40 (1989): 120.

36. Though I have chosen here to focus on the *Apocryphon of John* and the figure of Sophia, other so-called gnostic texts invite similar analysis in terms of shame, e.g., the *Tripartite Tractate*, where Logos plays an ambivalent role similar to that of Sophia in the *Apocryphon of John*. On the affinities of the texts at this point, see the brief discussion in my "Creatio Ex Libidine: Reading Ancient Logos Differantly," in *Derrida and Religion: Other Testaments*, ed. Yvonne Sherwood and Kevin Hart (New York: Routledge, 2005), 148–50.

37. Karen King notes that, although the theme of "female sexuality and reproductive power out of male control" is present in this narrative, greater emphasis is placed on "Sophia's disruption of harmony in the divine household through her reckless female daring and ignorance." Karen L. King, *The Secret Revelation of John* (Cambridge, Mass.: Harvard University Press, 2006), 90. She does, however, affirm Ingvild Gilhus's argument that the mimetic and reciprocal relation between pleroma and cosmos established by the *Apocryphon* "introduces sexual reproduction into the world above by making divine reproductivity the model for what goes on in the world below" (127).

38. Cf. King's assertion that the *Apocryphon of John* portrays "the creation of the world as a gross parody of divine perfection"; I do, however, read this text somewhat differently from King at the point where she emphasizes the text's "sharp and unbending use of oppositional logic" (*The Secret Revelation of John*, 88–89). My own position is that the aspect of mimicry or parody undercuts a strictly oppositional logic; see my "Creatio Ex Libidine," 146–48. I am grateful to Karen, whose knowledge of this text far exceeds my own, for being willing to engage with me in amicable dispute over such matters throughout the years of our scholarly friendship.

39. See King's rich discussion of the *Apocryphon*'s account of the creation of humanity (*The Secret Revelation of John*, 110–21). She emphasizes that the text presupposes two genealogies for every human—"one that stresses rupture and difference, and one that stresses likeness to the true God"—while affirming that "both the psychic and material bodies are perfectible, by conforming to a human being's true self, which is fashioned in true imitation of the Divine Image and has received the life-giving Spirit-breath of Sophia."

40. I realize that this strongly framed rhetorical question may seem to strain the text unfairly. Yet the subtleties of (erotic) reciprocity are not foreign to its myth. As Karen King has pointed out, Sophia's conception mimics Barbelo/Pronoia's conception of the Only-begotten, who is likewise imperfect but receives the perfection of anointing from the paternal Spirit. This parallel or precedent is even more marked in the short version of the *Apocryphon*, in which Barbelo initiates the con-

ception by gazing intently into the pure light of the Spirit. Karen L. King, "Christ and Sophia in the *Apocryphon of John*," in *Images of the Feminine in Gnosticism*, ed. Karen L. King (Philadelphia: Fortress, 1988), 158–76. If the Spirit allowed itself to be aroused by Barbelo's desire, it seems complicit in refusing to be aroused by Sophia's not dissimilar desire.

41. King, *The Secret Revelation of John*, 89–94.

42. Julia Kristeva, "Freud and Love: Treatment and Its Discontents," in *The Kristeva Reader*, 247. See also the helpful discussion of Kristeva's theory of metaphor provided by Kathleen O'Grady, "Sacred Metaphor: Julia Kristeva and Umberto Eco," in *Feminist Philosophy of Religion*, ed. Pamela Sue Anderson and Beverley Clack (London: Routledge, 2004), 153–69, as well as the subtle elaboration of her intuitions regarding the links between eros and metaphor offered by Elliot R. Wolfson, "Suffering Eros and Textual Incarnation: A Kristevan Reading of Kabbalistic Poetics," in *Toward a Theology of Eros: Transfiguring Passion at the Limits of Discipline*, ed. Virginia Burrus and Catherine Keller (New York: Fordham University Press, 2006), 341–65.

43. As Elizabeth Clark argues, "a major motif in his [Jerome's] attack on Origenism lay in his insistence that moral hierarchy must be preserved and gradations of status in the afterlife upheld." *The Origenist Controversy: The Cultural Construction of an Early Christian Debate* (Princeton, N.J.: Princeton University Press, 1992), 150–51.

44. J. Rebecca Lyman, *Christology and Cosmology: Models of Divine Activity in Origen, Eusebius, and Athanasius*, Oxford Theological Monographs (Oxford: Clarendon Press, 1993), 39.

45. E.g., Henri Crouzel, *Origen: The Life and Thought of the First Great Theologian* (San Francisco: Harper and Row, 1989), 248–57, who goes to great length to demonstrate the continuity of the earthly and ethereal bodies conveyed by Origen's controversial doctrines of pre-existence and resurrection.

46. As Lyman, *Christology and Cosmology*, 39, puts it, "The importance of the Logos paradigm in Origen's Christology can hardly be overstressed."

47. Mark Julian Edwards, *Origen Against Plato*, Ashgate Studies in Philosophy and Theology in Late Antiquity (Aldershot: Ashgate, 2002). John David Dawson, *Christian Figural Reading and the Fashioning of Identity* (Berkeley: University of California Press, 2002), 52, similarly emphasizes the extreme revisionism of Origen's Platonism, as evidenced by his hermeneutics: "For while there is no question about the Platonic character of Origen's thinking, the extent to which an 'unchristianized' Platonic metaphysics grounds, founds, or otherwise determines his biblical interpretation is precisely the question at issue."

48. See Patricia Cox Miller, *The Poetry of Thought in Late Antiquity: Essays in Imagination and Religion* (Aldershot: Ashgate, 2001), 247–70. It is also an insight found across a spectrum of ancient Jewish texts, from the philonic to the rabbinic corpora.

49. Ibid., 183.

50. Ibid., 184.

51. There are striking affinities here not only with the association of divine withdrawal and fecundity in a gnostic text such as the *Tripartite Tractate* (see Miller,

Poetry of Thought, 248) but also with the later Jewish mystical concept of *ṣimṣum*. See Elliot R. Wolfson, "Divine Suffering and the Hermeneutics of Reading: Philosophical Reflections on Lurianic Mythology," in *Suffering Religion*, ed. Robert Gibbs and Elliot R. Wolfson (London: Routledge, 2002), 101–62, and *Venturing Beyond: Law and Morality in Kabbalistic Mysticism* (Oxford: Oxford University Press, 2006), 304–16.

52. This is admittedly a "strong" reading of Origen, who is inclined to attribute the fall into difference to the souls' negligence or lapse in desire, in a context in which desire can only be for God. Yet this perspective remains in perhaps productive tension with the implication that God always already desired difference, as reflected in his particular understanding of Sophia and the eternity of creation. Human desire, participating in divine desire, is the desire for the difference that is God but also the difference that reflects the transformative capacity of humans.

53. Edwards, *Origen Against Plato*, 89–97.

54. Ibid., 105.

55. As Lyman, *Christology and Cosmology*, 55, notes, Origen's doctrine of eternal creation "might be similar to divine foreknowledge" but "the deeper issue is the congruence of divine will and divine nature," which "results in God's continuous salvific and creative action." Regarding his concept of a pre-cosmic fall, Lyman likewise argues that Origen's doctrines must always be interpreted within the particular contexts in which they are conceived: "Origen's concept of the pre-existence of souls seems to be a way of understanding the inequality of present existence and the collective effect of the Fall, rather than an assertion of the soul's immortality or a previous spiritual life" (60).

56. Desire is arguably the more primary site of human participation in the divine than is nature. See Lyman, *Christology and Cosmology*, 48: "Origen used the common Platonic idea of participation not as an abstract relation to a constitutive Form, but rather to express a state or condition of individual relationship to an active, intentional divine being."

57. Cf. Edwards, *Origen Against Plato*, 93–94. Edwards does not find the notion of a pre-existent soul of Jesus any more supportable by Origen's text than the notion of pre-existent souls more generally. Here again I find myself partly sympathetic with Edwards's critical intervention while also inclined to seek a different resolution via a more nuanced interpretation of Origen's conception of time.

58. Love or desire is crucial. As Lyman, *Christology and Cosmology*, 74–75, emphasizes, the mediation of the Word is not sheerly metaphysical; it also, and more importantly, occurs through the manifestation of a divine volition or intentionality in which the cosmos participates, albeit imperfectly.

59. Miller, *Poetry of Thought*, 213.

60. Note that Dawson, *Christian Figural Reading*, 15, is inclined to deny Origen's supersessionism vis-à-vis Jewish interpretation altogether, which is not a position that I find tenable.

61. Elliot R. Wolfson, *Through a Speculum That Shines: Vision and Imagination in Medieval Jewish Mysticism* (Princeton, N.J.: Princeton University Press, 1994), 329–30, 355. Also strikingly relevant to Origen's hermeneutics are Wolfson's more recent hermeneutical reflections on the paradoxical relation of disclosure and

occlusion: "every act of revealing is a concealing, for the truth cannot be revealed unless it is concealed." *Language, Eros, Being: Kabbalistic Hermeneutics and Poetic Imagination* (New York: Fordham University Press, 2005), 17.

62. See Joseph W. Trigg, "Divine Deception and the Truthfulness of Scripture," in *Origen of Alexandria: His World and His Legacy*, ed. Charles Kannengiesser and William L. Petersen (Notre Dame, Ind.: University of Notre Dame Press, 1988), 147–64.

63. I am persuaded by Dawson's argument that one ought not read Origen's claim that some passages of scripture lack a literal or "fleshly" meaning as evidence that the corporeality of the text can or should be overcome or superseded: "all passages of Scripture (presumably including those that have no bodily meaning) are parts of the single body of the text" (Dawson, *Christian Figural Reading*, 76). I would add that the very passages that, according to Origen, have no bodily meaning, nonetheless signify—paradoxically, via the very jamming of signification that occurs within the "literal" (non)sense of the text.

64. See Miller, *Poetry of Thought*, 214–15.

65. Ibid., 218.

66. Koetschau frag. 40.

67. Dawson, *Christian Figural Reading*, 65.

68. Ibid., 74–80.

69. Kristeva, *Powers of Horror*, 1.

70. Ibid., 13.

71. See my *"Begotten, Not Made": Conceiving Manhood in Late Antiquity*, Figurae: Reading Medieval Culture (Stanford, Calif.: Stanford University Press, 2000) for a comparative account of Athanasius's and Gregory's christologies pursued from a slightly different angle, namely, theological constructions of masculinity. Note that I have here chosen here to focus on Gregory's *Catechetical Oration* because of its central focus on incarnational Christology, matching that of Athanasius in *On the Incarnation of the Word*. In my earlier work, I consider a slightly broader set of texts from each of these writers, ones that disclose both Athanasius's significant turn from the trope of Word to that of Son and Gregory's characteristic displacement of "christological" issues onto figures of virginity.

72. Kristeva, *Powers of Horror*, 54.

73. Ibid., 54.

Chapter 3. The Desire and Pursuit of Humiliation

Epigraph. Emmanuel Levinas, *On Escape*, 1935, trans. Bettina Bergo (Stanford, Calif.: Stanford University Press, 2003), 60, 64.

1. Edward Gibbon, *The History of the Decline and Fall of the Roman Empire*, vol. 2 (Philadelphia: Abraham Small, P.H. Nicklin, & Isaac Bilby, 1816), 424.

2. E. R. Dodds, *Pagan and Christian in an Age of Anxiety: Some Aspects of Religious Experience from Marcus Aurelius to Constantine* (New York: Norton, 1965), 34.

3. Dodds, *Pagan and Christian in an Age of Anxiety*, 33.

4. Dodds, *Pagan and Christian in an Age of Anxiety*, 36.

5. Note that his equation of "plenitude" with "totality" clearly distinguishes it from construals of the pleromatic as expansion or overflow.

6. Levinas, *On Escape*, 69.

7. Cf. Lacan's punning proposal of *une hontologie* as a way out of ontology via shame (*honte*) in the final lecture of his 17th seminar, *The Underside of Psycho-analysis*, in which he suggests provocatively that shame is not only the "underside" but also the final product of psychoanalysis. Jacques Lacan, *L'Envers de la psychana-lyse*, Séminaire de Jacques Lacan (Paris: Éditions du Seuil, 1991), 209.

8. Levinas, *On Escape*, 64, 67.

9. Ibid., 64.

10. Ibid., 73.

11. As Edith Wyschogrod frames the thought, the origins of shame are in the experience of "the nudity of the Other's look." *Emmanuel Levinas: The Problem of Ethical Metaphysics* (New York: Fordham University Press, 2000), 100.

12. Emmanuel Levinas, *Totality and Infinity: An Essay on Exteriority*, trans. Alphonso Lingis (Pittsburgh: Duquesne University Press, 1969), 84.

13. Emmanuel Levinas, *Otherwise Than Being or Beyond Essence*, trans. Alphonso Lingis (The Hague: Martinus Nijhoff, 1981), 114.

14. Arguably neither Levinas nor the ancient Christian ascetics develop an adequate theory of inter-subjectivity, though both open up such a path.

15. See Georgia Frank, *The Memory of the Eyes: Pilgrims to Living Saints in Christian Late Antiquity* (Berkeley: University of California Press, 2000).

16. Patricia Cox Miller, " 'Differential Networks': Relics and Other Fragments in Late Antiquity," *Journal of Early Christian Studies* 6, no. 1 (1998): 135–36. See also her "Strategies of Representation in Collective Biography: Constructing the Subject as Holy," in *Greek Biography and Panegyric in Late Antiquity*, ed. Tomas Hagg and Philip Rousseau (Berkeley: University of California Press, 2000), 209–54.

17. David Brakke, *Demons and the Making of the Monk: Spiritual Combat in Early Christianity* (Cambridge, Mass.: Harvard University Press, 2006), 134–44.

18. As is subtly argued by Brakke, *Demons*, 157–81, by appeal to postcolonial theories of mimicry. He shows that the figure of the Ethiopian, culturally stereotyped as hypersexual, is particularly expressive of the affinity between the demon and the monk who "must simultaneously concede and disavow" sexual desire (167).

19. See, e.g., Clement of Alexandria, *Instructor* 2.10.

20. Cf. Brakke, *Demons*, 174: "Is she the only thing that Pachon's madness has led his hand to touch?"

21. Elizabeth Clark, "Sex, Shame, and Rhetoric: En-Gendering Early Christian Ethics," *Journal of the American Academy of Religion* 59 (1991): 221–45.

22. See the nuanced discussion of authorial humility and hagiographic writing in Derek Krueger, *Writing and Holiness: The Practice of Authorship in the Early Christian East*, Divinations: Rereading Late Ancient Religion (Philadelphia: University of Pennsylvania Press, 2004), 94–109. Especially relevant here is his discussion of deliberate stylistic humiliation: "As an instrument of ascetic praxis, the text functions as an extension of the author's body. Mortified, stigmatized by its own remarks about its inadequacy, the text suffers humiliation in order to save" (106).

23. Cf. David Brakke's comment regarding Evagrius's own thought: "although Athanasius's Antony moves past fornication rather quickly (albeit with struggle), Evagrius appears to think that even advanced monks have difficulty doing so: he offers numerous biblical passages to help monks who are in danger of losing hope that they will ever get past this demon" (*Demons*, 59–60).

24. See my "Praying Is Joying: Musings on Love in Evagrius Ponticus," in *Toward a Theology of Eros: Transfiguring Passion at the Limits of Discipline*, ed. Virginia Burrus and Catherine Keller (New York: Fordham University Press, 2006), 194–204.

25. Brakke, *Demons*, 64.

26. For an admirably clear and concise synthetic account of Evagrius's views on vainglory and pride, see Brakke, *Demons*, 67–69.

27. Levinas, *On Escape*, 67.

28. Ibid., 62–63.

29. See Brakke, *Demons*, 54.

30. A. S. E. Parker, "The Vita Syncletica: Its Manuscripts, Ascetical Teachings, and Its Use in Monastic Sources," *Studia Patristica* 30 (1997): 232.

31. Elizabeth A. Castelli, "Mortifying the Body, Curing the Soul: Beyond Ascetic Dualism in the Life of Saint Syncletica," *Differences* 4, 2 (1992): 138.

32. Krueger, *Writing and Holiness*, 149.

33. Castelli, "Mortifying the Body," 138.

34. Krueger, *Writing and Holiness*, 149.

35. E.g., Macrina.

36. Castelli, "Mortifying the Body," 146–47, comments on the conventionality of the image of the holy woman as athlete or soldier.

37. Brakke, *Demons*, 191.

38. Krueger, *Writing and Holiness*, 141–49.

39. Brakke, *Demons*, 189.

40. As Castelli, "Mortifying the Body," 142, notes: "There is certainly a tension in this text between a kind of dualism which understands material life in this world to be of no consequence, and a kind of embeddedness or interwovenness of spirituality and embodiedness which undercuts simple dualisms of body/spirit."

41. See Susan Ashbrook Harvey's nuanced discussion of sanctity and stench in *Scenting Salvation: Ancient Christianity and the Olfactory Imagination* (Berkeley: University of California Press, 2006), 201–21. She suggests that saintly stench "profoundly challenged the entire system of olfactory codes by which the ancient world was ordered" (201) and that "Christian ascetic practices required a certain reconfiguration of the categories 'good' and 'bad' odors" (204). Hagiographers might downplay the unpleasant odors that often attend ascetic life, or they might perform a reversal by reconstruing an unpleasant smell as a pleasant one. In the case of Syncletica, the endurance of stench becomes part of the holy person's ascetic practice, but ultimately the smell of putrefaction gives way to the fragrance of sanctity, on Harvey's reading (217). I am here pushing the argument a bit further in proposing that the intensity of Syncletica's stench *is* the fragrance of her sanctity, her fleshly corruptibility her self-transcendence.

42. Julia Kristeva, *Powers of Horror: An Essay on Abjection*, trans. Leon S. Roudiez (New York: Columbia University Press, 1982), 3.

43. Levinas, *On Escape*, 68.

44. Dorothy Allison, *Skin: Talking About Sex, Class, and Literature* (Ithaca, N.Y.: Firebrand Books, 1994), 250–51.

45. Allison, *Skin*, 179, 217, 219.

46. Geoffrey Galt Harpham, *The Ascetic Imperative in Culture and Criticism* (Chicago: University of Chicago Press, 1987), 61, emphasis original.

Chapter 4. Shameful Confessions

Epigraphs. Michel Foucault, "Sexuality and Solitude," 1980, in *Ethics: Subjectivity and Truth*, ed. Paul Rabinow, trans. Robert Hurley et al. (New York: New Press, 1997), 178; Jacques Derrida, "Typewriter Ribbon: Limited Ink (2)," in *Without Alibi*, ed. and trans. Peggy Kamuf (Stanford, Calif.: Stanford University Press, 2002), 109.

1. Michel Foucault, "About the Beginning of the Hermeneutics of the Self," 1980, in *Religion and Culture: Michel Foucault*, ed. Jeremy R. Carrette (New York: Routledge, 1999), 178–79.

2. Ibid., 179.

3. On the profound and revealing ambiguities regarding the relation of confession to volition as this is reflected in U.S. legal practice and theory, see Peter Brooks, *Troubling Confessions: Speaking Guilt in Law and Literature* (Chicago: University of Chicago Press, 2000).

4. Derrida, "Typewriter Ribbon," 134. The notorious problem of false confession is also handled sensitively by Brooks, *Troubling Confessions*.

5. Jacques Derrida, "Composing 'Circumfession,'" in *Augustine and Postmodernism: Confessions and Circumfession*, ed. John D. Caputo and Michael J. Scanlon (Bloomington: Indiana University Press, 2005), 25.

6. J. M. Coetzee, "Confession and Double Thoughts: Tolstoy, Rousseau, Dostoevsky," in *Doubling the Point: Essays and Interviews*, ed. David Atwell (Cambridge, Mass.: Harvard University Press, 1992), 272.

7. Paul de Man, "Excuses (Confessions)," in Paul de Man, *Allegories of Reading: Figural Language in Rousseau, Nietzsche, Rilke, and Proust* (New Haven, Conn.: Yale University Press, 1979), 285.

8. de Man, "Excuses (Confessions)," 299.

9. Derrida, "Typewriter Ribbon," 159.

10. Brooks, *Troubling Confessions*, 13.

11. Derrida, "Composing 'Circumfession,'" 24.

12. Derrida, "Typewriter Ribbon," 101. Emphasis added.

13. Coetzee, "Confession and Double Thoughts," 292.

14. Derrida, "Typewriter Ribbon," 128.

15. Derrida, "Composing 'Circumfession,'" 24.

16. Foucault, "Hermeneutics of the Self," 170.

17. Derrida, "Typewriter Ribbon," 111.

18. Derrida, "Composing 'Circumfession,' " 25.

19. Leo C. Ferrari, "The Boyhood Beatings of Augustine," *Augustinian Studies* 5 (1974): 7. Ferrari documents helpfully the prevalence of references to the scourging God in *Confessions*. As Theodore de Bruyn demonstrates, a significant shift in representations of flogging is already evident in earlier fourth-century Latin Christian authors, e.g., Ambrose: "The *flagellum* is no longer—or rather not merely—the cultural sign of servitude. It has become the cultural sign of sonship." He notes further, "But, as so often with Augustine, ideas that are not in themselves unique are developed and articulated with an insistence that has not only caught the attention of modern scholars but also invited reaction from Augustine's contemporaries. These reactions—or what Augustine anticipates as reactions—are incorporated into Augustine's representation of paternal discipline." "Flogging a Son: The Emergence of the *Pater Flagellans* in Latin Christian Discourse," *Journal of Early Christian Studies* 7, 2 (1999): 259, 264. What particularly interests me here is Augustine's intimate incorporation of the resistance that attends submission to acute shame—shame that results not only from the school master's beating but also from its apparent endorsement by both paternal and divine authorities.

20. Jean Jacques Rousseau famously recounts his own theft of a ribbon, as discussed by de Man, "Excuses (Confessions)," and subsequently by Derrida, "Typewriter Ribbon," who notes the curious absence in both Rousseau and de Man of any reference to Augustine. "Has anyone ever noticed, in this immense archive, that both Augustine and Rousseau confess a theft? And that both do so in Book 2 of their *Confessions*, in a decisive or even determining and paradigmatic place? This is not all: in this archive that is also a confession, both of them confess that, although it was objectively trifling, this theft had the greatest psychic repercussions on their whole lives. A propos, this apparently insignificant theft was committed by each of them at the precise age of sixteen" (80). Derrida, for his part, also admits in his own explicitly Augustinian confessional narrative to "a stolen pleasure, for example those grapes from the vineyard of the Arab landowner, one of those rare Algerian bourgeois in El-Biar, who threatened to hand us, Claude and me, we were eight or nine, over to the police after his warden had caught us with our hands on the grapes, and there was a nervous burst of laughter when he let us run off." "Circumfession," in Geoffrey Bennington and Jacques Derrida, *Jacques Derrida* (Chicago: University of Chicago Press, 1993), 159–60.

21. Jean Baudrillard, *Seduction*, 1979, trans. Brian Singer (New York: St. Martin's Press, 1990), makes a sharp distinction between the exposure of pornography and the secrecy of seduction. Citing Baudrillard, Karmen MacKendrick points toward both a theory and a practice of seduction at work in Augustine's text. "Carthage Didn't Burn Hot Enough: Saint Augustine's Divine Seduction," in *Toward a Theology of Eros: Transfiguring Passion at the Limits of Discipline*, ed. Virginia Burrus and Catherine Keller (New York: Fordham University Press, 2006), 205–17. Cf. the more austerely ascetic reading of Augustine offered by Mark Jordan in the same volume, "Flesh in Confession: Alcibiades Beside Augustine," 32–37.

22. As Mark Jordan puts it: "Augustine is bound by the lust of marriage" (Jordan, "Flesh in Confession," 34).

23. See MacKendrick, "Augustine's Divine Seduction."

24. Dennis Trout, "Re-Textualizing Lucretia: Cultural Subversion in the *City Of God*," *Journal of Early Christian Studies* 2, 1 (1994): 70.

25. E.g., Tertullian, *To the Martyrs* 4, *Exhortation to Chastity* 13, *On Monogamy* 17; Jerome, *Against Jovinian* 1.46, 49; Paulinus of Nola, *Poem* 10.192 to Ausonius. See Trout, "Re-Textualizing Lucretia," 61–62.

26. See my "Reading Agnes: The Rhetoric of Gender in Ambrose and Prudentius," *Journal of Early Christian Studies* 3, 1 (1995): 25–46.

27. Trout, "Re-Textualizing Lucretia," 62.

28. Anders Nygren finds the Augustinian synthesis of what are for him two contradictory notions of love ("agape" and "eros") deeply troubling; see his *Agape and Eros*, trans. Philip S. Watson (Philadelphia: Westminster Press, 1953), 556–58. Others of us may find it deeply attractive.

29. Karmen MacKendrick, *Counterpleasures*, SUNY Series in Postmodern Culture (Albany: State University of New York Press, 1999), 132.

30. Coetzee, "Confession and Double Thoughts," 271–72.

31. On the association of the figure of the Ethiopian with hypersexuality, see David Brakke, *Demons and the Making of the Monk: Spiritual Combat in Early Christianity* (Cambridge, Mass.: Harvard University Press, 2006), 157–81.

32. On Evagrius's confessional theory and practice in relation to Cassian's, see David Brakke, "Making Public the Monastic Life: Reading the Self in Evagrius Ponticus' *Talking Back*," in *Religion and the Self in Antiquity*, ed. David Brakke, Michael Satlow, and Steven Weitzman (Bloomington: Indiana University Press, 2005), 222–33.

33. Peter Brown, *The Body and Society: Men, Women, and Sexual Renunciation in Early Christianity*, Lectures on the History of Religions (New York: Columbia University Press, 1988), 421–22.

34. Brown, *The Body and Society*, 420 n. 127.

35. Michel Foucault, "The Battle for Chastity," 1982, in *Religion and Culture: Michel Foucault*, ed. Jeremy R. Carrette (New York: Routledge, 1999), 189–90.

36. Here as elsewhere he follows Evagrius's lead; see Brakke, *Demons*, 56.

37. Actually, Cassian's exegesis is more complicated than this, for he offers readings of the three temptations that suit both Luke's and Matthew's differing sequences.

38. David Brakke, "The Problematization of Nocturnal Emissions in Early Christian Syria, Egypt, and Gaul," *Journal of Early Christian Studies* 3, 4 (1995): 449. Note that Conrad Leyser, "Masculinity in Flux: Nocturnal Emission and the Limits of Celibacy in the Early Middle Ages," in *Masculinity in Medieval Europe*, ed. D. M. Hadley (London: Longman, 1999), 103–20, gently resists what he takes to be Brakke's overemphasis on both the interior and monastic aspects of Cassian's confessional practice, suggesting a more fluid and blatantly political setting for his discourse on nocutral emissions. I am not convinced that these arguments are mutually exclusive.

39. Brakke, "Nocturnal Emissions," 447.

40. For Augustine, such perfect chastity does not manifest this side of the res-

urrection; for a discussion of Augustine's views of wet dreams, see Brakke, "Nocturnal Emissions," 457.

41. Brakke, "Nocturnal Emissions," 450.

42. Lynda L. Coon, *Sacred Fictions: Holy Women and Hagiography in Late Antiquity*, Middle Ages Series (Philadelphia: University of Pennsylvania Press, 1997), 84. I have commented at greater length on this text in my *The Sex Lives of Saints: An Erotics of Ancient Hagiography*, Divinations: Rereading Late Ancient Religion (Philadelphia: University of Pennsylvania Press, 2004), 147–55.

43. Judith Butler, *Giving an Account of Oneself* (New York: Forham University Press, 2005), 39–41.

44. MacKendrick, "Augustine's Divine Seduction."

45. Butler, *Giving an Account of Oneself*, 11.

Afterword: Shame, Politics, Love

Epigraph. Martha C. Nussbaum, *Hiding from Humanity: Disgust, Shame, and the Law* (Princeton, N.J.: Princeton University Press, 2004), 17.

1. Nussbaum, *Hiding from Humanity*, 17.

2. Roger Kimball, "Does Shame Have a Future?" *New Criterion*, September 2004, 5.

3. Christina Tarnopolsky, "Prudes, Perverts, and Tyrants: Plato and the Contemporary Politics of Shame," *Political Theory* 32, no. 4 (August 2004): 469.

4. Kimball, "Does Shame Have a Future?" 9.

5. Nussbaum, *Hiding from Humanity*, 216.

6. Nussbaum, *Hiding from Humanity*, 208.

7. Nussbaum, *Hiding from Humanity*, 213.

8. Carlin Barton, *Roman Honor: The Fire in the Bones* (Berkeley: University of California Press, 2001), 288.

9. Nussbaum, *Hiding from Humanity*, 172, 217, 222.

10. Kimball, "Does Shame Have a Future?" 5.

11. On ancient Christianity and the history of tattooing, see my "Macrina's Tattoo," in *The Cultural Turn in Late Ancient Studies: Gender, Asceticism, and Historiography*, ed. Dale B. Martin and Patricia Cox Miller (Durham, N.C.: Duke University Press, 2005), 103–17.

12. Judith Butler, *Excitable Speech: A Politics of the Performative* (New York: Routledge, 1997), 2.

13. Nussbaum, *Hiding from Humanity*, 270–71.

14. Jean Bethke Elshtain, *Democracy on Trial* (New York: Basic Books, 1995), 55.

15. Barton, *Roman Honor*, 284.

16. Judith Butler, *Giving an Account of Oneself* (New York: Fordham University Press, 2005), 42.

17. Elliot R. Wolfson, "Secrecy, Modesty, and the Feminine: Kabbalistic Traces in the Thought of Levinas," *Journal of Jewish Thought and Philosophy* 14

(2006): 209. Wolfson here gives voice to a Levinasian sensibility that also pervades Butler's reflections on the epistemological limits that condition ethics. See also his reflections on the links between extreme humility and an ethics of compassion that exceeds even the dichotomy of good and evil, thereby closing the distance between ethics and eros, in *Venturing Beyond: Law and Morality in Kabbalistic Mysticism* (Oxford: Oxford University Press, 2006), 286–316.

Bibliography

Ancient Works

Acts of Paul and Thecla. English translation R. McL. Wilson and Wilhelm Schneemelcher. In *New Testament Apocrypha*, vol. 2, *Writings Related to the Apostles, Apocalypses, and Other Subjects*. Philadelphia: Westminster Press, 1965. 353–64. Greek edition R. A. Lipsius, *Acta Apostolorum Apocrypha, Part 1.* Hildesheim: Georg Olms, 1959. 235–72.

Apocryphon of John. English translation Frederik Wisse. In *The Nag Hammadi Library*, ed. James M. Robinson, rev. ed. San Francisco: Harper, 1990. 104–23. See also Karen L. King, *The Secret Revelation of John* (Cambridge, Mass.: Harvard University Press, 2006), 26–81. Coptic edition with English translation Michael M. Waldstein and Frederik Wisse, *The Apocryphon of John: Synopsis of Nag Hammadi Codices II.1; III.1; and IV.1 with BG 8502.2.* Nag Hammadi and Manichaean Studies 33. Leiden: Brill, 1995.

Athanasius. *Life of Antony.* English translation Robert C. Gregg. Classics of Western Spirituality. New York: Paulist Press, 1980. Greek edition *Vie d'Antoine*, ed. G. J. M. Bartelink. Sources chrétiennes 400. Paris: Cerf, 1994.

———. *On the Incarnation of the Word.* English translation and Greek edition Robert W. Thomson. Oxford: Clarendon Press, 1971.

Augustine. *Confessions.* English translation R. S. Pine-Coffin. New York: Penguin, 1961. Latin edition Corpus Christianorum, Series Latina 27. 3 vols. Oxford: Clarendon Press, 1992.

———. *City of God.* English translation Henry Bettenson. New York: Penguin, 1984. Latin edition Corpus Christianorum, Series Latina 47, 48.

Evagrius of Pontus. *The Praktikos* and *Chapters on Prayer.* English translation John Eudes Bamberger, OCSO. Cistercian Studies Series 4. Kalamazoo, Mich.: Cistercian Publications, 1981. Greek edition of *Praktikos* in *Traité pratique, ou, le moine*, edited by A. and C. Guillaumont, 2 vols, Sources chrétiennes 170, 171 (Paris: Cerf, 1971). Greek edition of *Chapters on Prayer* in *Patrologia Graeca*, ed. J. P. Migne, vol. 79, cols. 1165–1200.

Gregory of Nyssa. *Catechetical Oration.* English translation Cyril Richardson in *Christology of the Later Fathers*, ed. Edward R. Hardy. Philadelphia: Westminster Press, 1954. 268–325. Greek edition J. H. Srawley, Cambridge Patristic Studies. Cambridge: Cambridge University Press, 1903.

Ignatius of Antioch. *Letter to the Romans.* In *The Apostolic Fathers: Greek Texts and*

English Translations, updated edition, ed. and rev. Michael W. Holmes. Grand Rapids, Mich.: Baker Books, 1999. 166–67.

John Cassian. *Conferences*. English translation Boniface Ramsey. Ancient Christian Writers 57. Mahwah, N.J.: Paulist Press, 1997. Latin edition Corpus Scriptorum Ecclesiasticorum Latinorum 13.

———. *Institutes*. English translation Boniface Ramsey. Ancient Christian Writers 58. Mahwah, N.J.: Paulist Press, 2000. Latin edition Corpus Scriptorum Ecclesiasticorum Latinorum 17.

Leontius of Neapolis. *Life of Symeon the Fool*. English translation Derek Krueger, *Symeon the Holy Fool: Leontius's Life and the Late Antique City*. Berkeley: University of California Press, 1996. 131–11. Greek edition *Vie de Syméon le Fou et Vie de Jean de Chypre*, ed. with translation and commentary A. J. Festugière. Bibliothèque archéologique et historique 95. Paris: Geuthner, 1974. 1–222.

Letter of the Churches of Vienne and Lyons. In Eusebius, *Ecclesiastical History* 5.1. English translation and Greek text Kirsopp Lake. New York: G.P. Putnam's Sons, 1926.

Life of Mary of Egypt. English translation of the Latin text Benedicta Ward in *Harlots of the Desert: A Study of Repentance in Early Monastic Sources*. Kalamazoo, Mich.: Cistercian Publications, 1987. 26–56. Latin text *Patrologia Latina*, ed. J. P. Migne, vol. 73, cols. 671–90. Greek text *Patrologia Graeca*, ed. J. P. Migne, vol. 87, cols. 3693–3726.

Life of Syncletica. English translation Elizabeth A. Castelli in *Ascetic Behavior in Greco-Roman Antuqiuity: A Sourcebook*, ed. Vincent L. Wimbush. Minneapolis: Fortress, 1990. 265–311. Greek edition *Patrologia Graeca*, ed. J. P. Migne, vol. 28, cols. 1487–1558.

Martyrdom of Polycarp. In *The Apostolic Fathers: Greek Texts and English Translations*, updated edition, ed. and rev. Michael W. Holmes. Grand Rapids, Mich.: Baker Books, 1999. 226–45.

Origen. *On First Principles*. English translation G. W. Butterworth. New York: Harper and Row, 1966. Greek edition *Traité des principes*, ed. Henry Crouzel and Manlio Simonetti. 5 vols. Sources chrétiennes 252, 253, 268, 269, 312. Paris: Cerf, 1978–1984.

Palladius. *Lausiac History*. English translation Robert T. Meyer. Ancient Christian Writers 34. New York: Newman, 1964. Greek edition Cuthbert Butler. 2 vols. Texts and Studies: Contributions to Biblical and Patristic Literature 6. Cambridge: Cambridge University Press, 1898–1904.

Passion of Perpetua and Felicitas. English translation and Greek text Herbert Musurillo in *Acts of the Christian Martyrs*. Oxford: Clarendon Press, 1972. See also J. Armitage Robinson. Texts and Studies: Contributions to Biblical and Patristic Literature 1. Cambridge: Cambridge University Press, 1891.

Tertullian. *On the Flesh of Christ*. English translation P. Holmes. Ante-Nicene Fathers 3. Latin edition *La chair du Christ*, 2 vols., ed. Jean-Pierre Mahé. Sources chrétiennes 216, 217. Paris: Cerf, 1975.

———. *On the Resurrection*. English translation and Latin edition Ernest Evans. London: S.P.C.K., 1960.

Modern Works

Adamson, Joseph, and Hilary Clark. "Introduction: Shame, Affect, Writing." In *Scenes of Shame: Psychoanalysis, Shame, and Writing*, ed. Joseph Adamson and Hilary Clark, 1–34. Albany: State University of New York Press, 1999.

Allison, Dorothy. *Skin: Talking About Sex, Class, and Literature*. Ithaca, N.Y.: Firebrand Books, 1994.

Bader, Michael J. "The Psychodynamics of Cynicism." *Tikkun* 11 (May-June 1996).

Barton, Carlin. *The Sorrows of the Ancient Romans: The Gladiator and the Monster*. Princeton, N.J.: Princeton University Press, 1993.

———. "All Things Beseem the Victor: Paradoxes of Masculinity in Early Imperial Rome." In *Gender Rhetorics: Postures of Dominance and Submission in History*, 83–92. Binghamton, N.Y.: Center for Medieval and Early Renaissance Studies, 1994.

———. "Savage Miracles: The Redemption of Lost Honor in Roman Society and the Sacrament of the Gladiator and the Martyr." *Representations* 45 (1994): 41–71.

———. *Roman Honor: The Fire in the Bones*. Berkeley: University of California Press, 2001.

Bataille, Georges. *Erotism: Death and Sensuality*. 1957. Trans. Mary Dalwood. San Francisco: City Lights, 1986.

Baudrillard, Jean. *Seduction*. Trans. Brian Singer. New York: St. Martin's Press, 1979.

Beacham, Richard C. *Spectacle Entertainments of Early Imperial Rome*. New Haven, Conn.: Yale University Press, 1999.

Benedict, Ruth. *The Chrysanthemum and the Sword: Patterns of Japanese Culture*. Boston: Houghton Mifflin, 1946.

Boyarin, Daniel. *Dying for God: Martyrdom and the Making of Christianity and Judaism*. Stanford, Calif.: Stanford University Press, 1999.

———. *Border Lines: The Partition of Judaeo-Christianity*. Divinations: Rereading Late Ancient Religion. Philadelphia: University of Pennsylvania Press, 2004.

Bradley, K. R. *Slaves and Masters in the Roman Empire*. Oxford: Oxford University Press, 1987.

Brakke, David. "The Problematization of Nocturnal Emissions in Early Christian Syria, Egypt, and Gaul." *Journal of Early Christian Studies* 3, 4 (1995): 419–60.

———. "Making Public the Monastic Life: Reading the Self in Evagrius Ponticus' *Talking Back*." In *Religion and the Self in Antiquity*, ed. David Brakke, Michael L. Satlow, and Steven Weitzman, 222–33. Bloomington: Indiana University Press, 2006.

———. *Demons and the Making of the Monk: Spiritual Combat in Early Christianity*. Cambridge, Mass.: Harvard University Press, 2006.

Brooks, Peter. *Troubling Confessions: Speaking Guilt in Law and Literature*. Chicago: University of Chicago Press, 2000.

Brown, Peter. *The Body and Society: Men, Women, and Sexual Renunciation in Early Christianity*. Lectures on the History of Religions. New York: Columbia University Press, 1988.

Burrus, Virginia. "Reading Agnes: The Rhetoric of Gender in Ambrose and Prudentius." *Journal of Early Christian Studies* 3, 1 (1995): 25–46.

———. *"Begotten, Not Made": Conceiving Manhood in Late Antiquity.* Figurae: Reading Medieval Culture. Stanford, Calif.: Stanford University Press, 2000.

———. *The Sex Lives of Saints: An Erotics of Ancient Hagiography.* Divinations: Rereading Late Ancient Religion. Philadelphia: University of Pennsylvania Press, 2004.

———. "Creatio Ex Libidine: Reading Ancient Logos Differently." In *Derrida and Religion: Other Testaments,* ed. Yvonne Sherwood and Kevin Hart, 141–56. New York: Routledge, 2005.

———. "Macrina's Tattoo." In *The Cultural Turn in Late Ancient Studies: Gender, Asceticism, and Historiography,* ed. Dale B. Martin and Patricia Cox Miller, 103–17. Durham, N.C.: Duke University Press, 2005.

———. "Praying Is Joying: Musings on Love in Evagrius Ponticus." In *Toward a Theology of Eros: Transfiguring Passion at the Limits of Discipline,* ed. Virginia Burrus and Catherine Keller, 194–204. New York: Fordham University Press, 2006.

Butler, Judith. *Excitable Speech: A Politics of the Performative.* New York: Routledge, 1997.

———. *Giving an Account of Oneself.* New York: Fordham University Press, 2005.

Castelli, Elizabeth A. "Mortifying the Body, Curing the Soul: Beyond Ascetic Dualism in the Life of Saint Syncletica." *Differences* 4, 2 (1992): 134–53.

———. *Martyrdom and Memory: Early Christian Culture Making.* New York: Columbia University Press, 2004.

Clark, Elizabeth A. "Sex, Shame, and Rhetoric: En-Gendering Early Christian Ethics." *Journal of the American Academy of Religion* 59 (1991): 221–45.

———. *The Origenist Controversy: The Cultural Construction of an Early Christian Debate.* Princeton, N.J.: Princeton University Press, 1992.

Coetzee, J. M. "Confession and Double Thoughts: Tolstoy, Rousseau, Dostoevsky." In J. M. Coetzee, *Doubling the Point: Essays and Interviews,* ed. David Atwell, 251–93. Cambridge, Mass.: Harvard University Press, 1992.

Coon, Lynda L. *Sacred Fictions: Holy Women and Hagiography in Late Antiquity.* Middle Ages Series. Philadelphia: University of Pennsylvania Press, 1997.

Crouzel, Henri. *Origen: The Life and Thought of the First Great Theologian.* San Francisco: Harper and Row, 1989.

Dawson, John David. *Christian Figural Reading and the Fashioning of Identity.* Berkeley: University of California Press, 2002.

de Bruyn, Theodore. "Flogging a Son: The Emergence of the *Pater Flagellans* in Latin Christian Discourse." *Journal of Early Christian Studies* 7, 2 (1999): 249–90.

de Man, Paul. "Excuses (Confessions)." In Paul de Man, *Allegories of Reading: Figural Language in Rousseau, Nietzsche, Rilke, and Proust,* 278–301. New Haven, Conn.: Yale University Press, 1979.

Delaney, Carol. "Seeds of Honor, Fields of Shame." In *Honor and Shame and the Unity of the Mediterranean,* ed. David D. Gilmore, 35–48. Washington, D.C.: American Anthropological Association, 1987.

Derrida, Jacques. "Circumfession." In Geoffrey Bennington and Jacques Derrida, *Jacques Derrida*, 3–315. Chicago: University of Chicago Press, 1993.

———. "Typewriter Ribbon: Limited Ink (2)." In Jacques Derrida, *Without Alibi*, ed. and trans. Peggy Kamuf, 71–160. Stanford, Calif.: Stanford University Press, 2002.

———. "Composing 'Circumfession.'" In *Augustine and Postmodernism: Confessions and Circumfession*, ed. John D. Caputo and Michael J. Scanlon, 19–27. Indiana Series in the Philosophy of Religion. Bloomington: Indiana University Press, 2005.

deSilva, David A. *Honor, Patronage, Kinship, and Purity: Unlocking New Testament Culture*. Downers Grove, Ill.: InterVarsity Press, 2000.

Dodds, E. R. *The Greeks and the Irrational*. Berkeley: University of California Press, 1951.

———. *Pagan and Christian in an Age of Anxiety: Some Aspects of Religious Experience from Marcus Aurelius to Constantine*. New York: Norton, 1965.

duBois, Page. *Torture and Truth*. New York: Routledge, 1991.

Edwards, Mark Julian. *Origen Against Plato*. Ashgate Studies in Philosophy and Theology in Late Antiquity. Aldershot: Ashgate, 2002.

Elshtain, Jean Bethke. *Democracy on Trial*. New York: Basic Books, 1995.

Ferrari, Leo C. "The Boyhood Beatings of Augustine." *Augustinian Studies* 5 (1974): 1–14.

Foucault, Michel. "About the Beginning of the Hermeneutics of the Self." 1980. In *Religion and Culture: Michel Foucault*, ed. Jeremy R. Carrette, 158–81. New York: Routledge, 1999.

———. "The Battle for Chastity." 1982. In *Religion and Culture: Michel Foucault*, ed. Jeremy R. Carrette, 188–97. New York: Routledge, 1999.

———. "Sexuality and Solitude." In *Ethics: Subjectivity and Truth*, ed. Paul Rabinow, trans. Robert Hurley et al., 175–84. New York: New Press, 1997.

Frank, Georgia. *The Memory of the Eyes: Pilgrims to Living Saints in Christian Late Antiquity*. Berkeley: University of California Press, 2000.

Frilingos, Christopher A. "Sexing the Lamb." In *New Testament Masculinities*, ed. Stephen D. Moore and Janice Capel Anderson, 297–318. Atlanta: Society of Biblical Literature, 2003.

———. *Spectacles of Empire: Monsters, Martyrs, and the Book of Revelation*. Divinations: Rereading Late Ancient Religion. Philadelphia: University of Pennsylvania Press, 2004.

Futrell, Alison. *Blood in the Arena: The Spectacle of Roman Power*. Austin: University of Texas Press, 1997.

Gibbon, Edward. *The History of the Decline and Fall of the Roman Empire*. Vol. 2. Philadelphia: Abraham Small, P.H. Nicklin, and Isaac Bilby, 1816.

Gilmore, David G. "Introduction: The Shame of Dishonor." In *Honor and Shame and the Unity of the Mediterranean*, ed. David G. Gilmore, 2–21. Washington, D.C.: American Anthropological Association, 1987.

Gleason, Maud W. *Making Men: Sophists and Self-Presentation in Ancient Rome*. Princeton, N.J.: Princeton University Press, 1995.

Hanson, K. C. "How Honorable! How Shameful! A Cultural Analysis of Matthew's Makarisms and Reproaches." *Semeia* 68 (1994): 81–111.

Harpham, Geoffrey Galt. *The Ascetic Imperative in Culture and Criticism*. Chicago: University of Chicago Press, 1987.

Hart, Lynda. *Between the Body and the Flesh: Performing Sadomasochism*. Between Men—Between Women: Lesbian and Gay Studies. New York: Columbia University Press, 1998.

Harvey, Susan Ashbrook. *Scenting Salvation: Ancient Christianity and the Olfactory Imagination*. Berkeley: University of California Press, 2006.

Irigaray, Luce. *An Ethics of Sexual Difference*. Trans. Carolyn Burke and Gillian C. Gill. Ithaca, N.Y.: Cornell University Press, 1993.

Jansen, John F. "Tertullian and the New Testament." *Second Century: A Journal of Early Christian Studies* 2, 4 (1982): 191–207.

Jennings, Theodore W. *The Man Jesus Loved: Homoerotic Narratives from the New Testament*. Cleveland: Pilgrim Press, 2003.

Jordan, Mark D. "Flesh in Confession: Alcibiades Beside Augustine." In *Toward a Theology of Eros: Transfiguring Passion at the Limits of Discipline*, ed. Virginia Burrus and Catherine Keller, 22–37. New York: Fordham University Press, 2006.

Kaster, Robert A. *Emotion, Restraint, and Community in Ancient Rome*. Oxford: Oxford University Press, 2005.

Keller, Catherine. *Apocalypse Now and Then: A Feminist Guide to the End of the World*. Boston: Beacon Press, 1996.

———. *The Face of the Deep: A Theology of Becoming*. London: Routledge, 2003.

Kimball, Roger. "Does Shame Have a Future?" *New Criterion* (September 2004): 4–9.

King, Karen L. "Christ and Sophia in the *Apocryphon of John*." In *Images of the Feminine in Gnosticism*, ed. Karen L. King, 158–76. Philadelphia: Fortress, 1988.

———. *The Secret Revelation of John*. Cambridge, Mass.: Harvard University Press, 2006.

Kristeva, Julia. *Powers of Horror: An Essay on Abjection*. Trans. Leon S. Roudiez. New York: Columbia University Press, 1982.

———. "Freud and Love: Treatment and Its Discontents." Trans. León S. Roudiez in *The Kristeva Reader*, ed. Toril Moi, 238–71. Oxford: Blackwell, 1986.

———. "Stabat Mater." Trans. León S. Roudiez in *The Kristeva Reader*, ed. Toril Moi, 160–86. Oxford: Basil Blackwell, 1986.

Krueger, Derek. "The Bawdy and Society: The Shamelessness of Diogenes in Roman Imperial Culture." In *The Cynics: The Cynic Movement in Antiquity and Its Legacy*, ed. R. Bracht Branham and Marie-Odile Goulet-Cazé, 222–39. Berkeley: University of California Press, 1996.

———. *Symeon the Holy Fool: Leontius's Life and the Late Antique City*. Transformation of the Classical Heritage. Berkeley: University of California Press, 1996.

———. *Writing and Holiness: The Practice of Authorship in the Early Christian East*. Divinations: Rereading Late Ancient Religion. Philadelphia: University of Pennsylvania Press, 2004.

Kyle, Donald G. *Spectacles of Death in Ancient Rome*. London: Routledge, 1998.

Lacan, Jacques. *L'Envers de la psychanalyse.* Séminaire de Jacques Lacan. Paris: Éditions du Seuil, 1991.

Levinas, Emmanuel. *Totality and Infinity: An Essay on Exteriority.* Trans. Alphonso Lingis. Pittsburgh: Duquesne University Press, 1969.

———. *Otherwise Than Being or Beyond Essence.* Trans. Alphonso Lingis. The Hague: Martinus Nijhoff, 1981.

———. *On Escape.* 1935. Trans. Bettina Bergo. Stanford, Calif.: Stanford University Press, 2003.

Lewis, Helen Block. "Introduction: Shame—The 'Sleeper' in Psychopathology." In *The Role of Shame in Symptom Formation,* ed. Helen Block Lewis, 1–28. Hillsdale, N.J.: Erlbaum, 1987.

Leyser, Conrad. "Masculinity in Flux: Nocturnal Emission and the Limits of Celibacy in the Early Middle Ages." In *Masculinity in Medieval Europe,* ed. D. M. Hadley, 103–20. London: Longman, 1999.

Loraux, Nicole. *Tragic Ways of Killing a Woman.* Cambridge, Mass.: Harvard University Press, 1987.

Lyman, J. Rebecca. *Christology and Cosmology: Models of Divine Activity in Origen, Eusebius, and Athanasius.* Oxford Theological Monographs. Oxford: Clarendon Press, 1993.

MacKendrick, Karmen. *Counterpleasures.* SUNY Series in Postmodern Culture. Albany: State University of New York Press, 1999.

———. *Word Made Skin: Figuring Language at the Surface of Flesh.* New York: Fordham University Press, 2004.

———. "Carthage Didn't Burn Hot Enough: Saint Augustine's Divine Seduction." In *Toward a Theology of Eros: Transfiguring Passion at the Limits of Discipline,* ed. Virginia Burrus and Catherine Keller, 205–17. New York: Fordham University Press, 2006.

Maier, Harry O. *Apocalypse Recalled: The Book of Revelation After Christendom.* Minneapolis: Fortress, 2002.

Malina, Bruce. *The New Testament World: Insights from Cultural Anthropology.* Louisville, Ky.: Westminster/John Knox Press, 1993.

Matthews, Rupert. *The Age of the Gladiators: Savagery and Spectacle in Ancient Rome.* Edison, N.J.: Chartwell Books, 2004.

Miller, Patricia Cox. "Desert Asceticism and 'the Body from Nowhere.'" *Journal of Early Christian Studies* 2 (1994): 137–53.

———. *Dreams in Late Antiquity: Studies in the Imagination of a Culture.* Princeton, N.J.: Princeton University Press, 1994.

———. "'Differential Networks': Relics and Other Fragments in Late Antiquity." *Journal of Early Christian Studies* 6, 1 (1998): 113–38.

———. "Strategies of Representation in Collective Biography: Constructing the Subject as Holy." In *Greek Biography and Panegyric in Late Antiquity,* ed. Tomas Hagg and Philip Rousseau, 209–54. Berkeley: University of California Press, 2000.

———. *The Poetry of Thought in Late Antiquity: Essays in Imagination and Religion.* Aldershot: Ashgate, 2001.

———. "Relics, Rhetoric and Mental Spectacles in Late Ancient Christianity." In

Seeing the Invisible in Late Antiquity and the Early Middle Ages, ed. Giselle de Nie, Karl F. Morrison, and Marco Mostert, 25–52. Turnhout: Brepols, 2005.

Moore, Stephen D. *Poststructuralism and the New Testament: Derrida and Foucault at the Foot of the Cross*. Minneapolis: Fortress, 1994.

———. *God's Gym: Divine Male Bodies of the Bible*. New York: Routledge, 1996.

Moore, Stephen D. and Janice Capel Anderson. "Taking It like a Man: Masculinity in 4 Maccabees." *Journal of Biblical Literature* 117, 2 (1998): 249–73.

Moxnes, Halvor. "Honor and Shame." In *The Social Sciences and New Testament Interpretation*, ed. Richard L. Rohrbaugh, 19–40. Peabody, Mass.: Hendrickson, 1996.

Nathanson, Donald L. "Foreword." In *Scenes of Shame: Psychoanalysis, Shame, and Writing*, ed. Joseph Adamson and Hilary Clark, vii–viii. Albany: State University of New York Press, 1999.

———. "Preface." In *The Many Faces of Shame*, ed. Donald L. Nathanson, vii–xiii. New York: Guilford Press, 1987.

———. "The Shame/Pride Axis." In *The Role of Shame in Symptom Formation*, ed. Helen Block Lewis, 183–205. Hillsdale, N.J.: Erlbaum, 1987.

———. *Shame and Pride: Affect, Sex, and the Birth of the Self*. New York: Norton, 1992.

———. "A Timetable for Shame." In *The Many Faces of Shame*, ed. Donald L. Nathanson, 1–63. New York: Guilford Press, 1987.

Neyrey, Jerome H. *Honor and Shame in the Gospel of Matthew*. Louisville, Ky.: Westminster/John Knox Press, 1998.

Niehues-Pröbsting, Heinrich. "The Modern Reception of Cynicism: Diogenes in the Enlightenment." In *The Cynics: The Cynic Movement in Antiquity and Its Legacy*, ed. R. Bracht Branham and Marie-Odile Goulet-Cazé, 329–65. Berkeley: University of California Press, 1996.

Nussbaum, Martha C. *Hiding from Humanity: Disgust, Shame, and the Law*. Princeton, N.J.: Princeton University Press, 2004.

Nygren, Anders. *Agape and Eros*. Trans. Philip S. Watson. Philadelphia: Westminster Press, 1953.

O'Grady, Kathleen. "Sacred Metaphor: Julia Kristeva and Umberto Eco." In *Feminist Philosophy of Religion*, ed. Pamela Sue Anderson and Beverley Clack, 153–69. London: Routledge, 2004.

O'Malley, T. P. *Tertullian and the Bible: Language, Imagery, Exegesis*. Utrecht: Dekker & Van de Vegt, 1967.

Osborn, Eric. *Tertullian, First Theologian of the West*. Cambridge: Cambridge University Press, 1997.

Otten, Willemien. "Christ's Birth of a Virgin Who Became a Wife: Flesh and Speech in Tertullian's *De Carne Christi*." *Vigiliae Christianae* 51 (1997): 247–60.

Parker, A. S. E. "The Vita Syncletica: Its Manuscripts, Ascetical Teachings, and Its Use in Monastic Sources." *Studia Patristica* 30 (1997): 231–34.

Peristiany, J. G., ed. *Honour and Shame: The Values of Mediterranean Society*. London: Weidenfeld and Nicholson, 1966.

Peristiany, J. G., and Julian Pitt-Rivers. "Introduction." In *Honor and Grace in An-*

thropology, ed. J. G. Peristiany and Julian Pitt-Rivers, 1–17. Cambridge: Cambridge University Press, 1992.

Perkins, Judith. *The Suffering Self: Pain and Narrative Representation in the Early Christian Era*. London: Routledge, 1995.

Pippin, Tina. *Death and Desire: The Rhetoric of Gender in the Apocalypse of John*. Louisville, Ky.: Westminster/John Knox Press, 1992.

Pitt-Rivers, Julian. "Postscript: The Place of Grace in Anthropology." In *Honor and Grace in Anthropology*, ed. J. G. Peristiany and Julian Pitt-Rivers, 215–46. Cambridge: Cambridge University Press, 1992.

Plass, Paul. *The Game of Death in Ancient Rome: Arena Sport and Political Suicide*. Madison: University of Wisconsin Press, 1995.

Satran, David. "Fingernails and Hair: Anatomy and Exegesis in Tertullian." *Journal of Theological Studies* n.s. 40 (1989): 116–20.

Sedgwick, Eve Kosofsky. *Touching Feeling: Affect, Pedagogy, Performativity*. Durham, N.C.: Duke University Press, 2003.

Sedgwick, Eve Kosofsky, and Adam Frank. "Shame in the Cybernetic Fold: Reading Silvan Tomkins." In *Shame and Its Sisters: A Silvan Tomkins Reader*, ed. Eve Kosofsky Sedgwick and Adam Frank, 1–28. Durham: Duke University Press, 1995.

Seesengood, Robert. *Competing Identities: The Athlete and the Gladiator in Early Christian Literature*. London: Continuum, 2007.

Seim, Turid Karlsen. "Descent and Divine Paternity in the Gospel of John: Does the Mother Matter?" *New Testament Studies* 51 (2005): 361–275.

Sider, Robert Dick. *Ancient Rhetoric and the Art of Tertullian*. Oxford: Oxford University Press, 1971.

Tarnopolsky, Christina. "Prudes, Perverts, and Tyrants: Plato and the Contemporary Politics of Shame." *Political Theory* 32, 4 (August 2004): 468–94.

Tilborg, Sjef van. *Imaginative Love in John*. Leiden: Brill, 1993.

Tomkins, Silvan S. *Affect, Imagery, Consciousness*. Vol. 2, The *Negative Affects*. New York: Springer, 1963.

Trigg, Joseph W. "Divine Deception and the Truthfulness of Scripture." In *Origen of Alexandria: His World and His Legacy*, ed. Charles Kannengiesser and William L. Petersen, 147–64. Notre Dame, Ind.: University of Notre Dame Press, 1988.

Trout, Dennis. "Re-Textualizing Lucretia: Cultural Subversion in the *City Of God*." *Journal of Early Christian Studies* 2, 1 (1994): 53–70.

Valantasis, Richard. "Constructions of Power in Asceticism." *Journal of the American Academy of Religion* 63, 4 (1995): 775–821.

Webster, Jane S. *Ingesting Jesus: Eating and Drinking in the Gospel of John*. Atlanta: Society of Biblical Literature, 2003.

Wiedemann, Thomas. *Emperors and Gladiators*. London: Routledge, 1992.

Williams, Bernard. *Shame and Necessity*. Berkeley: University of California Press, 1993.

Wolfson, Elliot R. *Through a Speculum That Shines: Vision and Imagination in Medieval Jewish Mysticism*. Princeton, N.J.: Princeton University Press, 1994.

———. "Divine Suffering and the Hermeneutics of Reading: Philosophical Reflections on Lurianic Mythology." In *Suffering Religion*, ed. Robert Gibbs and Elliot R. Wolfson, 101–62. London: Routledge, 2002.

———. *Language, Eros, Being: Kabbalistic Hermeneutics and Poetic Imagination.* New York: Fordham University Press, 2005.

———. "Secrecy, Modesty, and the Feminine: Kabbalistic Traces in the Thought of Levinas." *Journal of Jewish Thought and Philosophy* 14 (2006): 193–224.

———. "Suffering Eros and Textual Incarnation: A Kristevan Reading of Kabbalistic Poetics." In *Toward a Theology of Eros: Transfiguring Passion at the Limits of Discipline*, ed. Virginia Burrus and Catherine Keller, 341–65. New York: Fordham University Press, 2006.

———. *Venturing Beyond: Law and Morality in Kabbalistic Mysticism.* Oxford: Oxford University Press, 2006.

Wurmser, Leon. "'Man of the Most Dangerous Curiosity': Nietszche's 'Fruitful and Frightful Vision' and His War Against Shame." In *Scenes of Shame: Psychoanalysis, Shame, and Writing*, ed. Joseph Adamson and Hilary Clark, 111–46. Albany: State University of New York Press, 1999.

———. *The Mask of Shame.* Baltimore: Johns Hopkins University Press, 1981.

———. "Shame: The Veiled Companion of Narcissism." In *The Many Faces of Shame*, ed. Donald L. Nathanson, 64–92. New York: Guilford Press, 1987.

Wyschogrod, Edith. *Emmanuel Levinas: The Problem of Ethical Metaphysics.* New York: Fordham University Press, 2000.

Index

Acknowledgments

Where to begin, where to end, in acknowledging my many debts? I remain grateful to Drew University's Theological School—wonderful colleagues and students, an enabling administration and staff—for supporting my work in so many and such improbable ways. Beyond Drew, I also owe gratitude for hospitality and critical engagement to those who have both invited and generously received my thoughts about shame at Cambridge University, Cornell University, Harvard Divinity School, Rutgers University, the University of California at Berkeley, the University of Michigan, and the University of Oslo. Dear friends who have listened and responded with both tact and wisdom include Sharon Betcher, Daniel Boyarin, Catherine Keller, Derek Krueger, Rebecca Lyman, Karmen Mac-Kendrick, Stephen Moore, and Karen Torjesen; Daniel, Derek, and Karmen actually read the whole manuscript, as did an unusually insightful and generous anonymous reader for the press. Jennifer Glancy also gave helpful commentary. Erika Murphy, in her capacity as student research assistant, offered aid and encouragement at every step along the way. My editor Jerry Singerman, whom I also count as a friend, treats me better than I deserve; he is a joy to work with, as is the staff at the University of Pennsylvania Press.

Where to begin, where to end? James and Mary Kelly have been more indulgent of my quirky obsessions than I could ever have expected: astonishingly, for teenagers, they are not particularly ashamed of their mom. Elliot Wolfson encouraged me from the beginning to write what was on my heart and to write from the heart; later, he read what I'd written. It is from my heart that I dedicate these pages to him.